MW01224548

Negotiated Memory

Julie Rak

Negotiated Memory: Doukhobor Autobiographical Discourse

UBCPress · Vancouver · Toronto

For Joan

15   14   13   12   11   10   09   08   07   06   05   04   5   4   3   2   1

Printed in Canada on acid-free paper

National Library of Canada Cataloguing in Publication

Rak, Julie, 1966-
  Negotiated memory : Doukhobor autobiographical discourse / Julie Rak.

  Includes bibliographical references and index.
  ISBN 0-7748-1030-0 (bound)

  1. Dukhobors – Canada – Biography – History and criticism.
2. Autobiography. I. Title.

FC106.D76R34 2004   305.6'89071   C2003-907326-2

Canadä

UBC Press gratefully acknowledges the financial support for our publishing program of the Government of Canada through the Book Publishing Industry Development Program (BPIDP), and of the Canada Council for the Arts, and the British Columbia Arts Council.

This book has been published with the help of a grant from the Canadian Federation for the Humanities and Social Sciences, through the Aid to Scholarly Publications Programme, using funds provided by the Social Sciences and Humanities Research Council of Canada.

A reasonable attempt has been made to secure permission to reproduce all material used. If there are errors or omissions, they are wholly unintentional and the publisher would be grateful to learn of them.

UBC Press
The University of British Columbia
2029 West Mall
Vancouver, BC V6T 1Z2
604-822-5959 / Fax: 604-822-6083
www.ubcpress.ca

Contents

Acknowledgments

I am glad to say that my list of acknowledgments for this project is long. I am very conscious of producing this work standing, as it were, on the shoulders of many people whose encouragement, example, and sometimes collaborative effort have made it possible for me to do it at all.

Completion of this work has been made possible by Support for the Advancement of Scholarship and Humanities and Fine Arts Research grants provided by the University of Alberta, 1998-2001, and by a grant from the Aid to Scholarly Publications Programme. I thank the Honourable Lois Hole, lieutenant-governor of Alberta, for her financial support. I thank Koozma Tarasoff, Jim Popoff, the staff of *Iskra,* Mike Chernenkoff, Steve Lapshinoff, Vi Plotnikoff, Jim Kolesnikoff, Jan Kabatoff, and John MacLaren, who provided me with much valuable information, assistance, and encouragement at key stages of my research. Many Doukhobor people have invited me into their homes and made me feel welcome during this project. There are too many of you to mention here, but please know that I am very grateful to all of you. I thank Jack MacIntosh of Special Collections at the University of British Columbia Main Library for his invaluable assistance. Thanks to Edward Hickcox for acting as an on-site research assistant during the final stages of the project. I am very grateful to my mentors and colleagues who have either read this manuscript or have had to hear me talk about it: Lorraine York, Daniel Coleman, Nina Kolesnikoff, Heather Zwicker, Shirley Neuman, Daphne Read, Dianne Chisholm, my graduate research assistant Karen Clark, and, of course, the Wriot Grrrls writing group – Cecily Devereux, Andie Palmer, Aara Suksi, and Heather YoungLeslie. I thank all of the students who took my course Subjectivity, Identity, and Autobiography between 1998 and 2001. They have helped to form my thinking about the issues I deal with here. I would also like to thank all of my translators: Elena Ilina, for the material from A.M. Bodianskii's collection and A. Efanow's diary; Jim Kolesnikoff, for all the oral narratives and for reading manuscripts with me; and Carol Theal, for the material from the Agassiz diary.

Portions of this book have appeared in somewhat different forms. Part of Chapter 3 has appeared as "'*Vechnaja Pamjat*' in the Diaspora: Community Doukhobor Autobiography" in *The Doukhobor Centenary in Canada* (Ottawa: Slavic Research Group at the University of Ottawa and the Institute for Canadian Studies at the University of Ottawa, 2000), 322-41. Some of Chapter 5 has appeared as "Doukhobor Autobiography as Witness Narrative" in *Biography: An Interdisciplinary Quarterly* (Special Issue: Autobiography and Changing Identities) 24, 1 (2001): 226-41. Another part of Chapter 5 is forthcoming as "One Hybrid Discourse of Doukhobor Identity: The Freedomite Diary from Agassiz Prison" in *Adjacencies: Minority Writing in Canada,* ed. Lianne Moyes, Domenic Beneventi, and Licia Canton (Montreal: Guernica Editions).

I gratefully acknowledge the following sources for permission to reproduce material previously published elsewhere:

To Elaine Makortoff for her poem "Of Other Generations," *Mir* 2, 3-6 (1974): 44.

To D.E. (Jim) Popoff for the interview with Nick D. Arishenkoff and Cecil W. Koochin, "Life in the Doukhobor Commune – (CCUB)," *Mir* 2, 3-6 (1974): 3-50.

To Eli Popoff for his transcription and translation of material from the Joint Doukhobor Research Committee, *Report of the United Doukhobor Research Committee in the Matter of Clarification of the Motivating Life-Concepts and the History of the Doukhobors in Canada (Symposium Meetings, 1974-1982)* (Castlegar, BC: Selkirk College, 1997).

To University of Toronto Press for the passage from William Janzen, *Limits on Liberty: The Experience of Mennonite, Hutterite and Doukhobor Communities in Canada* (Toronto: University of Toronto Press, 1990).

To the Writer's Trust of Canada for excerpts from George Woodcock and Ivan Avakumovic, *The Doukhobors* (Toronto: McClelland & Stewart, 1977).

The cover image was graciously provided by Jan Kabatoff. This is what the artist has to say about the image: "The 'I Remember, I Forget ... ' monoprint uses acrylic paint, silk-screened historic photograph and heirloom imagery, and collage on paper. It is part of a series of monoprints that are one-of-a-kind, even though they share similar elements. The 'I Remember, I Forget ... ' series speaks of memory fragments, history, loss of cultural identity and the passage of time. The identity of the Doukhobor women is unknown, but this image is important to Doukhobors because the women in it symbolize the feminine strength and stoicism that was too long undervalued in Doukhobor culture."

Introduction

When the first Doukhobor immigrants stepped onto a pier in Halifax in 1899 as refugees from tsarist religious persecution in Russia, they began a chapter in the history of the development of Canada as a nation that is still being written and that, at times, is still under erasure. The story of the Doukhobors in Canada remains one of the most unusual stories of mass migration because the Doukhobors arrived at a time when ideas about Canada's position in the British Empire were still debated and the position of migrants was not yet fully worked through. Soon after the Doukhobors began to live in Canada their belief in pacifism, anti-patriotism, communal living, and vegetarianism, along with their desire to retain their own language and their deep suspicion of institutionalization of any kind, proved to be threatening to many who were developing ideas about Canada and what it should mean to be Canadian. This resulted in a struggle that highlights what type of nation Canada was at the turn of the last century, and why, until very recently, the Doukhobors have had so much difficulty living in it.

Doukhobors, out of all proportion to their rather small numbers, have played a large part in the othering of certain kinds of ethnicity and religious expression in Canada. This is because they have been, in Louis Althusser's words, "bad subjects." Not only did they resist the institutions, laws, and beliefs that would have made them into "good" immigrants and docile citizens but they also refused to recognize the terms of recognition that would have made them like most other migrants. Althusser (1990, 135) says that subjectivity works through the recognition of an already-existing state of affairs rather than through choice: good subjects "work all right 'all by themselves'" because they recognize their own positionality, but bad subjects are bad because they cannot recognize themselves inside the mechanisms that produce personhood. Therefore, the State cannot recognize them either and can only inculcate its goodness and the rightness of its practices by repressing their ways of knowing. So-called good

nations need bad subjectivity in order to point the way to good and obe-
dient citizenship. Bad subjects cannot be treated as people who have histories and knowledges of their own because the history of the bad subject
cannot be recounted or written inside of the State. Bad subjects are people
who are treated as if they are without their own cultural sense of memory,
without full personhood, and, at times, without the rights and privileges
that are extended to other citizens in a liberal state.

The questions that I address in this book are: if the Doukhobors have
been bad subjects in Canada and must live within systems that cannot recognize them as anything else, then what happened when some of them
used a discourse of the "good subject" – like autobiography? And why
would they have used it? In order to answer these two questions, critical
thinking about autobiography needs to change. Autobiography must be
thought of as a discourse rather than as a genre, and as a discourse that
is sustained by the trappings of identification that have underwritten
what the self is and how it has been seen in much of the Western world.
When autobiographical discourse is used by writers or speakers who do
not have access to the privileges of autobiographical identity – such as
print literacy, a sense of one's "place" in history that others will recognize,
or the leisure time to write a book – then that discourse changes as it is
used, even as it brings certain advantages. Autobiographical discourse can
surface in places where it normally is not seen, such as legal records, newspaper articles, prison narratives, and ethnographic recordings. And when
it appears in such places the discourse itself alters so that it can be appro-
priated for use by those who are not powerful or whose version of events
cannot be allowed to have validity. In this more flexible way of understanding what autobiography is and how it can be used, autobiography
can become a point of negotiation between good subjects and bad, and
it can be a way for those who are bad to become visible – regardless of
whether the outcome is an identity win or an identity loss.

Doukhobor history and cultural context must be considered as key to
the ways in which autobiography can be used to achieve visibility. During
their 100 years in Canada the Doukhobors have not often been remembered for their pacifist principles, their commitment to types of communal living, or even for their non-institutionalized religious expressions.
Usually they are remembered, inaccurately, for nude protests and arson in
British Columbia. This is a result of negative press coverage and, in particular, of the success of *Terror in the Name of God* (Holt 1964), a sensationalist
account of the protests and depredations by *Vancouver Sun* reporter Simma
Holt. Complex relations inside of Doukhobor groups have meant that,
while some historical studies have been written by Doukhobors, like other
ethnic minority or religious sectarian groups, much more information has
been written about them by outsiders than by Doukhobors themselves.

This makes it all the more imperative to study what has happened when Doukhobors have written and spoken about themselves and about Doukhobor identity, and to see the very act of entering autobiographical terrain as an attempt to negotiate what will be remembered about Doukhobor history as well as what position Doukhobors will have in Canada both now and in the future.

Even now, Doukhobors who refer to themselves as "Canadians," and who had the right to vote restored to them in 1962, do not call themselves Doukhobor-Canadians. They do not hyphenate their identities, and for many of them the terms of this non-hyphenation are still being thought through. Thus, Doukhobors who live in Canada have negotiated between Homi Bhabha's (1994) idea of nation as the pedagogical and the performative without accepting either the formulation of the nation as the nation-state or the belief in the nation as a group of people.

Doukhobor beliefs and practices were always radically anti-national and anti-institutional, and then they were combined with their commitment to oral traditions, their history of conflict with secular and church authorities, and their conviction that they were destined to be exiles and wanderers until a prophesied return to Russia. Not only were Doukhobors opposed to a separation of church and state, but they also opposed the ideas of church and state in and of themselves. This meant that Doukhobors effectively became subjects who could not be written into the Canadian national script except as curiosities or as a threat to nationhood. They literally had no way to recount their own histories because they had little legitimacy within Canada as subjects. Therefore, when, by the 1950s, many of them had partially assimilated, some Doukhobors began to combine their oral traditions with written forms in order to write as what I term "hybrid subjects." Their sense of who they were and how to tell their life story falls somewhere between the ideals of Doukhoborism and the idea of Canada. As they either wrote autobiographically or responded to ethnographers or interviewers who asked them to tell their life stories, these Doukhobors turned a discourse that normally excluded them and their concerns into a point of negotiation between their sense of their history, community, and identity (on the one hand) and the Canadian version of history, identity, and nationality (on the other). They tried to use the power inherent in autobiographical discourse for their own ends.

When they have needed to become visible as subjects in the Althusserian sense, either outside their own contexts or, in later cases, to each other, Doukhobor writers and speakers have also used aspects of autobiographical discourse as a way to figure out how Doukhobor identity works for them in their own terms. At times they have also used this alternative identity construction to resist assimilative discourses that anxiously seek to erase the differences between Doukhobor ways of understanding the world and non-Doukhobor ways of doing so. Finally, autobiographical forms have helped some Doukhobors to recover alternate memories of their struggle in Russia and Canada. As I mentioned, these can take on the character of a refusal as Doukhobors use autobiography to criticize the liberal idea of citizenship embedded in the idea of hyphenating one's cultural identity with one's citizenship. However, at other times, they use aspects of autobiographical discourse as a way of negotiating with non-Doukhobors, thus recasting the individuation of autobiographical discourse as a communal effort that non-Doukhobors might be able to understand. Sometimes these negotiations were successful, and some Doukhobors were able to become visible within Canadian narrative forms in ways that did not sacrifice their identities and concerns. At other times, these negotiations were not successful, and narrative control remained in the hands of non-Doukhobor interpreters who could not hear, understand, or respect what Doukhobors might have to say about their history and experiences within a wider Canadian context.

Even though autobiography has not always been successful, many Doukhobors have written or spoken autobiographically in order to employ the subject of autobiography for their own ends. Since the construction of autobiography is not a "natural" process for them in Doukhobor culture, autobiographical discourse in a Doukhobor context has a special power when it surfaces in other kinds of texts, or in interviews, in part because it only appears when it is *not* part of autobiography as it is most commonly understood. In fact, the very idea of "Doukhobor autobiography" may seem unusual in itself since there are no "conventional" written autobiographies by Doukhobors in existence. Most of the material I examine here is not found in conventionally published books but, rather, in archived Doukhobor magazines, legal testimony, tape recordings, and prison diaries. Some of the material was originally written or spoken in a Doukhobor form of Russian, which is not widely understood outside of Doukhobor communities. Moreover, none of the three major prevailing Doukhobor groups in Canada (the Independents, the Community Doukhobors, and the Freedomites) seem to have the conditions that create autobiographical writing. Until the 1930s (and in some groups much later) most Doukhobors were part of a primarily Russian language oral culture and many were not print literate in Russian or English. Therefore, for much of their history, Doukhobors would not have had access to written autobiographies that would have provided models for them. Doukhobor subjectivity also generally seems to operate less on an individual than on a group level, perhaps due to Doukhobor beliefs about equality and the sanctity of communal living. One of the ironies of my research has been that, although I have found autobiographical writing by almost everyone who worked with Doukhobors or who came into contact with them –

including early advocates (such as Aylmer Maude and Leopold Sulerjit-skii), writers of Canadian travel narrative (like Emily Murphy), Stephan Sorokin (a non-Doukhobor Freedomite leader), Hazel O'Neal (who wrote the xenophobic memoir entitled *Doukhobor Daze*), and an RCMP officer (who wrote a memoir based on his attempt to round up stripping Free-domite protesters and try to dress them) – I have found no book-length, published autobiographical accounts by Doukhobors themselves.

I found that if I were willing to adjust my ideas about what constitutes autobiographical discourse, and to look beyond the constraints of main-stream publishing, then Doukhobors can and do produce autobiography. However, the autobiography they produce contests all three aspects of the definition of the genre suggested by James Olney (1980): that autobiog-raphy is, literally, "auto-bio-graphe" – self, life, and writing – a genre in which individual authors create narratives of their lives that reflect a pre-occupation with self, a unique creative representation of self, and their lived experience in the world. What I have also found is that the Dou-khobors produce unconventional autobiography *because* they are uncon-ventional subjects who refused to be made into hyphenated subjects and then into citizens. This situation has meant that a consideration of Doukhobor autobiographical discourse (which includes writing and speak-ing) actually means that commonly accepted ideas about autobiography, written representation, and the self need to be revised to take Doukhobor conceptions of identity into account.

This revision of what autobiography is "supposed" to be occurs because the Doukhobors have had to turn to alternate strategies to retell their own histories, both orally and in writing, against the grain of the sensationalist image of Doukhobors propagated by government commissions and by the Canadian media. They are not the only group to do this. The Doukhobors' appropriation of some (but not all) aspects of Western autobiographical discourse has utilized autobiography as testament and testimony, as a form of alternative memory for an entire people. This has been studied in Hertha Dawn Wong's (1992) work on precontact and postcontact autobio-graphical discourses by Native Americans, Genaro Padilla's (1993b) study of Chicano/Chicana autobiography after the American conquest of north-ern Mexico, and Anne Goldman's (1996) study of ethnic working-class women in America. My study of Doukhobor autobiographical discourse shares similarities with this work.

This means that the Doukhobors use autobiography in ways similar to those used by other marginalized groups – to challenge what a self might be. Anne Goldman's (1996, ix) call "for a wider autobiographical field [so that] we describe a wider spectrum of the ways and means by which people in the twentieth century speak themselves into existence" recog-nizes how minority autobiographical writings can result in new forms that blend fiction and fact, memoir and autobiography, and diary and memoir to result in new ways to make identity. My project joins this emerging scholarship about autobiography as a discourse that can be used outside the Western narratives of the subject, and it does so by looking at Doukhobor texts produced from 1900 to the present – texts that come from a variety of oral and written, singular and collaborative, sources.

To examine how and why Doukhobors have used autobiographical discourse in the ways that they have, I suggest in Chapter 1 that, when its forms begin to change, autobiography should be rethought as a series of discursive moves rather than renamed as something "other" than autobiography (e.g., life writing or manifesto). This means that autobiography can be considered as a set of identity-building strategies that help to make Doukhobor resistance to the Canadian state's conceptions of identity possible. I also suggest that Doukhobor autobiographical discourse does not erase the power to refer that is inherent in the discourse of autobiography; rather, it makes use of that very power in order to negotiate identities and to gain visibility for them within a public sphere. Thus, I look at theoretical work concerning the connections between subjectivity and identity within and without autobiography theory in order to show how Doukhobor identity, like other types of collective identity formations, can remake some of what has been understood to be classic *techne* for constituting identity.

In Chapter 2 I review key moments and places in Doukhobor history in order to provide a context for the primary source material I examine and to indicate how developing imperialist ideas about what Canadian identity was quickly came into conflict with Doukhobor ways of imagining and using. These conflicts appear as motifs and as identity touchstones in subsequent autobiographical writing by Doukhobors.

In Chapter 3, using the figure of *vechnaiia pamit* (eternal memory/ eternal consciousness), a Doukhobor phrase that conflates memory and spiritualized history, I examine identities constructed in transcribed Doukhobor psalms. I then look at the relationship between these psalms and collected memoirs and interviews from *Mir* and *Iskra* as instances of identity construction. The construction of these identities and the figures they use recover Doukhobor history as a set of reactions to the wounded ideas of home sustained in what I call the Doukhobor diasporic imaginary, a set of tropes that figures home as both Russia and the memory of resistance to oppression in Russia.

Through an examination of transcribed and oral accounts of migration and life in Canada, Chapter 4 deals with the construction of Doukhobor oral identities. I look at the complexities of these texts as oral and sometimes written collaborations with reference to debates about orality and literacy. Chapter 5 examines Freedomite Doukhobor narratives that contain collective Doukhobor subject performatives in Bakhtin's sense – public identities inside a hybridized discourse that falls between memoir, autobiography, and diary. The materials here include Freedomite prison diaries by Mikhail Chernenkoff i drugie (1993) and Alexander Efanow (1930) as examples of first-person plural "witness" records. In these, the writers record an alternative history of their imprisonment using the proper name of one person as a way of combining many accounts of an event in the form of a diary-cum-memoir. Peter Maloff's (1957) work on legal testimony is another example of autobiographical hybridity, this time conflating the formats of legal document and autobiography, respectively. I also look at the autobiographical writing produced by Fred Davidoff (1964) when Simma Holt asked him to contribute to her book *Terror in the Name of God*. I evaluate the differences between this work and the unpublished autobiography Davidoff wrote in prison as a response to it.[1]

My decision to collect Doukhobor autobiographical work and to subject it to contemporary theory opens up some possibilities for analysis while it closes down others. I do hope to make Doukhobor autobiographical writing and speaking in previously untranslated and archived forms more accessible, both to Doukhobors and to non-Doukhobors. However, the theoretical basis of this book may make some aspects of the analysis inaccessible to non-specialists in the field of autobiography. The question of theory's "place" in the analysis of materials that often fall outside of the assumptions made by the philosophic tradition that informs much of Western literary theory problematizes the question of access. Am I, as a non-Doukhobor, recovering narratives from what Caren Kaplan (1992, 115) calls an "out-law genre" just so that I can recoup the resistant elements of these narratives into reassuring objects of study that bolster the very Western institutions of "self" that they critique? These questions, summarized in Peter Dickinson's (1994) questioning of the commodifying of Aboriginal oral narratives by non-Aboriginal scholars, add a political layer to the reading of such narratives.

However, the debate about whether the subaltern can ever speak, or whether she or he is always made to speak by dominant discourse, only seems to be raised in absolute terms, which assume that writers and speakers not operating purely within Western traditions of subject representation cannot ever occupy hybrid positions themselves and cannot themselves theorize. This approach would seem to deny members of oppressed groups the ability to change the terms of representation while it also renders invisible the genealogy of alternative representation used by those not immersed in dominant ways of representing subjectivity. The Doukhobors, for example, regard Leo Tolstoy as a philosopher and a cultural theorist because his ideas inspired Doukhobor leaders and because he was directly responsible for the Doukhobor migration from Russia to

Canada. Doukhobors actively reproduce (and read) his writings as well as those of their own leadership. Comments on literacy by Doukhobors themselves, which appear in many of the narratives that I examine, often refer to alternative Doukhobor learning practices that do not make use of print literacy. These examples indicate that Doukhobor writers and speakers are aware of and use other ways of thinking about theoretical issues; while they do not operate within the trajectories of Western metaphysics, they do make theory of their own. This other set of practices, which sometimes does use aspects of non-Doukhobor epistemology, should be considered valid in its own right and should be able to interact with other types of theorizing, as an alternative to it and, at times, as a critique of it. Therefore, Doukhobor autobiographical discourse should be seen as a challenge to autobiography theory (and some of the assumptions made by theories of the subject) rather than as a defeated discourse. This concern for revision has been taken up by other scholars as well. Genaro Padilla (1993b, 8), for instance, makes a similar call for revision when he states that alternate ways of representing oneself autobiographically are "owned neither by Western culture nor by writing" and should also be studied. Ownership is not to be assumed.

While there is always a danger that my work will reify the work Doukhobors have done, I emphasize that it is not intended to be the last word on Doukhobor autobiographical discourse. In fact, I hope that readers of the narratives I discuss will be encouraged to look at the primary materials and make their own decisions about what may be found there and whether or not my own commentary is helpful. Readers who are interested in primary source material and who are conversant with Doukhobor history should pay particular attention to Chapters 3 to 5, where readings of primary texts and recordings are integrated with theoretical commentary.

I recognize that there may be those who wonder why I rely upon contemporary theory about identity when talking about Doukhobor materials. As I have said, I do view Doukhobor materials as themselves constituting a type of theory that can engage in dialogue with contemporary non-Doukhobor theory. But contemporary theory about identity must be used in a book that links the production of autobiography with cultural identity. By striking a balance between Doukhobor materials and contemporary theory, I believe that each can be used to inform and revise the other.

This is why I join other critics in pointing out that autobiography produced by minority writers and speakers is often the product of people who have not been part of the dominant narratives of subjectivity in North America. This view that autobiography sometimes functions as a political mark of difference does not dispense with the genre entirely. In fact, work by Doukhobors can help to revise the meaning of the term "autobiography" so that it can be understood not just as a collection of resistant narratives but also as an important way for people without power to make positions for themselves, to ensure that their cultural memories are not erased or disregarded but, rather, are used as points of negotiation. This is a mark of the will many of these Doukhobor writers and speakers have had to remain visible and to survive within an environment that has not always been hospitable. The determination of many Doukhobor writers, speakers, and narrative collectors exemplifies what Koozma Tarasoff (1982), quoting from the Doukhobor psalm "Tsar David Oseevich" in the Doukhobor Living Book, has called *plakun trava*. The *plakun trava* is a riverbed plant that thrives by growing upstream. In the psalm, *plakun trava* defines itself by the current it grows against, for "*Plakun trava* is here because / it floats against the current of the water" (*Book of Life of the Doukhobors* 1978, 107-9). *Plakun trava* can be recast as a figure that marks the work of identity negotiation and preservation in Doukhobor autobiographical discourse, which defines itself by working against the prevailing discursive current.

Negotiated Memory

1
Beyond Auto-Bio-Graphe: Autobiography and Alternative Identities

Q. Is it possible for one person to save another?
A. If the other person listens, it is possible.

— Psalm 12, The Living Book

The passage from the Doukhobor psalm cycle *Zhivotnaiia Kniga* (The Living Book) contains several important assumptions about what it is to be a (Doukhobor) person. Personhood is interdependent rather than independent since knowledge progresses as part of a question-and-answer pairing between people. Salvation is part of everyday living: it does not come from a divine source outside people but from a divine source found in others. It could also signify a material type of "salvation" which is not necessarily unlike the more spiritual ways of understanding the term found in major religious traditions. Most important of all, "salvation" can only happen if the relationship between people is cooperative. The other must listen in order for change to occur, while "saving" is associated with an/other speaking. These lines show that Doukhobor epistemology is verbal, embodied, and dialogic: it requires more than one person to transmit knowledge and to make change, whether that change is spiritual, material, or both. This view of the interdependence of people implies a version of personhood rooted in ideas about community and collectivity that do not presuppose the existence of people as free, independent subjects who can learn silently from books or media (or from their own experiences) without "help" from others. It is hard for people raised in liberal traditions that assume that all people are unique and should exist as individuals, or who believe implicitly that spiritual matters are separate from material ones, to imagine this other set of ideas about what the production of knowledge and personhood itself can mean. This is the challenge that Doukhobor identities present when they appear in a discourse that, since the eighteenth century, has in Western societies most often been associated with the development of liberal subjectivity: the discourse of autobiographical writing.

The history of autobiography theory and criticism is also bound up with the development of theories about subjectivity and, to a lesser extent, about identity in the humanities and social sciences more generally. There have even been times when the debates about genre and what roughly could be called the idea of the self in the relatively obscure area of auto-biography studies have influenced theoretical enquiry about subjectivity more generally, particularly in the areas of deconstruction, women's stud-ies, and African-American studies. Autobiography as a genre has been closely allied with the development of certain types of Western subjectiv-ity, although many recent critiques of autobiographical discourse have contested earlier attempts to place autobiography at a stable centre of identity formation accessible only to those who hold various kinds of dis-cursive privileges (i.e., those that give them the right to write in the genre) (Gilmore 2001, 2). But as critical enquiry has shifted to considerations of autobiography produced by people who do not have access to some or all of these privileges, there has been some danger of renaming these other modes of autobiographical representation as something other than autobiography. Many critics, including myself, have looked for ways to describe these alternative forms, and in some cases they have made argu-ments for dispensing with autobiography as a term altogether.[1]

Whether autobiography critics want to admit it or not, the "traditional" discourse of autobiography still carries much cultural capital in the West. People who have historically been unable to secure representation inside of the fields that guarantee authenticity and legitimacy in Western discourse are often very much aware of the power of autobiographical dis-course when they choose to enter it. This makes it important to under-stand why people who do not enjoy the automatic assumptions of the representability of their lives in texts use the forms that may seem to exclude them. What happens to the autobiography's assumed power to record and shape individual lives when people who do not think of them-selves primarily as individuals write it for political reasons? What happens when people without print literacy use the conventions of the genre that are based on assumptions about print and the leisure time to write? When autobiography is cut loose from the history of book production and sur-faces in legal documents, video, or popular songs, why does it do so? These questions show the importance of looking at autobiography's power to refer as well as at how ideas about identity and subjectivity are also chang-ing, at times hand-in-hand with autobiography's changing status as a *techne* for representation.

For many writers who belong to minority groups, including the Dou-khobors, alternative forms of autobiographical representation make "auto-biography" operate as a discursive field where issues about ethnic identity, alternative historicity, and the relationship of a minority subjectivity to the ideas associated with being a nation (which exclude minority subjects as other, as surplus, and as excess) can be addressed. Doukhobor autobio-graphical discourse is one of those in-between places where Doukhobor identity, which, in Canada, has for the most part been considered to represent the exotic, pathological, or threatening, is under negotiation. To prepare for a more detailed look at how some Doukhobors have used autobiography to do this, I begin with a look at what "identity" has come to mean. Identity has long been paired with ideas about subjectivity, but the term itself can be thought of as operating in ways that do not presuppose the liberal inheritance of thinking about the freedom and autonomy of the individual or about the ability of the individual to either recall or construct narratives about his or her "self."

Subjectivity, Identity, Autobiography

My subheading is based on the title of Sidonie Smith's (1993) book *Subjectivity, Identity, and the Body*. This book has been widely influential in autobiography studies and in women's studies because it develops her earlier idea (presented in *A Poetics of Women's Autobiography*) that discussions of autobiography need to take account of the discourse of androcentrism at work in what she refers to as "the universal subject" (Smith 1987, 9-10). While Smith's argument helped to push autobiography studies in many new and exciting directions, she forgoes the promise of a discussion of identity in favour of an extended discussion of the history of subjectivity.[2] Although this may seem odd, it is hardly uncommon. Raymond Williams (1976, 260) describes the history of the word "subjective" as a nightmare from which "we might feel we shall never wake up." Despite this daunting description of the term, if one looks at the *Oxford English Dictionary*, then it is still possible to trace its path from its earlier sense of one who is under the dominion of a monarch or government, to the subject of enquiry, to the mind, to (in psychological terms) the ego (*OED Online* 2001b). However, the word "identity" is more difficult to pin down, even though much contemporary cultural theory uses it frequently and often, as does Smith, in concert with the term "subject." The term "identity," like the term "subject," developed as an idea in a variety of disciplines, including mathematics, philosophy, theology, and what became anthropology; but it also developed as a set of practices that attached some of its more abstract meanings to developing theories of the personality and the individual. Identity in mathematics and in nineteenth-century metaphysics is "the quality or condition of being the same" in substance, nature, or properties (*OED Online* 2001a). It is still understood this way in mathematics, as it is in the word "identical."

The second sense of the word in the *Oxford English Dictionary* contains one of the cornerstones of the development of human psychology as a discipline: "the sameness of a person or thing at all times or in all circumstances" (*OED Online* 2001a). This sense comes from Locke's *Essay on Human Understanding,* in which he says that the unity of person is the same as the unity of other bodies in space because "consciousness" accompanies thinking and guarantees the "Sameness of a rational Being" (Locke 1980, 246-47). Locke's understanding of identity connects it first to sameness generally and then to a unity of consciousness, and it does so in a way that is fundamental to understanding how identity became linked to the emergence of individuality – and the idea that each person has a personality that does not fundamentally alter – in its modern sense. To a point, Raymond Williams's (1976) discussion of "individuality" as a keyword follows a similar trajectory: individuality developed as an idea during the Enlightenment, where Leibniz and Hobbes (among others) argued that laws and forms of society were based on a notion of the individual's *primary* existence apart from social, economic, or religious obligations. Therefore, identity is about the primacy of consistency in one's personhood, which is guaranteed by the assumption that consciousness of self exists *a priori*. Identity became linked to the belief that consciousness (an inner imperative) implies both human consistency and human individuality. The idea of "identity crisis" in psychology signifies this idea as such a crisis is, in part, a crisis of inconsistency, which occurs when someone does not "know" who they are or cannot integrate the various aspects of his or her personality. In Freud's (1991, 135) view, for example, identity is bound up with difference within communal affiliations in the sense that it is not only about identifying with an other but also about subsuming or even consuming the other to make it part of one's own ego. In other words, identity in this version of psychoanalysis acknowledges difference, but this difference is surmounted in order to ensure inner consistency. Subsequent psychoanalytic investigations of identity are either founded on this belief in identity as a marker of psychological consistency or they critique it (e.g., Jacques Lacan and Julia Kristeva).

But unlike the more abstract concepts of subjectivity and individuality, identity did not become part of political theories of the social order because its scientific meaning of "sameness" affixed it, as a term, to what Foucault might call *techne* – minor practices that, at the beginning of the twentieth century, signified what kind of subject one was and what one's place in the world was (as indicated by one's external affiliations). So we find that, by 1900, identity is signified by an attribute that serves to show that a person is the *same* person as is indicated by certain means of identification – such as an identity bracelet, identity papers, or a patch (*OED Online* 2001a). Therefore, identity became part of a series of metonymic substitutions that tie material facts of belonging to consciousness. The proper name or photograph of a person *is* the essence of that person because it makes his/her body *authentic;* it returns the name of a person to his/her body because the thing stands in for the body itself. That is why *techne* of identity make it possible to know the place of a person in the social order and to identify that with his/her "inner" self or consciousness of self: his/her signature, social insurance number, or yellow star of David *stands in* for the self within a web of social markers. The marks of identity either make it possible for a person to have agency in a given system, or – in the case of the star of David during the Nazi regime – make it impossible. This metonymic property of identity signifies essences while relying on non-essential modes of signification to claim that essences and their material guarantees have the same effects. This is how identity is understood to be connected to the material conditions that determine the existence of a person.

These two senses of identity now create a certain amount of confusion. Locke's original sense of identity as the essential sameness of a person and the sense of identity as part of the external factors that tie inner consciousness to the outer world work to confuse the meaning of "identity." This is particularly true as poststructuralist critiques of the Romantic idea of a unified self, unique and existing separately from cultural conditions, have asserted either (1) that the self is determined by social practices or (2) that language does not "reflect" or "reveal" a self but, rather, constructs it (Pile and Thrift 1995). Poststructuralist critiques of this type would seem to indicate that what is being discussed is identity; however, they also call into question identity's other meaning (as "identical" in a psychological sense). Therefore, unlike the term "subjectivity," which has been associated with a specific critique of how personhood is understood in philosophy and the social sciences (see Foucault, Althusser, Lacan, Derrida, de Man, and others), the term "identity" has been used by critics who want to unite materialist political critiques with psychoanalytic or metaphysical ideas about desire and personhood. This is an attempt to "return" identity to a discussion of the social order and how one "knows" oneself within that order. Identity's metonymic function serves to explain how different "identity categories" (such as race, gender, class, sexuality, and religion) can work in non-essentialist ways to construct personhood. The concept of identity can also be used as a way to explain how a person can be formed by social forces and yet have the agency to be able to work against social inequities. Judith Butler's (1990, 24-25) discussion of gender identity is an example of this: for her, gender identity is innately performative because it involves a repetition of norms that act as returns, rather than exact identifications, and these effects are what produce identity. Therefore, identity "feels" essential but is in fact discursive and, therefore, open to a questioning of norms that can facilitate political change (Butler 1993, 30).

This type of move, however, places identity on the same plane as subjectivity, which means that at times these terms are used interchangeably despite the confusion involved in identity's double meanings. This confusion raises the problem of agency: how can a person "choose" identities when identity itself is constructed? Is identity formed outside the body by others, or is it still related to Locke's "unity of consciousness," now understood as the ability to construct it? For example, Teresa de Lauretis argues for a non-essentialist understanding of identity as a group of elements that do not cohere. In other words, she argues for "a multiple, shifting and often self-contradicting identity, a subject that is not divided in, but rather at odds with, language; an identity made of heterogeneous and heteronomous representations of gender, race, and class and often indeed across languages and cultures; an identity that one decides to reclaim from a history of multiple assimilations and that one insists upon as strategy" (de Lauretis 1986, 9). De Lauretis refers to identity as consisting of multiple, shifting, and inconsistent elements, but she also refers to dis/identification as connected to the relationship between the subject and language, and, via an agency that makes one "reclaim" identities as a strategy, she returns identity to the idea of sameness. In order to make identity part of politics, its quality as a collection of *practices* fits well. Still, it is hard to let go of identity's association with verisimilitude because, without it, identity cannot be understood to be a strategy within multiple positions created by difference.[3]

So, with Stuart Hall (1996), we could ask, "who needs 'identity'" in the wake of anti-essentialist critiques of ethnic, racial, and national conceptions of identity and its vicissitudes? Hall's answer to this question, although he too admits that the complex histories of identity as a concept are yet to be fully worked out (16), is to affirm the political importance of identity and to talk about it as a set of regulating practices for subjectivity that create temporary affiliations within it: "I use 'identity' to refer to the meeting point, the point of *suture,* between on the one hand the discourses and practices which attempt to 'interpellate,' speak to us or hail into place as the social subjects of particular discourses, and on the other hand, the processes which produce subjectivities, which construct us as subjects which can be 'spoken.' Identities are thus points of temporary attachment to the subject positions which discursive practices construct for us" (5-6). However, as Hall says later, during his discussion of Althusser and interpellation, efforts to see identity as fractured and yet as part of a necessary fictive and temporary unity with subject positions do little to resolve the ambiguity inherent in the term's uneasy position between psychoanalysis and social theory.

One other way to work through "identity" as a term is to acknowledge that its ambiguity is part of its advantage if it is unhooked from the Western preoccupation with identity as part of the creation of individual, free "selves." Outside of the West's assumption that "everyone" has an unconscious in a way that is both the same as but different from that of all others, how does identity function? Are there, in Althusser's sense, "bad subjects"[4] that cannot be interpellated because they cannot hear the call of (Western) ideologies concerning what it is to be a person? In anthropology, the work of Marcel Mauss represents an early way to think about how the idea of personhood need not depend on psychic relations between inside and outside, consciousness and the unconscious, but, rather, on other articulations of identity that depend on group affiliation and recognition that exist *before* individual identities. Mauss works out a way to understand what he calls *personnage* (role or persona) as the way in which many societies understand essence. A person is a person in a given society because of the role that he or she plays (Mauss 1985, 12) not because of any pre-given essence. Mauss goes on to say that he thinks that selfhood worked in ancient India and China in this performative way. He then discusses how the Etruscans and then the Romans developed the idea of a "persona," or mask, which they associated with naming practices, with people being acknowledged to be human because of the names and titles they held (12-16). Mauss's view of selfhood-in-relation altered with the influence of Christianity and, later, psychology, changing the import of *personnage* to *moi* (the self). This change shows how, in the West, individualism became associated with personhood (22). The purpose of Mauss's discussion is to show that the development of Western thinking about the person is just as affected by communal and institutional ways of understanding selfhood as is the development of thinking about the person in other cultures. What is important here is that Mauss indicates, long before poststructuralism, that psychology has a history and that there are ways of understanding how identity works that do not depend on psychic relations between outside and inside. In fact, he clearly states that psychological notions related to individuality and personhood are recent developments (3). Although he makes very broad generalizations about the Zuñi, the people of ancient China, and the Haida, his assumption that all people have ways of formulating what an individual is and how individuals should interact appears to be a way of understanding how identity can work as a way of recognizing otherness and communal relations without assuming that otherness must be subsumed. In Mauss's sense, institutions such as proper names, religious ceremonies, and other external identity markers can construct identity as *techne*, while "consciousness" can be located in these *techne* (or in group recognition of the work that such *techne* performs) rather than in an unconscious (or "personality") that exists outside of cultural considerations.

As Stuart Hall (1996) suggests, much of the theorizing about identity and its relationship to the subject could be the result of a "compulsive Eurocentrism." Identity, in its dual senses of identification within difference and identification against it, is a term that can be used to look at how identity has been thought outside the dualities of psychological and social identity formation upon which so much Western thought depends. If autobiography is an identity technology that has been thought to depend upon those very Western formations of "personality," "the self," and "personhood," then what happens when people who are not formed primarily by these discourses decide to use them? What other kinds of agency are there, and what kinds of negotiation with dominant epistemologies do their practitioners undertake? When is autobiography used by people with conceptions of identity that do not hold individuality as primary? What is won and what is lost in the negotiation for identity? I now turn to a discussion of the complex history of autobiography criticism in order to show how critical discourse about autobiography, and the difficulty of understanding how autobiography works generically, has both participated in and critiqued identity's difficult history in the West. It is this history into which, as "bad subjects" who do not play by the rules of Western consciousness or Western economics, the Doukhobors enter and find tools for negotiating identity and what can be remembered.

The Order of Things: Unpacking (My) Library

One day, while I was researching autobiography theory in a university library, I discovered a relationship between the way autobiography has been catalogued and the critical shifts in theory and criticism of autobiography during the last twenty-five years. Tired of running up and down flights of stairs searching for books that seemed to be shelved all over the building, I went to the Library of Congress classification index to find out how autobiography, a genre that has resisted many attempts at definition, has been classified. I found that a shift in library classification mirrored a disciplinary shift in autobiography studies – autobiography as part of historical inquiry had shifted to autobiography as part of literary studies. This can be seen in the movement of major critical texts on autobiography since the 1970s: from the CT 25 section of the Library of Congress classification system (under history), to the HQ section (women's studies), to the PR section (under British literature) and, in large numbers, to the earlier PS sections (under American literary criticism).

The move of texts from history to literary studies and, especially, to American literary studies reflects a change in the way theorists have conceived the relationship of subjectivity to text. The epistemology that informs these changes in classification has generated a cycle of inquiry that led autobiography studies away from history, where the subject of autobiography was assumed to have value only because it was a "real" subject discussing actual events, to literary studies, where the "ordering imperative" of the subject assumed primary importance and the text of autobiography no longer seemed to be the unreflective product of its author (although the "self" of the author still seemed to some to be the subject and the object of narrative). Since the advent of politically motivated forms of inquiry in the fields of women's studies, African-American studies, and Native studies (to name only a few), the study of autobiography is once again returning to historical epistemologies. But this return is not a "pure" return to the discipline of history. Informed by interdisciplinary approaches that reference developments in cultural studies and critical theory, this return not only questions the ahistorical and apolitical relationships of autobiographical subjects to narrative but also questions autobiography's economy of "auto-bio-graphe" (self-life-writing), which James Olney (1980, 19) suggests is the only form that autobiographical discourse can take.

This last shift towards radicalizing the politics of autobiographical form coincided with autobiography's movement to certain areas of American studies and the study of subjectivity and its relationship to the making of nations. PS 366, the designation for American autobiography, also records this shift. PS 366 occupies a subsection called "American Literature – Special Topics." Other topics in the classification include: Afro-Americans, Mentally Handicapped, Sexual Perversion, Social Problems, Mexican-Americans, Swindlers and Swindling, and Wisdom. The Library of Congress's decision to classify autobiography as an other among these "others" serves to reinscribe its status as a marginal literature about (and by) people whose work would also fall under the other designations in "Special Topics." It also defines autobiography studies as American, which makes it hard to take account of the development of autobiography studies in other countries, including China, Germany, Canada, and Australia.[5]

Despite the proliferation of theory and criticism of autobiography since the mid-1980s, much of it challenging the idea that autobiographical writing can ever constitute an agreed-upon genre, autobiography theory still occupies a minor place in the general theory and criticism of literary studies. It is a blurry field that exceeds the boundaries of what is acceptable to studies of literature. Autobiography, as it is now studied, is neither history nor fiction. It is also both.

The Publicly Private Subject:
Autobiography Criticism and Its Origins

Because of the emergence of politically aware theories of identity, Olney's (1980, 22) dream of autobiography as a territory that can be "secured" for literary studies and rescued from history has not materialized. This emergence occurred because autobiography studies shifted from a dependence on earlier, canonized models of a psychologized, internalized "self" that can represent the consciousness of an epoch to an understanding of identity as positional, political, and contextual. Following initial work by feminist scholars, theorists are now examining autobiography by autobiographers who have not been part of the naturalization of Western "selfhood" constructed by conditions including (but not limited to) property ownership, masculinity, whiteness, European languages, an assumption of a shared Christian heritage, and literacy. These studies are beginning to change what has been considered legitimate autobiography, who autobiographers can be, and how what Linda Hutcheon has called "ex-centric" national subjects[6] use aspects of autobiographical discourse in order to write and speak themselves (often under the mark of difference) as subjects into the very discourse that excludes them.

This study of Doukhobor autobiographical discourse situates itself within the context of these developing areas of inquiry without cancelling out the work on the subject of autobiography that the more recent approaches critique. Thus I move beyond Olney's figure of "auto-bio-graphe" as the pure discourse of a single author's written life "captured" for literary study without denying the power of that discourse in the Western world. This is important because, as Laura Marcus (1994, 223) has observed, the recent accommodations that autobiography theory has made for complex models of identity from identity politics may be able to make use of the previous debates about the ideal subject in deconstructionist and humanist critical discourse concerning autobiography. As poststructural theory becomes more closely associated with other inquiry in postcolonial studies, feminist theory, sexuality studies, and race/ethnicity theory, considerations about subjectivity within deconstruction and psychoanalysis can be placed in critical tension with considerations about group identity, politics, and culture in ways that are able to recast what can be thought about the inheritance of metaphysics and its relationship to the flow of power. Autobiographical discourse, whether it is part of a "canon" of study or whether it is on a type of margin, is a place where the genealogy of the liberal subject can be tracked, challenged, and remade as autobiography, and where the conditions of its production are taken up by a variety of writers and speakers for tactical purposes.

Autobiography Theory and Power

When James Olney (1988, 8) says, "in the beginning, then, was Georges Gusdorf," he imparts the authority of the Judeo-Christian creation story to a European philosopher who also owes a profound debt to Dilthey and Misch. Other critics, with the qualified exception of Sidonie Smith,[7] accepted Olney's statements without questioning them. Subsequent critiques tend to reinculcate the generic foundations of autobiography because it is assumed that the connection between self and text still holds; it is just that the wrong selves have been given primacy. The result can be an essentialism of autobiography which only recognizes that writers of autobiography write *themselves* into existence in certain ways. An assumption like this does not call into question the properties of genre which made the autobiography canon and its margins real to critics in the first place. Leigh Gilmore's (1994a, xiii) point that writers placed outside the genre "are always somehow 'found' on the margins, the margins being construed as a 'place' quite literally without a history," should serve as a warning to critics who wish to recoup so-called marginalized writers into a genre without thinking about the implications of marginality for autobiography itself. The critical terrain of autobiography must be recognized as a place that has not remained static.

This autobiographical selfhood, which must underwrite autobiography in the mould of Augustine, Rousseau, Goethe, and Montaigne (to name a few), is *not* described as public in the way that Sidonie Smith and others have assumed; instead, Georg Misch, one of the earliest theorists of autobiography, assumes that good autobiography features a radical interiority of the subject influenced by Romanticism, with its emphasis on self-discovery and self-reflection.[8] Memoirs, he concludes, "offer a passive relation to the world," while in autobiographies the life story is central and active (Marcus 1994, 149), a distinction repeated often in autobiographical criticism. Most feminist critics have assumed that traditional autobiographical discourse is masculinist because it is public, the record of great men. This understanding of women's writings as irreducibly private if they do not repeat this masculinist discourse conflicts with the conflation of autobiography with Romantic subjectivity – a conflation made by Misch (1950) and, after him, by Gusdorf (1980; 1991). The difficulty is that the interiority of the Romantic subject, who turns away from historical concerns in order to "reflect" on the self's uniqueness and, in so doing, captures through its coherence (not correspondence) the spirit of the age, is an elite subject whose being is guaranteed not by the writing of a text but, rather, by social conditions that allow such a narrative of interiority to take place.

This is why memoir has not been discussed much in autobiographical criticism and theory until recently. Its very publicity has been held by some to be creatively inferior within a cultural milieu in which the assertion of subjectivity is held to be paramount, while narratives of interiority are critiqued as public narratives of worthy authors whose lives guarantee the success of their writings. However, memoir's tendency to not be just about an individual may make it the most important autobiographical form at the millennium in what Gilmore (2001) refers to as the American "culture of confession." It may even be an important form for women because, as Helen Buss (2001) has recently claimed, it does not rely on the notion of the individual as sealed off from historical influences.

When ethnic minority writers and speakers use the memoir form, the publicity of memoir discourse can work to eliminate the division between self and other that forms the basis for gendered, racial, and cultural exploitation as part of discourses about difference. Because subjectivity in a memoir is constructed in terms of the *events* a subject witnesses or affects rather than in terms of a radical interiority guaranteed by "culture" or "history," memoir forms can allow for constructions of subjectivity that differ from those usually authorized by dominant discourses. The memoir form can combine with what Caren Kaplan has called "outlaw" narrative forms to create new forms that strategically construct alternative public subjects visible to non-members of the oppressed group – forms that do not compromise that group's difference. Examples of these are the Latin American *testimonio* described by John Beverly (1992), the Holocaust survivor narrative, and the Doukhobor witness narrative.

As Leigh Gilmore (2001, 38) says, memoir does not have to be resolved into the confessional form, although this can leave the readers without an "authority" whose version of events can be trusted. I would add that the memoir form's history as a "public" form gives people who have been denied the right to interiority – who would be considered unable to confess anything or whose testimony would not be believed – access to authority in the public sphere without the need of a private self that must make the journey from private to public in order to be believed.

The "Problem" of Genre, the Subject of Autobiography
In autobiography theory, Roy Pascal, along with Wayne Shumaker, is credited as one of the first theorists to construct a systemic view of the genre along with a historically based canon of texts and an understanding of autobiography's aesthetic properties. His work *Design and Truth in Autobiography* (Pascal 1960) is positivist in that it is based on a large list of texts that he arranges into rigid categories. Although Pascal has been criticized for creating a critical hierarchy of autobiography that uses as models narratives by Western men, his most difficult legacy is something else. What is problematic about Pascal's study is its construction of an epistemology that "admits" certain autobiographers into the charmed circle of typology excluding, not on the direct basis of gender, race, nation, and class, but on the *body of knowledge* a writing subject was supposed to produce as part of autobiography's formation as a genre. These knowledge structures become increasingly ritualized after Pascal's initial work in the area. In his work we see the struggle for an epistemology that represents dominant discourse so that autobiography can "be" a genre; we also see clear evidence of the subsequent difficulties critics had with the relationship between the writer of autobiography and the subject of autobiographical narrative.

Pascal begins with his concern that the form of autobiography needs to be defined – a clear act of genre building in order to place autobiography on par with forms such as poetry or the novel (2-3). Following Misch (1950), Pascal decides that the source of individual life is spiritual and is found in the identification of "personality." Autobiography is a record of the personality rather than of verisimilitude (Pascal 1960, 7-8). Like Gusdorf, Pascal is able to lift autobiography from the realm of history so that autobiographical success (truth) can be found in the structure of the narrative (design) and its evocation of "personality," which happens wherever humanist constructions of subjectivity occur. "Personality" is communicated successfully through the text when the reading public can discern a correspondence between inner and outer life. In a statement that encapsulates the struggle autobiography critics have had when they have tried to define (or deconstruct) autobiography as a genre, Pascal refers to the correspondence between design and truth as a correspondence between the written subject of autobiography and the "non-textual" subject. He attempts to resolve the disjuncture as an instance of doubling when he says that "the autobiographer has in fact a double character. He exists to some degree as an object, a man recognisable from outside ... but he is also the subject" (Pascal 1960, 71). Here, Pascal admits – although he does not inquire much further – that once the historicity of a subject is questioned, the problem of autobiography becomes the unmanageability of the "inside" narrative and the "outside" subject. How can one keep the "inside" inside and the "outside" outside so that "truth" is communicated? Pascal decides that this balance is achieved by means of three things: critical judgement, "correct" publicity, and the need for a narrative shape determined by publicity. Critical judgement, which also serves to enshrine the importance of the autobiography critic, depends on an awareness of inside/outside communications between text and life and an ability to "choose" the classics in terms of this balance and coherence, a re-reading of Dilthey in terms of critical taste. Therefore, autobiographies by mystics fail as "true" autobiography because their composition of the subject is too "interior," while memoirs fail, predictably, because they are too public and are not focused enough on the personality (Pascal 1960, 9). The best autobiographies, it seems, are by men and women "of outstanding achievement in life" (10) who communicate an understanding of the subject as formed by history but grounded in narrative design.

This opens the way for an autobiographical canon to be constructed in which the texts may refer to each other and to Pascal's aesthetic categories without reference to the historic sets of authorizations that enable these autobiographers to write themselves as subjects. Pascal's canon, therefore, begins with Augustine and then moves to Benjamin Franklin, to Rousseau, to Wordsworth, and culminates with Goethe, from whom he borrows the title of his own study. Although Pascal leaves room for women "of achievement" in his bibliography, which concludes *Design and Truth,* the requirements for a balance between reflection and public activity, on the one hand, eliminate alternative autobiographical forms, while on the other hand the model for public activity – "achievement" – becomes conflated with a cultural memory of achievement that excludes women. Women enter this retrospective discourse of fame not as women but, rather, as those who have negotiated this discourse successfully due to other "advantages." Therefore, after Pascal, autobiographies by Virginia Woolf, Mary MacCarthy, Gertrude Stein, Zora Neal Hurston, Saint Theresa, and Maxine Hong Kingston do get discussed by autobiography critics but not in terms of the epistemological specificity (and struggle) bound up with issues faced by those who do not wholly participate in the dominant narratives of Western identity outlined by Pascal.

Finally, Pascal's (1960, 185) requirement for coherent narrative, although it has been read as an endorsement of the untroubled liberal subject, points out the difficulties of asserting narrativity and experience as mutually determinate: "what is important [in autobiography is that it] has to have a shape, an outward shape in the narrative, and this shape is the outcome of an interpenetration and collusion of inner and outer life, of the person and society. The shape interprets both." Pascal's insistence on shape as the way to heal the inner/outer split between text and life only serves to problematize the split for, in his formulation, it is the shape that somehow "interprets": there are no reading communities and no difficulties with the transference of "experience" into writing, difficulties that are raised by later critics concerned with psychoanalysis, textuality, and the gender of autobiographical subjects. At the moment of canon building, when the referentiality of the autobiographical subject should be the most secure, Pascal's resolution serves to undermine that referentiality since it gives the power of interpretation to form, not content, and to the text only. Subsequent movements in critical theory would further undermine this attempt to keep inside and outside, self and community, text and life, writer and reader firmly in their places, and this made the creation of fixed autobiography canons impossible while also frustrating attempts to codify autobiography as a genre.

One of the results of this difficulty with the referentiality of the autobiographical text was what is now known as the work of the New Model theorists. Although their work does not amount to that of a critical school, New Model theorists, including John Sturrock, James Olney, Paul Jay, Paul John Eakin, Janet Varner Gunn, and, most recently, Robert Folkenflik, have stressed that autobiography study should not be tied to history but, rather, to the process of memory and its written reproductions. This position stresses that the narrative of autobiography does not and should not represent historically received models of life narrative but, rather, should correspond ontologically with the experience of "life as lived" (Eakin

1985, 5). Sturrock (1977, 54), for example, claims that autobiography "has everything to learn" from psychoanalysis and therefore should depart from historical chronology to take on the trappings of fiction, while Paul Jay (1984, 25) claims that autobiography is a "talking cure," a therapeutic narrative that elides the split between self and text through the act of narration. James Olney (1980, 19) summarizes this move when he explains that New Model critics have shifted the focus from "bios," a reflective telling of the life story, to "auto," the autobiographical self created/discovered/reflected through the telling of life as story.

But "graphe," the problem of writing and referral, largely remains untheorized in Olney's reading, and with good reason. The insistence of some New Model theorists that some type of autobiographical "consciousness" could be accurately communicated via narrative does not usually include a discussion of language's power to refer. This difficulty raises a series of questions about narrativity, genre, and subjectivity, which, with varying degrees of success, New Model theorists have attempted to resolve. Does, for example, the structure of narration "reproduce" autobiographical memory from a pre-existing subject, or does the narrative itself "produce" autobiographical identity, which corresponds to an extratextual self, through patterns of experience only? And if autobiography is really about consciousness and the manipulation of quasi-fictive elements, is it a true genre separate from fiction? Here is where the interests of the New Model theorists combine with aspects of phenomenology in complex attempts to resolve the splits between narrative, self, and life. Some critics grounded the autobiographical self in a type of "consciousness," although it became difficult to say whether consciousness was located in "experience" or narrative. Grounding consciousness in experience led to phenomenological readings that created essentialist relationships between self and form: form is ontological function (Eakin 1985, 34). Grounding consciousness in "narrative" led critics such as Janet Varner Gunn and James Olney to either affirm that consciousness *is* narrative but not in a poststructuralist sense (Olney 1972, 30-34) or that narrative manifests the same "deep structures" found in consciousness, a turn towards phenomenology that attempts to mend the gap between fictional and autobiographical structures by stating that autobiography is an act of reading (Gunn 1982, 15-17).

However, as in the case of phenomenological readings in other areas, this type of approach depends upon a subject insulated from a contextual set that constructs it. The self always operates independently of place or time, while it insists on absolute agency through consciousness: the self knows itself, understands itself, and acts independently of textual constructions that "it" also creates. And in autobiography theory generally, this type of phenomenological reading has given rise to debates about the "fictionality" of autobiography. If autobiography is really about the self constructing a narrative of its own symbolizations, then what is the difference between autobiography and fictional first-person narratives? This is one of the reasons that Olney makes a case for autobiography's undecidability as a genre, a position taken up by many subsequent theorists (Olney 1980, 4-5).

Autobiography as Product

One of the more rigorous ways in which the questions of narrative, subjectivity, and genre have been addressed in New Model theory occurs as part of structuralism. In *Le pact autobiographique,* a term that supports Benveniste's contention that the writing subject and the written subject of autobiography may not entirely refer (1971), Philippe Lejeune (1989) attempts to narrow the question of autobiographical genre to a matter of the validity of the author's "signature." Although humanists and post-structuralists have criticized Lejeune for doing this, he remains the only theorist to deal with autobiography as a mode of identity production tied to the realm of publishing. This consideration is important since it stresses the fact that autobiography is not only a literary enterprise but also a discourse that participates in capitalist enterprise. Although Lejeune did not pursue this line of inquiry, his study of the signature does indicate that autobiographical identities have a use-value that enables autobiographical narrative to circulate in the public realm. This aspect of autobiographical discourse has been useful for minority writers and speakers who can use the publicity of the discourse to gain visibility as subjects. But the use-value of autobiography can potentially work against these subjects by constructing their identities as exotic, "other" commodities. This difficulty can be found in Doukhobor autobiographical discourse.

Like Lejeune, Elizabeth Bruss (1976, 11) uses aspects of linguistic theory, in her case taken from Austin and Searle, to create a definition of autobiography as an illocutionary act in which the author and the protagonist are the same person. Bruss's formalist stance with respect to genre obscures her interesting observations about autobiographical discourse as a cultural product. Her comments echo Lejeune's focus on autobiography as a cultural product. Bruss recognizes that "conceptions of individual identity are articulated, extended and developed through an institution like autobiography" (5). Her statement indicates that autobiography is an institution that has created discursive rules for identity formation at the same time as it has participated in identity constructions in Western cultures. In the same vein, Bruss observes that autobiography as a genre is produced by "implicit contextual conditions" circulating in culture, including the emergence of bourgeois subjectivity in the developing novel form during the eighteenth century in Britain and Europe. In a rare moment of cross-disciplinary thinking, which anticipates the role the study of auto-biography would play in the development of cultural studies, Bruss's discussion of autobiography as a cultural-linguistic act bridges the gap, articulated by the New Model theorists, between text and life by refiguring autobiography as an instance of linguistic identity formation occurring simultaneously in other discourses.

Bruss's and Lejeune's ideas about autobiographical discourse have not gained wide currency, perhaps because the referentiality of the autobiographical subject became the battle-ground between phenomenological/humanist approaches and poststructuralist approaches to the idea of the subject. Olney (1980) opposed poststructuralism in the introduction to his 1980 collection, following Gusdorf's (1975, 58) more blunt dismissal, in which he says that deconstructionist critiques of autobiography are conducting an autopsy on the death of liberal man. An important article by Paul de Man (1979), "Autobiography as De-facement," served to focus the debate in autobiography studies on the question of the ability of the autobiographical subject to refer. De Man dispenses with genre-construction, calling it an impossible task, and links deconstruction as firmly to the dissolution of the Romantic autobiographical subject as phenomenological humanists linked it to the Romantic subject's "discovery" of identity as a creative project. Most notably, de Man's essay records the subject/object split observed by other critics of autobiography, from Gusdorf to Lejeune; however, unlike other theorists, he refuses to resolve the split in terms of authorial intention, the operation of generic "types," or even, in the broad sense, the activity of the reader.

De Man begins his discussion by pointing out that attempts to make autobiography into a genre in order to give it a place "among the canonical hierarchies of the major literary genres" (19) fail in part due to the undecidability of autobiography's origins and to the intersection of other "laws" of genre concerning what constitutes poetic language and autobiographical form: "we assume that life *produces* the autobiography as an act produces its consequences, but can we not suggest, with equal justice, that the autobiographical project may itself produce and determine the life and that whatever the writer *does* is in fact governed by the technical demands of self-portraiture and thus determined, in all its aspects, by the resources of his medium?" (920).

If either aspect of the autobiographical "economy" can circulate an image of subjectivity, "autobiography, then, is not a genre or a mode, but a figure of reading or of understanding that occurs, to some degree, in all texts" – a figure that occurs as a specular moment of mutual substitution on the part of two subjects within a network of tropes signifying subjectivity even as they signify an attempt to escape the tropes that constitute it (de Man 1979, 921-23). For de Man, this set of ceaseless tropic substitutions prevents the possibility of referral. The figure of *prosopopeia,* the address to a voice-less or dead entity that posits the possibility of the reply of what is mute, is for him the trope of autobiography, making autobiography the sign not of life but, rather, of death due to the ceaseless circulation of life-tropes defacing any attempt to do anything but represent the un-representable (930). The moment of reading, therefore, occurs only in a recognition that one's own status in that economy is tropic because one's own figures of recognition are also tropic. Autobiography is mute. The split between sub-ject and object, the "I" who speaks and the "eye" that sees the "speaking," cannot be surmounted.

De Man's devastating critique of attempts to codify autobiography as a genre has been alternately welcomed, vilified, and ignored as naive be-cause it de-historicizes subjectivity at the expense of those whose repre-sentational status cannot be disfigured because it has never been figured. However, as Marcus (1994, 207) points out, Mary Jacobus has revised de Man's narrow paradigm of mutually displacing speculativeness to reading as a performative moment between reader and autobiographer that is also "an act of generic ascription whereby textual and epistemological instabil-ity or hybridity are neutralised, and, in the conflation of generic type and of character, the text is both given a recognisable generic home and at the same time stabilised as the utterance of a coherent subject, authorised by the proper name." Jacobus (1984) is actually revising Lejeune in order to revise de Man, thus linking autobiography as a discourse of the proper name to the act of reading. This grounds her discussion politically. *Pros-opopeia* is not the figure that operates as the abject preventing speech but a figure of correspondence that allows historically recognizable strategies of identity-formation to take place. In this way, reading does not guaran-tee genre but, rather, positions genre and subjectivity for strategic pur-poses within interpretive communities.

Mary Jacobus's reinterpretation of de Man's evocation of reading indi-cates what the legacy of deconstruction is in terms of current autobiogra-phy theory. When de Man's theory of reading is combined with Derrida's formulation of autobiography as guaranteed through the ear of the *other* – the reader, who signs and authorizes (Derrida 1985, 51) – it is possible to conceive of the existence of reading communities who read the tropes of autobiographical identity *differently* from the ways proscribed and pre-scribed by the canonic figures of Romanticism. The "auto" of autobiogra-phy cannot exist, not because it talks to itself but because it cannot exist without (an)other to authorize it. This difference changes the relationship between subjectivity and trope. For writers operating outside dominant identity discourses, this opens up the autobiographical subject to multiple readings and reconstructions since identity has been situated as other (or others) by the discourse of identity that de Man critiques. The legacy of deconstruction, then, is the possibility it offers of multiple subject positions constructed within autobiography rhetoric rather than its insistence on autobiographical tropism as the necessary death of all subjects. Marcus's (1994, 201) comments on the impact of 1970s deconstruction are appropriate here: "what seems to have emerged from this process [of poststructural critique of the subject] is a stronger sense of the plurality and the social construction of subjectivities and, possibly, a shift from concepts of 'subjectivity' to those of 'identity' and 'difference,' concepts less philosophically burdened and more overtly attuned to culture and history." This sense that the subject could be plural, multiple, and socially constructed has moved the study of autobiography away from attempts to bridge gaps between self, text, and life and linked it to other forms of cultural production. Kathleen Ashley's (1994, 7) statements reflect this shift when she observes that the "disappearance" of the subject may herald multiple tropic identifications in autobiography: "what writings of autobiography are possible when the autonomous self is not the privileged speaker, when the mark of autobiography – the I – may designate a place from which to speak, an authority in some discourses and not others, the signature of self-representation wherever it appears?"

Michael M.J. Fischer, an anthropologist who refigures anthropology's long use of the "life history" through postmodern theory, affirms the importance of multivocality in autobiography and its connection to other cultural forms. He refers to the use of a multiple subject as strategic: "But perhaps the most important use of life histories, increasingly so in the contemporary world, is the strategic use of a life frame that straddles major social and cultural transformations" (Fischer 1994, 82). When these observations about the possibilities of a multiple subject that can strategically occupy many discourses become combined with politically motivated theories of autobiography, autobiographical writing and speaking by those who have not been participants in grand narratives of self can be read as a series of identity-consolidation strategies that critique those narratives even as they make use of some of their elements. These developments mark autobiography theory's final move away from the "problem" of genre and classification and towards examinations of autobiography as part of culture – a discourse situated within other cultural discourses that construct and are constructed by many conditions of subjectivity.

The Subject of Gender, the Gendered Subject: Women's Autobiography Theory

In his introduction to his 1980 collection, *Autobiography: Essays Theoretical and Critical,* James Olney wrote that the advent of politically grounded interdisciplinary fields of enquiry should be linked to autobiography criticism and theory. For Olney (1980, 12-13), autobiography could even become the "focalizing literature" for these fields, which he decided needed a centre to provide privileged access to a unique experience. Since Olney assumed an unproblematized relationship between the subject and language, autobiography could function metonymically as national subjectivity. Although the difficulties with this thinking have become obvious, Olney makes a case for considering autobiography as a cultural product and, in its linkage of place and subject, a way of understanding the history of oppressed people: "To understand the American mind in all its complexity – so goes the argument – read a variety of American autobiographies ... the student who sees autobiography as the central document possesses something very like a key to all the other literature as well" (14). This view of autobiography's usefulness presents it as inextricably linked to an Americanist ideology of bourgeois individualism, self-reliance, and uniqueness, a view perpetuated in the work of many Americanists. Albert E. Stone (1982, 9), for example, links autobiography to American individualism: "the individualist ideal continues to inspire many twentieth-century Americans, especially when they participate in autobiographical occasions as authors and audiences. [These authors] therefore exhibit their shared belief not only in *individualism* as a common cultural value but also in *identity* as a vital personal achievement." Stone's belief that American individualism closely matches autobiographical imperatives neglects Robert F. Sayre's (1980, 147) point that autobiography in America is a commodity within an industry of identity within which citizenship and identity become part of the same ideal, creating "the identification of autobiography *in* America *with* America."

But Olney's list of "likely" texts for study does indicate that there will be room for contesting narratives, even contested "Americas," within the paradigm since he includes autobiographies of Booker T. Washington, Malcolm X, Frederick Douglass, Olaudah Equiano, Richard Wright, and Maya Angelou (among others). And in this sense, Olney was correct in thinking that autobiography would be pivotal, particularly within Americanist modes of inquiry in the disciplines of women's studies, American studies, African-American studies, Native-American studies, and Chicano/Chicana studies. What occurred, however, was a shift from the debates about the referentiality of the subject to politically contextualized readings of identity as it appears in narratives produced by writers whose identities exclude them from participating in dominant constructions of the subject.

In the area of women's autobiography, for instance, considerations of gendered subjectivity first meant that the autobiographical canon was revised and that an alternate tradition of women's autobiography was established, with the latter taking into account the position of women as other within Western traditions. Other scholars recovered non-traditional and "illegitimate" forms of autobiography or self-writing – letters, diaries, and memoirs – theorizing that women tend to choose disrupted, discontinuous, and private forms (such as diaries and letters) in which to express themselves rather than the public form of autobiography with its (ostensibly) centred subject (Walker 1988; Nussbaum 1988a). Consideration of these alternative autobiographical forms, as Celeste Schenck (1988) observes, led many critics to notice how divisions of genre are in fact gendered, marking off the "major" genres as the preserve of male writers. These latter genres are to be kept free of contamination by those "others" not authorized to participate in the discourse as valid subjects capable of using the accepted forms of expression.

Despite critiques of androcentric assumptions about the idea of genre that began to appear in some feminist work, much of the earlier feminist criticism of women's autobiography argued for the inclusion of women's autobiographical productions in the autobiography canon along with the alternative framings of knowledge they contained. At first, these were described by paradigms of lack or failure due to the gendered split between public and private spheres, with the autobiography criticism tradition presented as that of the single male author successfully surmounting, on his own, obstacles in public life without referring to private difficulties or to others (namely, women) who helped him on his vocational way. Mary G. Mason (1980, 210), for example, claimed that women's life-writing "seems to acknowledge the real presence and recognition of another's consciousness, and the disclosure of female self is linked to the identification of some 'other.'" And Carolyn Heilbrun (1988, 25) wrote that women who live the male "quest plot," which emphasizes public achievement alone, "succeed" in narrative only by chance or as exceptions to this (gendered) rule.

By the latter half of the 1980s, these paradigms of failure had been revised as an alternative set of narrations that indicate how women's essential nature is defined by means of interaction with others as community, which admits splits between self/other and subject/object that autobiographies by men do not. To this end, critics such as Susan Stanford Friedman (1988) and Shari Benstock (1988) use aspects of the psychoanalytic theories of Lacan and Chodorow, and theories of community by Rowbotham, to indicate how women experience split subjectivities that enable them to formulate alternatives to the Law of the Father as selves-in-community. The formation of these alternative "selves" went hand-in-hand with a critique of autobiography criticism that linked Gusdorf's, Pascal's, and Olney's version of autobiography with patriarchal discourse, as in the introduction of Brodzki and Schenck's (1988, 1) *Life/Lines*: "the (masculine) tradition of autobiography beginning with Augustine had taken as its first premise the mirror capacity of the autobiographer: *his* universality, *his* representativeness, *his* role as spokesman for the community." These critics make an important point: autobiographers whose subjectivities fall outside the singularity of the subject as a "self" can construct multiple identities, in community, against hegemonic (and in this case patriarchal) subject formations privileged in liberal discourses of the individual. Shari Benstock (1988, 19-20), for instance, attacks Olney and Gusdorf's investment in the coherence of the autobiographical subject and assumes that the stability they assign to autobiographies by men "stabilizes" over time. Her argument collapses autobiography theory and its texts into a single rhetoric of male selfhood. Friedman (1988, 34-35) also critiques Gusdorf and Olney for creating a "model of separate and unique selfhood" that "ignore[s] the role of collective and relational identities in the individuation process of women and minorities."

One of the most important contributions of feminist autobiography theory after this point is in the connection theorists have made between the genealogy of the discourse of the subject and issues of gender difference. The most sustained critique of autobiography criticism as masculinist is that of Sidonie Smith, the autobiography theorist who, arguably, has had the most impact on autobiography studies since the publication of her first book, *A Poetics of Women's Autobiography,* in 1987. Smith was the first feminist theorist to describe the poetics of autobiography theory and criticism as androcentric. And she did this not simply because the canon is incomplete but also because the historical elements that constructed the androcentric subject, from the European eighteenth century to the advent of Freudianism, precluded any other type of autobiography (Smith 1987, 4).

Smith's rapid overview of the making of this masculinist subject in autobiography theory traces the debates between New Model theorists, phenomenologists, and poststructuralists in order to ask "where in the maze of proliferating definitions and theories, in the articulation of teleologies and epistemologies ... is there any consideration of woman's *bios,* woman's *aute,* woman's *graphia,* and woman's hermeneutics?" (Smith 1987, 7). Smith uses this question to determine that questions like it cannot be answered by autobiography theory because it ignores and minimizes gender as an organizing category of knowledge. Like Benstock and Friedman, Smith turns to the work of Chodorow, Homans, and Irigaray in order to emphasize woman's essential nature as communal and her language as a work against silencing: "seemingly silent and repressed, woman comes to speak loudly as she intervenes in the phallic drive of masculine discourse with her alternative language of fluid, plural subjectivity" (Smith 1987, 13). Although her evocation of biological essentialism in terms of woman's absolute difference is now open to critique, Smith's analysis opened the field of feminist autobiography studies to a sustained critique of the subject using contemporary critical theory. Autobiography then becomes, in its refusal of androcentric subjectivity and its formation of alternative subjectivities, a politically motivated act that can be examined via poststructural feminisms that remain politically grounded in a re/viewing of the discourse of subjectivity (19).

In *Subjectivity, Identity, and the Body*, Smith's critique of what she called "the universal subject" became more pronounced. When combined with historic and philosophic movements such as empiricism, liberalism, the rise of the bourgeoisie, the impact of Darwinism, and the consolidation of Protestant ideology, the universal subject becomes the self-regulating, exclusionary province of those who have the power to set the epistemological terms of debate about what constitutes ontology. Women occupy the position of other and lack. According to Smith (1993, 18-19), this is the self that Western autobiographical practices purported to represent:

> a mimetic medium for self-representation that guaranteed the epistemological correspondence between narrative and lived life, a self-consciousness capable of discovering, uncovering, recapturing that hard core at the center ... selfhood and autobiography mutually implied one another ... and so, autobiography consolidated its status as one of the West's master discourses, a discourse that has served to power and define centers, margins, boundaries, and grounds of action in the West.

Smith's description of the inevitable, irresistible march of the universal subject into the centre of discourse is compelling, but it leaves many questions unanswered. Although she leaves some room for the interiority of the Romantic subject, she does not make connections between the way in which autobiography theory has been developed by scholars of Romanticism and the features of Romanticism itself. She also does not sufficiently historicize autobiography theory in terms of the texts used – *The Confessions* of Augustine surely cannot exist on the same ideological plane as *The Confessions* of Rousseau as one more manifestation of the universal subject, although the fact that they do so in some theories is significant. And what of autobiography's status as a "master" discourse that defines centres? The relationship between the growth of subjectivity in the West and the rise of autobiography are certainly linked, but the complexities of race, class, colonization, nationality, sexuality, and religion in addition to gender mark the participation of subjects in master narratives in a variety of ways, and all of these affect the circulation of autobiography as a commodity in popular culture as well as in "high" literary culture. Although autobiography has remained a popular commodity in this regard, as a critical discourse it remains on the margins of critical inquiry precisely because it does *not* feature the objectivity and impassivity of scientific discourse that Smith says is the domain of the universal subject, nor was it seen to participate in the realm of universality as (until recently) did the discourses of philosophy and history. It is more probable that the discourse Smith describes has been and is available to writers of autobiography but that its parameters shift constantly, allowing the people she calls "the working class and the colourful" (Smith 1993) to write themselves as alternative subjectivities into and against this "master" discourse.

Despite the difficulties associated with this aspect of Smith's work, it opened the way for materialist feminist inquiry to gain access to a genealogy of the subject using contemporary literary theoretical concepts. This has meant that some feminist critiques influenced by postmodernist readings of multiple identities, theories about race and power, and postcolonial readings of autobiography are beginning to challenge some of the assumptions of the earlier feminist criticism of autobiography. These critiques, when combined with other work on autobiography by ethnic minority writers and speakers, are useful for reviewing autobiography criticism's assumptions of a decontextualized, singular subject whose successful life (or successful craft) always produces a self-reflective text within generic confines.

The growing concern white, feminist critics had with other marginalized subjectivities and their own possible complicity in their marginalization led to their participation in what Laura Marcus (1995) has called "an autobiographical turn" in literary theory. Following Nancy K. Miller's (1991) call for an autobiographical, "personal criticism" that critiques the fantasy of objectivity found in patriarchal scholarship, Liz Stanley (1992), in *The Auto/Biographical 'I,'* grounds her readings in what she calls "accountable knowledge." Accountable knowledge calls attention to the context-dependent aspects of Stanley's own knowledge and understanding in order to critique the fantasy of objectivity and essentialism of the text as always-interpreted "other" into which feminist researchers from culturally dominant positions can be drawn (210). Stanley's position on context has implications for autobiography theory as well as for feminist epistemology since it reflects developments in anthropology and history that are moving towards greater visibility for the conditions of knowledge production and presentation. Autobiographical subjects who have had to occupy the position of "other" could potentially be writing to (an)other, Derrida's (1985) "ear of the other," who signs but who does not authorize.

Leigh Gilmore's critique of earlier essentialist tendencies in feminist autobiography theory also opens up possibilities for thinking of autobiography not as genre but, rather, as a discourse of identity production. In *Autobiographics,* Gilmore (1994a) critiques the essentialism of Jelinek (1980) and Mary G. Mason as a "psychologizing paradigm" that obscures how gender is produced, rather than discovered, through discourses of self-representation.

In autobiographical criticism, this results in writers whom are always found "somewhere on the margins, the margins being construed as a 'place' quite literally 'without history.'" Using aspects of Foucauldian theory, Gilmore suggests that "autobiography is positioned within discourses that construct truth, identity, and power, and these discourses produce a gendered subject" (xiv). She suggests that the genre of autobiography is actually a *techne* founded on principles of identity, a non-essentialist and regulating discursivity that depends on "a network of representational practices in which the production of truth is everywhere on trial" (19). Auto-biographers whose identities cannot be inscribed within dominant identity paradigms regulating what is true and what is knowable do not drop out of this formulation; rather, their alternate discourse "broadens our notion of 'discursive fact' to include the material consequences that precede, coincide with, and follow self-representation" (19). All moves within these alternate autobiographies are discursive and are made with reference to the relations between power, identity, and representation. This can include the refusal to speak within certain modes of address (20).

In this sense, the "I" of women's autobiography is not lost to historical considerations of the subject, but "the autobiographical 'I' is at home in both history and narrative because it is produced by the action that draws those fields together" (Gilmore 1994a, 86). Here, Gilmore opens a way for narrative to have political agency because of the power of reading communities who can recognize themselves in the life scripts they read about, thus making autobiography a potentially politically motivating form (27). She calls this "identification," a search for correspondence that does not occur between the reader and the autobiographer (which would downplay the role of the text) but, rather, between the reader, the text, and the *ideology* of the text, which allows the reader to place herself "in relation to other familiar positions within cultural scripts" (such as "woman" or "citizen") (23). Gilmore's use of this term also allows for potentially non-hierarchical readings that allow autobiography to be a discourse that represents political situations but that does not have to fully participate in universalist narratives of subjectivity and experience: "Imagine a reading practice that listens for another's voice, sees another's face even where sameness is sought, and searches not for the universal but for the specific, the unexchangeable. Identification, then, is contoured along the lines of the politics and possibilities in the cultural unfolding of self-representational writing" (24). Gilmore's reading of the relationships between discourses of subjectivity, identity, and identification provide a rich ground for considering other forms of alternate autobiography where autobiographers write themselves into and against autobiographical discourse in order to facilitate reader "identification."

African-American Autobiographical Discourse

African-American autobiography studies, like feminist studies, also represents a major mode of inquiry in autobiography, mainly because it has developed a parallel set of theoretical traditions and autobiography texts. This happened, Frances Smith Foster (1992, 32) observes, because many contemporary critics recognize autobiography to be central to African-American literary studies, from slave narratives to twentieth-century autobiographies. Although work on African-American autobiography is still concerned with historic recovery, that recovery is linked to identity issues and to the problems African-American writers have had representing themselves as subjects. The field of African-American autobiography criticism, therefore, has links to other emerging fields of enquiry about autobiography on the part of racial or cultural "others" in the United States. Like feminist scholarship, African-American autobiography critics began in the 1970s by recovering and theorizing about texts, most particularly conversion narratives (such as Jarena Lee's), antebellum slave narratives (including those by Frederick Douglass and Harriet Jacobs), postbellum narratives (such as Elizabeth Keckley's *Behind the Scenes*) and twentieth-century narratives.

Early work by Stephen Butterfield (1974) constructed the African-American tradition as articulating a strong sense of an individual's political responsibilities to his or her community. This feature is still central to black women's autobiography, in which the authors function – often ambiguously, as in the case of Zora Neale Hurston – as examples and models for later black women (Marcus 1994, 290). Subsequent work, such as William Andrews's (1986) collection *To Tell a Free Story*, describes African-American autobiography as writings that construct a set of identifiable tropes about blackness and racism in the United States. In a subsequent collection entitled *African American Autobiography*, Andrews (1993) maintains that, in an African-American context, language, rather than creating a screen between text and reality, consolidates reality and grounds identity. This is because African Americans use identity-tropes to create an alternative tradition that contests the history written for and about them in white American culture generally (Andrews 1986, 5).

To date, African-American autobiography studies still seems to be operating in the arena of historic recovery and the articulation of tropic narratives of racial identity, particularly in the area of black women's autobiography – an area about which Joanne Braxton (1989) published the first history in 1993. Critics are focusing particularly on African Americans who wrote or dictated antebellum slave narratives as they negotiate their identities with and often against the language and signs of their white oppressors/liberators (Andrews 1991, 210). Critics trace these negotiations in similar ways in the autobiographical writings of other ethnic minority authors.

Theorizing Border Subjects: Chicano/Chicana Autobiography
Questions of borderline representation, the power of the ethnologist, and
subject positioning have been considered in the recovery and theorization
of Chicano/Chicana life narratives. The work of critics in this area, particularly that of Genaro Padilla, is important for the study of alternative
autobiographical representations by other ethnic groups. In *Chicano Narrative,* Ramón Saldívar (1990) states that autobiography is a form of self-
definition used by Mexican Americans and that it can politicize them
as subjects even when they cooperate with an ethnographer. However,
self-definition in the case of Richard Rodriguez's *The Hunger of Memory*
(1982) also involves painful negotiations with a non-Chicano audience,
the "choice" to assimilate or acculturate in narrative and in life, and the
spectre of America as seen from the borders by the migrant who "trans-
gresses" the lines of geography, race, culture, and language (Saldívar 1990,
161-63). Raymund Paredes (1992, 283), by contrast, states that *The Hunger
of Memory* is a conversion narrative that moves from a Chicano identity to
an assimilated white identity, in contrast to Oscar Zeta Acosta's narratives
of ethnic "rebirth," here compared to Malcolm X's acceptance of his racial
identity as the beginning of his resistance to white hegemony.

The work of Genaro Padilla on Mexican-American autobiography from
the American conquest of northern Mexico in 1848 to ethnographic interviews with migrant farm workers during the 1930s is of great value
to my own work on Doukhobor autobiographical discourse because (1) he
makes similar arguments for a more inclusive understanding of autobiographical form within historical confines and (2) because he sees the
autobiographical "I" as, at times, a sign of the collective pain of a culture
in transition and undergoing deliberate erasure. Although Padilla does not
specifically discuss identity issues, what he refers to as "autobiographical
consciousness" could be construed as an identity construction that does
not resolve itself into ahistoric singularity. Significantly, Padilla (1993b, 8)
indicates that autobiographical discourse can be used by those not considered to be worthy subjects of autobiography when he says – as I have
mentioned earlier – that "autobiographical consciousness itself is culturally divergent, socially complex, and multiple in its articulations, owned
neither by Western culture nor by writing." This comment also highlights
the liberal-capitalist power (individuals can "own" a narrative and sell that
narrative of individuality) contained within the discourse. Padilla situates
his own desire to challenge autobiographical genre constraints within the
field of autobiography's movement towards examining plural, communal
subjectivity within cross-disciplinary formats:

> More and more autobiography scholars, especially feminist and Third
> World practitioners [sic] are arguing, traditional genre constraints have

been exclusionary and must be renegotiated, wedged open to alternate forms of self-representation – historiography, cultural ethnography, folkloristic narratives – that do not focus exclusively on the development of individual personality so much as on the formation, and transformation, of the individual within a community. (29)

Padilla's (1988, 287) own work traces the operation of the first-person in "untraditional" narratives by Mexican Americans that were not originally "meant to function as autobiography" but, rather, emerged in response to the changes Mexican Americans experienced after 1848. Narrative forms include unpublished "reminiscences" by upper-class Mexican Americans, a memoir by a Mexican Texas Ranger, oral accounts collected by a San Francisco bookseller, diaries, and journals (290-91). In other work, Padilla (1993a) examines the role of the ethnologist in creating and then editing a narrative set for the (dictated) life-stories of migrant farm workers, indicating that the migrating Mexican-American subject was constructed in the terms of a "scientific" discourse that places the speaker of the text under erasure, even replacing the speaker's name with an asterisk to deprive him or her of anything but typological identity as the object of study.

Native Autobiographies, Alternative Forms

Criticism of Native-American autobiography has also indicated that it widens the scope of autobiography as a genre. For example, Krupat points out that, before white contact, Native Americans had autobiographical traditions that ran parallel to but did not always refer to non-Native autobiographical forms or epistemologies. This reference to traditions has meant that non-Native ideas about Native "selves" can be seen to have been uncritically applied to Native peoples in a variety of contexts (Krupat 1991, 174). However, what Krupat calls "bi-cultural" ethnographic collaborations and written accounts by Native people who had converted to Christianity do exhibit tropes of negotiation with non-Native culture that can be read autobiographically because they operate with reference to both ways of representing identity (184-85).

The work of Hertha Dawn Wong (1992) addresses the role of alternative autobiographical technologies in the pictographs of Plains Indians imprisoned at Fort Wayne, Florida. The pictographs – a pre-white contact form of representation that features an individual's tribal affiliations and personal history – indicate how the artists depicted contact, the changing ways in which they named themselves, and how they were named by a white art teacher at the fort. These serve as examples of alternative autobiographical technologies in which the "self" is not the predominating referent. The circumstances of the pictographs' production indicate that these artists were able to use non-Native requests for representation to their own ends, mixing autobiographical forms. As Wong observes, these pictographs were "not an interiorized textual reenactment of Anglo domination. [These were] pictographic self-narration, an affirmation of a traditional self, constructed from the very materials of the oppressor" (87). This shows that the construction of alternative identities need not be a doomed project always already recouped by the colonizer; rather, it can be an example of a set of flexible negotiations against more unitary formations of identity, making use of the tools of identity that are available. For Wong, this type of adaptation refers not only to the resilience of the artists but also to a long tradition of autobiographical representation that operated before white contact under its own, often oral, traditions and rules (4). Like Padilla and Krupat, among others, Wong calls for a revision of what the boundaries of autobiographical representation are thought to be in order to take into account alternate technologies: "As we consider the autobiographical activities of non-Western cultures, however, it is crucial to reexamine our approaches" (4). This includes a critique of the assumption that autobiography is always about a written tradition produced by individual subjects and that subjects often considered "subaltern" or powerless can sometimes fashion their own narratives from the grand narratives of the oppressor. This last tendency, with its challenge to power imbalances that self/other designations are "supposed" to keep in check, marks many of the narratives examined by critics like Wong and Padilla as hybrid. These hybrid narrative forms can, at some points, work to produce hybrid identities that can allow their narrators to negotiate with the dominant discourses that threaten to enclose them.

Revising the Autobiographical Self: Hybrid Identities
The advent of identity politics and postcolonial theory has created separate but related areas of inquiry that are now, as in women's studies, causing a shift from a discussion of essentialized selves insulated from political history towards a discussion of politically motivated hybridized identity formations. These formations can be seen as what de Lauretis (1987) has called "technologies," rather than discrete categorizations of race/class/ gender that classify but do not have political consequences when the terms seem to stand in for groups of people who belong to minority groups. The idea of "technologies" has been combined with the work of Paul Smith (1988, 25), who has said that politically constituted subjects strategize from various positions.

In a feminist context, Sidonie Smith's and Julia Watson's important collection *De/Colonizing the Subject,* assesses postcolonial theory about colonization in a variety of contexts, critiques the idea of feminism as a transracial sisterhood based on the eternal sameness of subjects, and affirms the politicization of the sign of autobiography despite its double status as inscription of Western selfhood and possible space for liberation (Smith and Watson 1992). Smith and Watson equate this with a liberation of the genre itself from the constraints of purely textual parameters: "the autobiographical occasion (whether performance or text) becomes a site on which cultural ideologies intersect and dissect one another, in contradiction, consonance, and adjacency. Thus the site is rife with diverse potentials" (xix). This opening-up of autobiography as a politically motivated site is similar to Caren Kaplan's assertion that "out-law genres" can critique the hegemonic qualities of autobiographical discourse. According to Kaplan (1992, 119), they can also challenge the transnational assumptions of autobiography criticism as it constructs its object (autobiography) in order to incorporate exotic discourses into its own terms of subjective singularity, of the "I" as the privileged site of autobiographical rhetoric: "These emerging out-law genres require more collaborative procedures that are more closely attuned to the power differences among participants in the process of producing the text. Thus, instead of a discourse of individual authorship, we find a discourse of situation, a 'politics of location.'"

One way in which critique can occur without compromising the original discourse is by using the rhetorical tools of the oppressor to hybridize narrative. In autobiography, one example of this hybridization is Françoise Lionnet's (1989, 4-5) concept of *métissage*, or cultural braiding, which operates in autobiography as a kind of open collection of cultural and artistic forms that fall outside of "conventional" ways of remembering and recollecting. Hybridization in Mikhail Bakhtin's sense, however, signifies an even more radical mix of autobiographical forms than does "braiding." In Bakhtin's formation, dialogized hybridization means that, even at the level of an utterance, such as the use of the pronoun "I," different social languages create dialogic relationships that already contain (an)other language, such as an autobiographical utterance using "we."[9]

The work of Anne Goldman on ethnic working-class women's alternative autobiographical strategies brings these considerations together. The narratives of these women engage in identity productions using the materials at hand – in this case, the writing of cookbooks as an autobiographical strategy that resists essentialism while affirming collectivity. Thus, Goldman (1996, xxiv) argues for a return to historically grounded textual agency for ethnic autobiography in which a cultural plural is not conflated with a discrete "I"; rather, she advocates collective identification as a point along a continuum in which the "we" is metonymic of a collective at some, but not all, points (an application of Bakhtin's hybridized utterance). The cultural subject can be multiple and shifting, she says, which means that the articulation of identity in these non-traditional texts "takes different forms in different contexts" (xxx). This contests the idea that any one category of knowledge, whether race, gender, class, or whatever, is the prime categorization for identity, while it allows for a range of subject positions (both plural and singular) that an autobiographer could occupy. As Goldman says: "we [should] conceptualize race – and every other determinant of identity – not as a pure and irreducible category, but instead as formed by and informing the whole range of social, historical, political and cultural circumstances within which the subject locates herself" (xxxi). Goldman's continuum between "I" and "we" and her avoidance of "pure" categories for knowledge means that she can discuss alternative ethnic minority autobiography as an alternate technology for identity but not as a typology that either drains agency from the subjects who alter the discourse of autobiography and its ability to construct subjects or encloses subjects in the paradigms of "ethnic," "woman," or "immigrant." In this sense, Goldman represents the latest move in an effort to theorize immigrant identity not only in terms of the recovery of texts but also in terms of the paradigms that use and are used by migrant subjects.

Performativity and the Publicity of Autobiographical Discourse

It has become common to refer to the performativity of the (especially gendered) subject as a way of circumventing essentialist models of identity without conceding the subject's ability to choose between positions. Performativity does not necessarily have to be a trope of radical interiority where the object is language; rather, it can be a trope signifying *exterior* identity negotiation with others. To clarify how this happens, I now look at how, in autobiography, non-mainstream subjects who wish to negotiate their terms of identity in a public context can re-read performativity as a trope of visibility within difference.

According to Sidonie Smith (1995, 18) performativity in autobiography "constitutes interiority," and that interiority is an effect of autobiographical narrative. Smith assigns agency to the act of narration, and othering to the rhetoric of singularity produced in the narration, much as Judith Butler (1997a, 7) assigns agency (and historicity) to the act of language performing itself rather than to a subject who speaks or uses it. As an effect of language, performativity, for Smith (1995, 21), also constructs dis/continuous subjects within the "space" of interiority where identity becomes identification, a flexible dialectic of temporary correspondences that can unfix attempted identifications.

While Smith's and Butler's description of performativity seeks to retain agency within linguistic acts and so restore the possibility of political activity as part of decentred subjectivities, both of these versions of performativity rely on an idea of subjectivity as linked to interiority – an idea that owes something to the primal scenes of psychoanalysis, even if that link is eventually shown to be hallucinatory. What if the writing subject in an autobiographical formation does not acknowledge interiority or even his or her uniqueness as a subject? What if agency for these writers has never been assumed to be part of subjectivity but has always resided elsewhere, *and performativity is an act not of repetition but of necessary visibility?* Autobiographers who have had to construct their positionality as other inside another's discourses of self have not always experienced the luxury of assumed interiority and have often had to "perform" as other for those who possessed the power to represent them. The question of agency in language is crucial here.

For those autobiographers whose memories and collective histories have been treated as fictional, *as not being worthy of interiority* but, perhaps, as worthy of ethnographic curiosity, the "rules" of autobiographical discourse do not always apply. Models of self/other and of individuation may not assume primacy for these writers and speakers, and performativity may not just be an effect of language that decentres the subject but the strategy of a subject who has never been centred. Once thought of in this way, performativity takes on characteristics of exteriority. It does not so much tell the self to the self or heal the split between the lonely points of enunciation and utterance as it recovers the fractured memories of a community, operating as a means of telling the community's story to itself and to other communities.

Why Call It "Autobiography"?

It may seem strange that after challenging every part of Olney's exegeted auto-bio-graphe that I would want to keep using the term. Many critics who wish to mount a wholesale challenge to autobiography's critical discourse and who have called for a widening of its generic boundaries have coined new terms, such as "lifewriting," "lifestory," "biotext," *"testimonio,"* and "autoethnography." Others have borrowed terms (e.g., "personal narrative" and "life history") from other disciplines. However, I advocate using the term "autobiography" because it marks the genealogy of a discourse about genre that has never quite operated as a master narrative, although some critics have tried to make it work like one. In fact, one of the most significant aspects of the critical work on autobiography has been the shift from trying to locate what autobiography is generically (is it non-fiction using fictional techniques, is it an act of reading, is it an unbridgeable gap between written and "actual" subjects, is it about "truth" or "history" or "memory," is it transcultural?) in order to gain academic legitimacy to trying to locate it as a mainstream discourse of the subject (which "bad subjects" can use to critique discourses that construct them as powerless). Without such a genealogy, it might not be possible to understand the terms that have constructed master narratives of subjectivity in Western cultures, and so it might not be possible to adequately evaluate them. Hybrid discourses of autobiography still gain access to the power inherent in these narratives, while much work remains to be done on the residual impact these narratives have on popular autobiographical forms such as the ghost-written memoir or the "tell-all" memoir, which regularly appear on bestseller lists across North America. Although I am not comfortable with the term, for the foregoing reasons I think it is best to keep using it in critical discourse.

Where to Next? Autobiography and the Idea of Nation

As I complete this chapter, studies of autobiography that are beginning to look at new conceptions of identity proliferate, not in the least in my own country, Canada, where the rather meagre criticism on autobiography has, until recently, consisted of works by K.P. Stich (1988), Susanna Egan (1999), Shirley Neuman (1996), Helen Buss (2001), and a few others. In Canada, as elsewhere, emerging theories of postcoloniality, settler cultures, and identity politics are creating a dizzying array of new scholarship. These considerations are beginning to open up new possibilities for inquiry into the relationship of "citizenship," the idea that someone is a national subject belonging to an imagined community, to the discourse of autobiography. What is the relationship, hinted at by Benedict Anderson (1983, 204-5), of an identity in autobiography whose origins cannot be remembered and so must be narrated, and the need for national identities of origin that have become naturalized as part of "serial time"? How has Canada been narrated through autobiography? And, in "out-law" generic work by people like the Doukhobors (whose position in the nation has always been that of other), how has the idea of nation been resisted, accepted, negotiated? Is autobiography part of Bhabha's (1994) idea of "the pedagogical," a part of the narrated nation that tells the story of nation to itself institutionally? Or has it been part of what Bhabha calls the performative of "the people," part of those "rags and patches" of signification that turn a population into a body of citizens (144-45)? Is it both?

As Sidonie Smith (1987, 3) said more than a decade ago, "suddenly everyone in the universe of literary critics and theorists seems to be talking about autobiography." Evolving theoretical and critical emphases seem to have come full critical circle, from an emphasis on historicity, to a new set of subjectivities now referred to as "identities" that affiliate with interpretive communities rather than selves, and that engage in public acts of autobiographical formation that create hybrid forms that are written and spoken by autobiographers constructing hybrid identities. Although autobiography has been known as a genre in which the "I" is central, it is now necessary to theorize these collective identifications that take place outside traditional autobiographical strategies even as they critique them, collective identifications that can also signify a site of identity formation alive to its context and to the conditions of its production.

2
Doukhobor Beliefs and Historical Moments

For the sake of Thee, Lord, I loved the narrow gate; I left the
material life; I left father and mother; I left brother and sister;
I left my whole race and tribe; I bear hardness and persecution;
I bear scorn and slander; I am hungry and thirsty; I am walking
naked; For the sake of Thee, Lord.

— Doukhobor psalm sung at the
1895 Burning of Arms Resistance[1]

These words of the psalm "For the Sake of Thee" indicate that Doukhobor
identity is closely associated with pacifist resistance as a spiritual practice.
And each time this psalm is sung, this key event in Doukhobor history is
recalled in spiritual terms, which associates Doukhobor identity with the
continuous memory of this resistance. In this way, memory helps to keep
alive the Doukhobor identity as "Spirit Wrestlers," people who consider
part of their spiritual practice the obligation to work against injustice and,
often, against unjust authorities.

Doukhobor history has been marked by struggles with religious authorities (who disliked their refusal of institutional trappings) and with nation-
states (who found the Doukhobor combination of faith and political/
economic practices threatening). The challenge that Doukhobors have
posed to various types of authorities has sometimes meant that some
aspects of their history have been neglected or not understood by outsiders, while some of the activities of radical Doukhobors have become all
too "familiar" without being fully comprehended. Doukhobor autobiographical discourse constantly refers to key events in Doukhobor history
and links them closely to ideas about Doukhobor identity. In this chapter,
I begin with some information about Doukhobor beliefs and then move
on to some of the key events in Doukhobor history, providing some background about Doukhobor identity in the process.[2]

The Spirit Wrestlers: Identity in (as) Resistance

The name "Doukhobor" literally means *dukhoboretz*, or "Spirit Wrestler."
This name was considered to be derisive, and it was given to the
Doukhobors by the Archbishop Amvrosii Serebrennikov of Ekaterinoslav
in 1785. It signified that, in rejecting the rites of the Russian Orthodox
Church, the Doukhobors were wrestling with the Holy Spirit. Doukhobors

took this term and adapted it to mean that they were fighting *with* the Holy Spirit against the church and secular authorities (Woodcock and Ava-kumovic 1977, 19) – an early instance of Doukhobor resistance to author-itarianism. Doukhobors believe that all people bear the image of God within themselves. Jesus Christ himself is not God but, rather, a brother to human-kind who is on a par with other believers. Jesus is admired but not wor-shipped, and, because he or she bears the image of God, no believer is greater than another. All are equal. Instead of the trinity of Father, Son, and Holy Spirit found in classic Christianity: "for Doukhobors, there was one God, but in three parts: God the father was memory, God the son, intelli-gence, and the Holy Spirit, will. In that sense, *all* people were themselves the embodiment of the Trinity" (Breyfogle 1995, 28). The Doukhobor belief in universal equality forms the foundation of Doukhobor pacificism since to kill another person would be to kill someone who bears God's image. It is also the basis for the Doukhobors' belief that each person, be-cause she or he bears God's image, has divine reason within him or herself. It follows that, if one is open to this "internal light," then one will be guided by it. Religious ceremonies, church buildings, icons, feasts, sacraments, priests, and written liturgies are therefore held to be unnecessary. Strict reliance on the Bible is also thought to be unnecessary, although some teachings can be taken from it. Until recently, Doukhobors thought that the registration of births, deaths, and marriages was also unnecessary because it was not essential to accompany life passages (such as baptisms, weddings, or elab-orate funerals) with ceremonies. The only outward symbols Doukhobors use are the display of bread, salt, and water – the basic elements needed to sustain life – on a table at their meetings. The only religious custom at these meetings – which are called *molenie* when they are for spiritual pur-poses and *sobranie* when they are for decision making – occurs when each participant bows to the other in recognition of their respective divinity.

Instead of using a written text or catechism, Doukhobors sing unwrit-ten psalms and songs composed by themselves in Russian without accom-paniment or musical notation. The psalms use musical patterns found nowhere else. The sum total of these works, in addition to memorized prayers and "sayings," is called *Zhivotnaia Kniga,* or The Living Book. This "book" was not written down until the Doukhobors migrated to Canada at the end of the nineteenth century, and it was not transcribed by a Doukhobor. Doukhobor beliefs are passed on through the singing and reciting of The Living Book: to sing these songs is to attain mystical heights that mean more than does the literal meaning of many of the words and images (Breyfogle 1995, 27-28). Manual labour and life experience are thought to be spiritual and, particularly by older Doukhobors, more important than secular education. Until a few decades ago most Doukho-bors did not fully trust schools and universities because they are secular institutions that not only do not teach pacifism but also stress patriotism and secular worldviews. The slogan created by Doukhobor leader Peter Lordly Verigin in the nineteenth century remains central to Doukhobor ideas about their identity: "Toil and Peaceful Life." The exercise of "divine reason" is not seen as incompatible with a more millenarian belief in the spiritual value of dreams, prophecies, and visions, especially among those Doukhobors belonging to the more radical groups. Their commitment to hard (often rural) work, simplicity, and community, combined with mysticism, proved attractive to many Russian peasants who, during the eighteenth and nineteenth centuries, questioned the authority of the Orthodox Church.

But the Doukhobors' adherence to equality and fraternity, which attracted many of the idealistic people who helped them escape from Russia and come to Canada, includes another element that puzzled outsiders: the notion of divine, absolute leadership. Until the leadership of John J. Verigin in the 1960s, most Doukhobors regarded their leaders as being more spiritually adept than other people. Leaders were thought to have gifts of prophecy and to be capable of providing spiritually informed teaching. However, decisions made collectively in Doukhobor "business" meetings are based on the principle of the inner light, which, it is assumed, will bring all people into agreement, the leader (usually) being no exception: "the collective will expressed by the people in the sobranie, the meeting of the village or even the whole sect, emanates from the same inner spirit as the will of the inspired living Christ, and the times of harmony and even ... material prosperity among the Doukhobors have been those in which the leaders ... followed policies that found a ready response in the hearts of their followers" (Woodcock and Avakumovic 1977, 43).

The Burning of Arms

Throughout their history, the Doukhobors almost always had an uneasy relationship with the Russian tsars and, on two occasions, had been moved to remote areas of Russia. While under the leadership of Lukeri'ia (Luchechka) Kalmakova they were able to compromise with local government officials. By the end of her life, Luchechka prophesied that this compromise would end. Indeed, her belief that the spiritual glory of the Doukhobor people would return and, significantly, that they would again become pilgrims came about less than one-quarter of a century later, when her protégé, Peter Vasileyvich Verigin,[3] initiated changes to Doukhobor spiritual practices. From 1893 to 1894 Peter Lordly, in exile in Siberia, urged all his Doukhobor followers[4] to forgive their debts in the community, pay all outside debts, and make their land holdings common. Influenced by the writings of Tolstoy, Peter Lordly also asked Doukhobors to become vegetarians, to stop smoking and drinking, and to abstain from sexual intercourse until what he called "the time of tribulation" was over. Finally, he combined religious messianism with political radicalism when he began to preach against all governments, to encourage a type of anarchy, and to envision a Christian communist utopic community. To this end, Peter Lordly refused to swear an oath of loyalty to the State and told his followers not to swear oaths to the tsar, not to participate in any war, and, finally, to burn all of their weapons in public bonfires.

This last order, issued in strict secrecy and carried out on 29 June 1895, became known as the Burning of Arms. The event took place in three villages, where the Doukhobors piled up their swords, guns, and other weapons and burned them in large bonfires while they sang psalms. The strongest authoritarian resistance to this act took place in Goreloye, where the Small Party had warned the Russian military about what was going to happen. Soldiers on horseback attempted to trample the Doukhobors, who huddled together and shielded those who were wounded, refusing to salute the authorities or to speak of the tsar in worshipful terms. Some Doukhobors were maimed or killed by the hooves of the horses. An unnamed nobleman/official managed to stop the commander from ordering the mass execution of the resisters.

Shortly before the Burning of Arms and as part of the same resistance to tsarist authority, Doukhobors who had been conscripted into the tsarist army were asked to refuse to perform military service. On Easter 1895, ten of these soldiers, led by a young man named Matvei Lebedev, began to hand back their rifles. They were imprisoned, flogged, and semi-starved in an effort to bring them into submission. These methods were not successful, even though one young Doukhobor died as the result of maltreatment.[5] Meanwhile, after the Burning of Arms, the greater Doukhobor community was subjected to tortures of a different sort: in an attempt to force their compliance with authoritarian directives, Cossacks were billeted in Doukhobor villages, where they plundered and beat their Doukhobor hosts. Some Doukhobor women were raped, and 300 Doukhobors were exiled to Siberia. Finally, the remaining 4,300 followers of Peter Lordly were exiled to Batum in Georgia, where they were split up, given no land, and forbidden to work outside the region. Many fell ill or starved to death. Approximately 350 Doukhobors died at Batum. The often-sung Doukhobor psalm, "Sleep on, you brave fighting eagles," is dedicated to these early martyrs. As Woodcock observes, the words of this psalm have inspired many contemporary Doukhobors to resist secular authority (Woodcock and Avakumovic 1977, 100). They also form the basis in Doukhobor autobiographical discourse for a construction of Doukhobor identity as pacifist and as resistant to secular authority in all its forms.[6]

The Burning of Arms remains the single most important event in Doukhobor history, marking a return to the purity of Doukhobor pacifist practices. It also catapulted them onto the world stage when their struggle against one of the most powerful empires in the world became known to Tolstoy and his followers, who publicized it. Doukhobors commemorate this event every year at a ceremony called *Petrov Den* (Peter's Day) and treat it as central to their history. As Koozma Tarasoff (1982, 24) writes, "whether they knew it or not, the Doukhobors [at the Burning of Arms] were now no longer acting as a sectarian religious group. They had transformed themselves into a social movement."

Migration to Canada

When 7,500 Doukhobors migrated to Canada in 1899 as one group in order to avoid severe persecution in Russia, they were already beginning their unique relationship to the idea of Canada: once 500 more joined them later, this migration became the largest in Canada's history. By 1897 Prince Khilkov, a Russian nobleman who had been inspired to give his land to his peasants and to lead a life of political activism, found out what was happening to the Doukhobors and wrote Tolstoy for assistance. Tolstoy had already met three Doukhobor elders and had not realized that Peter Lordly had read his writings. He mistakenly believed that, in Doukhoborism, he had found a naive, pure form of the religious anarchism he advocated. Tolstoy's efforts to raise international awareness of the persecution of Doukhobors were particularly successful in England. English Quakers and Russian Tolstoyans, who shared some of the Doukhobor beliefs in pacifism, equality, and the indwelling of divine reason, became involved with the Doukhobor cause in 1897. They helped the Doukhobors ask the Empress Maria of Russia for permission to migrate.

In 1898 the Empress Maria granted permission for the Doukhobors to migrate on the condition that those who left never return to Russia. After a failed migration attempt in Cyprus, Tolstoyan and Doukhobor representatives visited Canada. Their meeting with Clifford Sifton, the minister of the interior, was successful. Sifton, who wanted to encourage a type of settler he had referred to as "the sturdy peasant in a sheepskin coat" to settle the Canadian West, agreed to three key terms that would guarantee Doukhobor migration and settlement: exemption from military service, no government interference with the internal organization of the sect, and the granting of blocks of land so that Doukhobors could continue to practise communal farming and living. The delegates found three separate areas of land in northern Saskatchewan, all consisting of unbroken prairie sod far north of the railway line. The Doukhobors received approximately 400,000 acres for cultivation. On 5 October 1898 an agreement was reached between the delegates and the Canadian government: 8,000 Doukhobors would migrate to the Canadian Prairies as soon as possible. This would be the largest planned mass migration to Canada ever undertaken.

The migration began shortly thereafter when the *Lake Huron,* a cargo ship, left Batum on 29 December 1899 with the first group of Doukhobors (from the Wet Mountains), accompanied by Tolstoyans and other people who wished to help with the migration. They landed in Halifax, were greeted warmly and with curiosity, and then went on to Winnipeg, where they initially stayed in large immigration halls and began their first painful adjustments to Canadian attitudes, climate, and economics before continuing on to Yorkton, Saskatchewan.[7] This first group was soon followed by two others: a large group on 29 December 1899 from Yelizavetpol and Kars and, on 27 April 1900, the surviving members of the Cyprus colony. When these settlers were joined by 500 followers of Peter Lordly, the total Doukhobor migration numbered approximately 8,000 people. Peter Lordly, for the time being, was not allowed to leave Russia. Twelve thousand Doukhobors, some from the Small Party and others who could not accept all of Lordly's changes to Doukhobor practices, also stayed behind.

Even though they did not have their leader with them and were forced to winter over in Saskatchewan without basic farming tools or farm animals, the Doukhobors persevered. Many found occasional work in Yorkton to generate cash, while the Quakers sent money, clothing, and food. Tolstoy donated the proceeds of his novel *Resurrection* to pay the expenses of the migration. In the spring the Doukhobors moved to the three settlement areas: the North Colony, the South Colony, and the Prince Albert Colony (north and west of Yorkton) and began to build sod huts. The younger men went to work constructing the railway for wages that they donated to the community. The women, elderly, and children built villages and broke the soil, at first without the help of farm animals. Following Peter Lordly's rather vague instructions by letter to live communally, the Doukhobors started a communal subsistence farming economy and shared any equipment they had. In this way, they quickly built decentralized settlements composed of fifty-house villages with wide streets (like those they had known in Russia). They made any objects they needed from wood, metal, and cloth. Even before Peter Lordly's arrival in 1902, relatively soon after migration Doukhobor self-sufficiency and dedication led to significant gains for the group. But conflict with non-Doukhobors on the Prairies and with government officials soon began.

Land and Identity: The Migration to British Columbia
The Doukhobors were already beginning to experience discrimination and distrust in Canada due to a series of misunderstandings with non-Doukhobor farmers, attempts by non-Doukhobors to squat on Doukhobor land, and pressure from non-Doukhobors to pay taxes for English schools that Doukhobors did not use. All of these factors combined to sour the

relationship between the Doukhobors and the immigration authorities so that when, in 1900, officials began to survey land, ask for the registration of vital statistics, and request that young men over eighteen sign individually for quarter sections of the land grant, they were met with resistance and refusal.[8] The struggle over land and identity had begun.

The Doukhobors saw individual ownership of land as a religious issue rather than as a matter of economic necessity. They had begun to prosper economically whether they worked communally or not, which caused Tolstoy to reproach them for abandoning communal land ownership: "to acknowledge property is to acknowledge violence" (qtd. in Maude 1904, 271). The government pressure on the Doukhobors to register their quarter sections individually caused vigorous debates about possible connections between the communal way of living and moral purity (Tarasoff 1995, 59). The debate about land registration quickly became a scene of conflict over competing visions of settler identity, with immigration officials and Anglo[9] settlers arguing that religious belief is separate from individual ownership, which must be paramount, while most Doukhobors argued that the land must be held in common because it belongs to God (Janzen 1990, 41-42). Arguments about land use helped to form the Independent Doukhobor movement, which was made up of Doukhobors who wanted to register their lands individually, and the millenarian Sons of God (the predecessor of the Sons of Freedom), who wanted to reject materialism and all aspects of Canadian life. To protest, more than 1,000 Sons of God went on a millenarian pilgrimage to "a land nearer the sun," where they would meet Jesus Christ and herald the return of their leader from Siberia.

The pilgrimage turned public opinion against the Doukhobors. The press had a field day debating whether the activity of the Sons of God was due to genetic abnormalities, mental aberrations, or character disorders. One article, for example, linked communal living and pilgrimages as part of a regrettable psychological condition, saying that the "Slavonic" mind had a "peculiar faculty for communal aberration, and a practical devotion to what it has accepted as true which would be sublime if it were not so pitiable" (qtd. in Tarasoff and Klymasz 1995, 128). But the trek of 1902 marked a lasting division between Doukhobors and Canadians. The press accused the radicals of moral and political coercion and refused to recognize that the religious basis for the protest was sincere (Woodcock and Avakumovic 1977, 179), while the censure of the general public, whose notions of religion and liberal control by the State did not include millenarian combinations of mysticism and wholesale protests against authority, contributed to misunderstandings of Doukhobor motivation. Such misunderstandings, deeply founded in liberal democratic ideas about land use, the separation of labour and religion, and the responsibility of individuals to the State, endured. Combined with their distrust of all governments and their refusal to perform military service, Doukhobor activity of any kind seemed to fly in the face of what most Anglo-Canadians considered to be the responsibilities adhering to Canadian identity: citizenship, patriotism, and the separation of faith and political activity. Thus, the 1902 trek became the first in a long series of nude protests and depredations intended to protest Canadian materialism, which marked these Doukhobors in particular and all Doukhobors in general as unassimilable. Consequently, they were encoded within Canadian history as bodies to be represented rather than as people who can speak and represent themselves. Years later, anger and incomprehension at Doukhobor approaches to the "sacred" areas of identity could still be found in numerous press articles and in such books as *Doukhobors at War* (Zubek and Solberg 1952) or, most notoriously, Simma Holt's (1964) spurious account of Doukhobor protest. This view of the Doukhobors still prevails: in the recent photographic coffee table book *Canada: Our Century*, the only photograph of the Doukhobors in what an editor of the collection says is a collection of "500 worlds" (Kingwell and Moore 1999, 21) is an enlarged photograph of a 1903 radical nude parade (41).

Stephen Leacock, in a pro-imperialist address to the Ottawa Canadian Club between 1903 and 1909, ridiculed an economic expansionist idea of nationhood that included any hint of non-Anglo otherness: "out of all these [migrants] we are to make a kind of mixed race in which is to be the political wisdom of the British, the chivalry of the French, the gall of the Galician, the hungriness of the Hungarian and the dirtiness of the Doukobor [sic]" (qtd. in Berger 1970, 151). The Doukhobors clearly function in this list as the symbol of an alliterative uncleanliness that will pollute Canadian nationhood. And, although Emily Murphy (1910, 61) thought that the Doukhobors could be assimilated, she concludes that this is true because their "fanatic" tendencies mean "we may safely say that any shortcomings these simple folk betray are mental rather than moral." For Murphy, the Doukhobors will make good Canadian citizens because they work hard, even though, due to their religious fervour, they are mentally unfit for anything else.

When Peter Lordly arrived and set up the Christian Community of Universal Brotherhood (CCUB)[10] as the communal administration for the Doukhobor settlements, tensions died down, at least temporarily. But the arguments caused by the government's pressure to register land did not disappear and, in reaction to the government's demands, the Doukhobors soon split into three broad factions: "a conservative centre, intent on communal institutions as a manifestation of the spiritual life; a radical left, intent on dramatic resistance to the world and on pursuing to a logical extreme the anarchistic implications of Doukhobor doctrine; and an assimilationist right, inclined ... to make its peace with authority and to revert to the individualism that characterized the laxer and more prosperous periods of Doukhobor history" (Woodcock and Avakumovic 1977, 192). These three broad orientations exist today as the moderate Union of Spiritual Communities of Christ (USCC) (or Community Doukhobor group), the remains of the factions in the Sons of Freedom group, and an Independent group. To this I must add that Woodcock's description of Doukhobor internal "political" leanings often translates into different emphases within a non-Doukhobor context. The "conservative" group, for example, contains a variety of Doukhobors who often differ with regard to the role that institutions should play in Doukhobor life, while the Sons of Freedom – despite anarchic tendencies – are often the most conservative in religious matters. The "right-wing" Independents have been active in the peace movement as well as in Canadian left-wing political parties such as the Co-operative Commonwealth Federation (CCF)/New Democratic Party (NDP). And members of Doukhobor groups have at times had a tendency to switch roles, as when the Independents of Saskatchewan refused to perform military service during the Second World War, or when their members occasionally switch group affiliations. Regardless of the group to which they belong, Dou-khobors usually have relatives in other groups, which can complicate their relationships. These complex relationships are often expressed in Doukhobor autobiographical discourse (sometimes indirectly as, for example, when Doukhobors describe moves from an area such as Blaine Lake, where there are many Independents, to Krestova, a Freedomite village in British Columbia).

Despite factionalism, the CCUB prospered from 1903 to 1907 under Peter Lordly's leadership. The achievements of the Community benefited the developing Canadian West as well: "arriving at a crucial time in the history of the prairies, the Doukhobors played a considerable part ... not only by breaking and cultivating large areas of land, but also by building many miles of the vital railway links, often under conditions that other workers were unwilling to accept. Though many Canadians were hostile from the beginning and others were rendered so by the eccentricities of the early Sons of Freedom, those who actually visited the Community and met Peter Lordly were more inclined to be impressed than otherwise" (Woodcock and Avakumovic 1977, 203). But the rising fortunes of the Doukhobors were quickly brought to an end when Clifford Sifton resigned from Laurier's cabinet and the more inflexible and conservative Frank Oliver took his place in 1904. Unlike Sifton, who was willing to take any immigrants who were willing to work hard and to populate the Canadian West quickly, Oliver represented a more conservative interpretation of Western settlement which, around the turn of the last century, was beginning to predominate in debates about the future of Canada as a participant in the British Empire.

In Jean Bruce's (1976) *The Last Best West* there is a photograph of a turn-of-the-century English literacy class run by Frontier College for immigrant railway workers – a photograph in which Doukhobor workers could never appear (see Figure 1). In the photograph, the workers sit at a table in a classroom. Their teacher stands at the head of the table. To his left, under a British flag, a large sign reads: "Our motto/No hyphenated Canadians." The meaning of the motto is clear. Immigrants taking classes at Frontier College were expected to learn English in order to become Canadian. To be Canadian, as the position of the flag indicates, is to be a subject of the British Empire. There were to be no "Ukrainian-Canadians," no "German-Canadians," no "Hungarian-Canadians" in this version of Canada. The text of J.S. Woodsworth (1909, 197) ties literacy programs to the national project because "ignorance of our language is a barrier that largely isolates those people from us and our institutions." "Our" institutions were interpreted by imperialist opponents of mass migration – not by Woodsworth and his supporters – as British institutions that support the British Empire. The purpose of choosing "the right" people for Canada clearly involved an anxious desire to direct the path from Woodsworth's "gates" to assimilation through institutional acceptance – in this case, via language instruction.

But, as I mentioned, this photograph is also important because of who cannot appear in it. There are no Sikh railway workers in this class, no Chinese migrants, no black workers from Oklahoma making extra money to pay for their new homesteads in Canada, and there are no Doukhobors working to make money for their developing communal living projects.

The reasons for this absence are also related to that imagined figure of the stranger, the migrant found within "our" gates who cannot be invited in. At a time when English Canadians were struggling with the relationship between migration and a developing sense of national identity, it was not possible to imagine that non-Caucasian, non-European people could ever really become Canadian, hyphenated or not. The prevailing opinion of the day was that what Howard Palmer (1994) has called "Anglo-conformity" would ensure the purity of the Canadian nation even as migration altered it. Anglo-conformity was based on a series of hierarchical classifications that, based on their physical and cultural distance from London, England, determined the suitability of ethnic minority people as residents in Canada. "Strange" religious sects placed low in the migrant hierarchy, and these included the Mennonites, the Hutterites, and the Doukhobors, who were somewhere below Jews and Southern Europeans, and somewhere above the "Asiatics" (Chinese, Japanese, East Indians) and black immigrants from the United States.

But Anglo-conformity was also fundamentally ambiguous, particularly when public opinion was directed at the members of groups thought to be religiously deviant. Within Anglo-conformity religion was read as ethnicity and then as a mark of unfathomable ethnic difference related to other cultural differences that could not be eradicated or anglicized. This slide from the characterizing of religious sects as deviant to ethnically other meant that most of the members of these groups were thought to be impossible to assimilate, although it was undeniable that they provided a workforce that Canada's expansionist settlement policy makers continued to require. Therefore, these migrants were the "strangers" who must remain on the edge of Canada's developing social borders, migrants who do not belong in Canada but who cannot be asked to leave. Their presence on the edge of what Canada would imagine itself to be as a nation, whether those who imagined were leftist reformers or imperialists, indicates much about the grounds for Canadian citizenship and about how otherness was to be managed in the service of national identity and nation building. The resulting struggles of Doukhobor groups with federal and provincial authorities about what it meant to live in Canada highlight national anxieties and convictions about national selves and immigrant others who refused discourses of liberal selfhood and entered into negotiations about identity and the ability of "others" to be part of the nation.

Frank Oliver, one of the most powerful politicians in Canada and an MP from the developing West himself, was one of the people who embodied the discourse of Anglo-conformity. He became responsible for turning

Figure 1   An early Frontier College class with Professor Gordon (c. 1907). *National Archives of Canada*, PA-139836

ideologies about what Canada would and would not include into policy, and the Doukhobors represented his test case for the proper management of settlement issues. Soon after he became minister of the interior, Oliver abolished the Doukhobor reserves and so, by 1906-7, the land crisis between Doukhobors and the Canadian government concerning land registrations in Saskatchewan came to a head. Oliver also began to insist that Doukhobors register marriages, births, and deaths; place their children in English schools; pay taxes; and – most disastrously for Doukhobors – swear an oath of allegiance to the Queen. Oliver insisted that the Oath, although it was not discussed in initial negotiations, was a prerequisite of Canadian citizenship, despite the fact that Doukhobors were categorically opposed to something that so openly contradicted their beliefs.

Under Oliver, the federal government reinterpreted the Dominion Land Act and began to insist that individual Doukhobor homesteads had to be registered. Public support was in Oliver's favour, particularly since a land rush in the Canadian West was fuelling English-Canadian resentment against the large land blocks in Saskatchewan held by a single, non-English-speaking group. The federal government no longer needed immigrants so badly that accommodations could be willingly made. Doukhobor territory, remote and part of an area that had not yet become a province in 1899, was highly prized by 1905, the year that Saskatchewan became a Canadian province. Already, squatters occupied some unfarmed Doukhobor reserves.

The government couched its demands in terms that directly linked questions of private property and ownership to Canadian identity discourses based on liberalism and individualism. Colonization agents sent to evaluate the Doukhobor situation reported unfavourably on Doukhobor communal values. For example, in 1905 C.W. Speers based his criticisms on his belief that individualism was lacking in Doukhobor communities, reporting to Oliver that "the individual [Doukhobor] homesteader had never been impressed with his rights as a settler nor his independence as an individual" (qtd. in Janzen 1990, 47). A Mr. McNab, a homestead inspector, recommended that Doukhobors be enticed to leave communal living since they are "rapidly absorbing Canadian sentiments" and otherwise behaving as good settlers (qtd. in Janzen 1990, 48). But communalism should be gently discouraged and the Community should cease to exist:

> it might here be suggested that the regulations re cultivation might be so amended as to assist in the development of individuality of action ... improvements [could] then be made on each individual homestead ... curiosity would then impel them to discover the possessor of each parcel. If the suggestion that upon each individual homestead some improvements be required were acted upon it would encourage those who have the inclination to leave the Community. (qtd. in Janzen 1990, 48)

McNab's recommendations assume that all good citizens must participate in a liberal capitalist system and that all settlers *desire this system* if they know what is "good" for them.

But the McDougall Commission, headed by a Protestant clergyman who had also negotiated with Aboriginal peoples on behalf of the government, had still more negative judgments to make. Oliver eventually followed this commission's recommendations, which stated that the Doukhobor reserves were "a most serious block and impediment to the natural and righteous growth of the country" and that the government, in allowing Doukhobors to have this land, was committing a "serious injustice to the general public" (qtd. in Janzen 1990, 48-49). McDougall equated communal life with pathological behaviour. He thought that communal living produced "extreme passivity and general lethargy ... a childishness in the performing of all labour." He added that "the individual having no special interest in the land or its product becomes extremely unstable," which equated capitalist productivity with mental health. One outcome of collectivity, McDougall concluded with obvious distaste, was that Doukhobors did not want to own land or become Canadian citizens since God alone was their king. McDougall finally recommended that the Doukhobor lands be taken from the Community and that all Doukhobors who would not register individually be forced to live on small reserves held for them "during the Government's pleasure" (49-50).

Oliver agreed with McDougall's analysis and recommendations, particularly since he assumed that many of the Doukhobor homesteads were not under cultivation. In fact, the Doukhobors were cultivating the land more quickly than the minimum rate required, but public pressure and the land rush encouraged Oliver to take drastic measures. First, he required that all Doukhobors register their homesteads individually or the land would be taken from them. Homesteads had to be located on the land the homesteaders farmed, which would effectively end village life and then spell the end of communal village labour. Sifton's more flexible agreements were annulled. The vast Doukhobor land grants were cancelled, with only a small amount of land around each village being retained by the Community Doukhobors. Oliver presented this last move as a concession that was made to the Doukhobors because they were such good settlers.

The Community Doukhobors protested when they heard of this plan. They summarized their objections in a letter to Frank Oliver, pointing to their productivity, their religious reasons for not taking an oath of allegiance, and the previous agreements with Sifton. In a conclusion that reflected their distrust of authority, they stated: "We will ask you very earnestly as we know we cannot do anything against you. You have the power. You are the Government. We have very kind and friendly wishes to you and are asking you to take our condition before your attention and let us have the land we have entered for, and we hope that you will never be disappointed that the Doukhobors will do any harm to you. All the Doukhobors say we hope the Canadian Government will continue to protect us in our religion" (qtd. in Janzen 1990, 55). Oliver replied that "the giving of public land is not a matter of religion but of law and fair play ... I have to deal with all the people in the same way" (qtd. in Janzen 1990, 55). The difference between the Doukhobors' view of identity and Oliver's is clear: for the Doukhobors, identity is collective, they have no power while "the Government," another collective, has it all, and land-holding is a religious matter that the government should protect. In exchange for protection, they promised not to harm the State, basically asking for the same situation that they had experienced under liberal tsars in Russia.

Oliver's use of terms such as "law" and "fair play" indicate that he and the government saw individual labour as existing on a "level" playing field and that the proper role of the State was to encourage uniformity in individual practices. Difference is not tolerated or even comprehended since it is seen as fundamentally unjust. Finally, religious matters are assumed to be part of the private sphere, while land-holding is assumed to be part of the public sphere. These spheres are mutually exclusive: to combine them is to violate both of them. Oliver's statements, and the reports of those who worked for him, were clearly part of a larger set of assumptions about Canadian identity that were popularly accepted by the press and by those who wanted Doukhobor land. J.S. Woodsworth's (1909, 234) comments about migration and integration summarize this view, which links citizenship to the connection between liberal individuality and uniformity:

> First of all, they [the new settlers] must in some way be unified. Language, nationality, race, temperament, training are all dividing walls that must be broken down ... There is a very natural tendency for people of the same nationality to settle in large colonies ... Such colonies are really bits of Russia or Austria or Germany transplanted to Canada. Not only are they less open to Canadian ideas, but closely united, they can control the entire community ... It would seem a wise policy to scatter the foreign communities among the Canadian, in this way facilitating the process of assimilation.

Oliver's ultimatum caused a variety of reactions inside the Doukhobor community. When the government took half of the Doukhobor lands in 1907, a land rush resulted. The rest of the land was either owned by Independent Doukhobors or was retained "in trust" by the government. One thousand Independents began to farm individually, while the Community Doukhobors were demoralized, particularly since Peter Lordly was visiting Russia at the time and offered no advice or comment. As for the Sons of Freedom movement, protest marches increased. Seventy marchers on one trek, who walked east (clad in blue gowns and straw hats), denounced Peter Lordly as a "machinery man" (Woodcock and Avakumovic 1977, 223). When they arrived in Winnipeg and stayed at J.S. Woodsworth's mission there, they invited him to join them in their trek eastward. Woodsworth, who would publish *Strangers Within Our Gates* two years later, declined, although he included photographs of the marchers in his book.

Once Peter Lordly came back to Canada, he realized that the situation in Saskatchewan would destroy the Community. After some unsuccessful inquiries in California, he bought land in Saskatchewan, where he established a brick factory. Then in 1908 he bought land in the Kootenay region of British Columbia. In 1909 5,000 Doukhobors – over half of the members of the Community and Sons of Freedom – moved to British Columbia where they once again combined manual labour for cash outside the Community with labour inside the Community. By 1912 8,000 men, women, and children were part of the CCUB in British Columbia, and in 1917 the Commune was incorporated by 5,880 adults. During the height of its efficiency during the First World War, the Community was the most successful communal experiment in North America. It prospered, and its members quickly planted orchards. They also built houses, barns, a brick works, a sawmill, a flour mill, and, eventually, a jam factory that, until the 1930s, produced the popular "KC Products" jam. Although Community members endured hardships and had little independence – they were not allowed to keep any money they made working outside, lived in "villages" consisting of two large houses for sixty people, and had to get their goods from the Community storehouses – Doukhobors who were part of the Community at that time remember it in autobiographical narratives as a secure environment, free from many of the concerns of the outside world. They often equate this communal living with spiritual purity – with a time before Doukhobors began to compromise with the outside world. Although the commune was hated by non-Doukhobors in British Columbia because it profited from the war effort even though it sent no soldiers to fight for Canada, and because there were ongoing problems with schooling and statistical registration, most Doukhobors remember the Community in a positive light. This was the case until Peter Lordly's death in 1924 in a train explosion.

Chistiakov, Growing Unrest, and the End of the CCUB
After Peter Lordly's death, the Sons of Freedom – active on a small scale during his lifetime – increased their activities. This time, their protests included more destructive acts. On 23 May 1923 the school in Brilliant was burned to the ground, the first of many Freedomite arsons. Arsonists followed this by burning Peter Lordly's house at Brilliant, a Doukhobor sawmill, and a poleyard in order to protest Community materialism and forced school

attendance. The government ignored Peter Lordly's plea to distance the orthodox Doukhobors from the zealots and to prosecute the culprits, instead choosing to force compliance with the school attendance laws. It seized CCUB property in response to the burnings and nude parades (McLaren 1999).

Despite the uneasy peace that resulted after this, patterns of relations between Doukhobors, non-Doukhobor residents of British Columbia, and the British Columbia authorities had been determined. British Columbia, a territory colonized by loyal British subjects, remained more colonial in outlook than the rest of the country and, therefore, was more intolerant of people who were not of English background, particularly people who were not enthusiastic about the British Empire. As a result, the Doukhobors encountered the same suspicion, intolerance, and outright racism as did Aboriginal peoples and Asian migrants. They were referred to as "blacks" because it was thought that they were not Caucasian – an ironic assumption since they migrated from the Caucasus. They were called (and are still called) "Douks" or "Dirty Douks," and they were (and in many cases still are) thought by the people of the British Columbia Interior to be generally unclean and ignorant. As recently as twenty-five years ago, Doukhobors were banned from some public pools and some public buildings in order to keep these places "pure."[11] Initially, the Doukhobors dealt with this situation by turning inward to the Community and away from the outside world, largely refusing to learn the language and customs of outsiders. Even by the 1960s, more than a generation after their arrival, all Doukhobors in British Columbia still spoke Russian as their first language, while many did not know how to speak English. As Woodcock observes, Doukhobors coped with outside pressures by hanging on to their mystic identity as sojourners: "Until the 1960s the Doukhobors in the Interior of British Columbia remained mentally unassimilated, retaining with extraordinary tenacity the sense of being transients who have paused – though it has been for sixty years – on their pilgrimage from one destination to the next" (Woodcock and Avakumovic 1977, 262). This identity regularly surfaces in Doukhobor autobiographical discourse when migration or Russia is discussed. Often repeating a prophecy by Luker'ia Kalmykova that the Doukhobors would migrate, build houses of glass, and then one day return to Russia, the Doukhobors retained a separate identity by viewing their trials in British Columbia as a preparation for that mystic journey. This refuge in an alternate version of their history and their future served to insulate them from any pressure to hyphenate their identities as "Doukhobor-Canadian." Even today they never use this term. With the exception of the Independent Doukhobors, Doukhobors generally maintained their identification with mystic history and their belief in the spiritual-material impermanence of their sojourn in British Columbia as a way of resisting the major institutional manifestations of their forced assimilation into another set of identities: education in the dominant language, individualism, participation in the building of imperial empire by means of war and patriotic commitment to war, and the conditions of visibility (registry, voting) required for citizenship. While the CCUB existed under Peter Lordly, this resistance to the secular authorities remained in uneasy balance with the desire to live out the meaning of "toil and peaceful life" in isolation from the secular world. However, after the events of 1924, this balance was forever disrupted.

Peter Chistiakov, Peter Lordly's son,[12] became the next Doukhobor leader. At Brilliant, during his introductory speech, he electrified Doukhobors with his long theological discussions and his slogan "Sons of Freedom cannot be slaves of corruption" (Woodcock and Avakumovic 1977, 287). Although his speech was meant to unite all three groups of Doukhobors, the Sons of Freedom interpreted his exhortation as indicating that they were the "ringing bells" who would recall the people to the true faith. Peter Chistiakov's subsequent pleas for them to stop radical protests were interpreted by them, using the Freedomite "upside-down" philosophy (where the opposite of what a leader said was taken to be true), as approval. Freedomite activity increased as they opposed the orders of the government to send their children to school: burnings and nude parades became more frequent.

Peter Chistiakov's subsequent mystical speeches also did much to further Doukhobor fusion of mystic identifications with worldly events, even as he turned Doukhobor fervour to his own ends. Consider his often-repeated migration model, which made sojourning central to Doukhobor identity. Chistiakov described migration as part of the Doukhobor history of resistance, envisioning it as a series of meals: "breakfast" is the Doukhobor struggle against icons and the Russian Orthodox Church, "dinner" is the rejection of militarism symbolized by the Burning of Arms, and "supper" is something that Chistiakov would not discuss but that he hinted was migration (Tarasoff 1982, 147).

Despite his strengths as a leader, Peter Chistiakov became more irrational in the years between 1931 and 1938. Not only did the Community lose large amounts of money due to the Depression, but the unsettling nature of Chistiakov's leadership and his large-scale evictions of Freedomites from Community land also caused a fall in membership dues. By 1931 these evicted Sons of Freedom, along with others who left voluntarily, had formed their own communities on poor land at the edges of the Doukhobor domain in the villages of Krestova and Gilpin. With these areas as their base, the Freedomites began large-scale nude protests and demonstrations that resulted in prison terms for them at Piers Island, when the maximum penalty in British Columbia for public nudity was raised from six months to three years.

By 1933 the Doukhobor communities were beginning to split in serious ways. The Independents became a stronger group and completely broke from the control of the Community, voting for Makaroff as a candidate for the CCF party. The Community, left without strong leadership and debt-laden in the midst of the Depression, began to founder. The Sons of Freedom, meanwhile, grew in numbers to several thousand, and their commitment to the protest against government control was only increased by the prospect of martyrdom at Piers Island: "whether [all Doukhobors] sought [a better way of life] by going on pilgrimages or by 'Toil and peaceful life,' such people were led by an almost superstitious belief in the possibility of attaining the kingdom of heaven on earth, and when this vision of the Community was broken, as happened during the 1930s, many of them were to follow the chialists among the Sons of Freedom, who offered an alternative vision" (Woodcock and Avakumovic 1977, 239). Between 1937 and 1939 the Christian Community of Universal Brotherhood went bankrupt for reasons that still anger Doukhobors today, many of whom see the events as a second land-grab by the Canadian government.[13] It is clear that the government could have bailed out the CCUB but chose not to do so, probably due to public antipathy towards the Doukhobors.

Peter Chistiakov died of liver and stomach cancer in 1939, the same year that the Community ended. Before his death, he dissolved the CCUB and formed the beginnings of the USCC as a spiritual equivalent to the old economic organization of the Community (Joint Doukhobor Research Committee 1997, 210). Peter Chistiakov's son, Peter Iastrebov (the Hawk), was named as leader, but he was somewhere in Stalinist Russia, which had been imprisoning and persecuting the Doukhobors for a decade. No one knew where he was. Therefore, the newly formed USCC decided to appoint John Voikin, Peter Chistiakov's grandson, as leader. He was renamed John J. Verigin and, at the age of eighteen, became the "secretary" of the USCC. His position at the time was temporary since most Doukhobors hoped that Peter Iastrebov would come from the USSR and restore the Doukhobor community to its former strength. This did not occur since Iastrebov probably died in the late 1930s. Under John J. Verigin the USCC did buy back land in the Kootenays, although the people did not resume communal living. The Independent Doukhobors began to assimilate more quickly after Peter Chistiakov's death. The Freedomites, divided into factions headed by a number of leaders, including the non-Doukhobor Stefan Sorokin, increased depredations (mostly against other Doukhobors in the Kootenays) as a protest against materialism and what they saw as other compromises with non-Doukhobor culture. Prejudice against all Doukhobors mounted due to Freedomite protests, and measures against Freedomites, including incarcerating their children for forced schooling in New Denver, increased. Freedomite activity peaked in 1962 after a mass imprisonment of Freedomite arsonists and bombers. At this time large numbers of Freedomites, led by Frances Storgeoff, marched to Agassiz prison (a fireproof facility for Freedomites serving jail terms), built a camp there, and, for several years, agitated for the release of prisoners.

Accommodation and Assimilation

After a large public outcry following the New Denver plan, the government of British Columbia legalized Doukhobor marriages, which meant that thousands of children were no longer considered illegitimate. The three-year prison term for nudity was dropped, and the right of Doukhobors to vote provincially was restored. Moreover, a compromise for citizenship was reached. Keeping in mind that Doukhobors considered themselves to be "citizens of the universe" who were technically citizens of Christ alone, they became "Canadian, subject to the law of God and Jesus Christ" (Woodcock and Avakumovic 1977, 347). The Community Doukhobors accepted this arrangement.

As for the Freedomites, the march to Agassiz represented the last mass protest by the Sons of Freedom. As Woodcock observes, assimilation has also affected this community, and "where decades of police and bureaucratic action failed, a few years of exposure to the affluent society have succeeded" (Woodcock and Avakumovic 1977, 356). Since that time, there have been no strong leaders and depredations were drastically reduced, although tensions between Freedomites and other Doukhobors – especially against John J. Verigin, the USCC organization, and some Freedomite radicals – were running high during the mid-1970s and 1980s, as is seen in confrontations described in the Joint Doukhobor Research Committee report of the period between 1974 and 1982.

The USCC, which remains the major organization of Community Doukhobors, was registered in 1954 and became a more formal organization in the 1960s. Its Russian/English magazine, *Iskra,* began as an all-Russian magazine in 1943, headed by Walter Lebedoff. By 1980 its circulation was approximately 1,500. Also in 1945 the Union of Youth, which included members from the ages of sixteen to forty, began. Although it operated as a social organization for younger Community Doukhobors, in the 1970s Doukhobors who had gone to Vancouver to be educated at the University of British Columbia used the organization to begin to discuss identity issues and to seek affiliations with Doukhobor youth of other groups. They started the *UYD Newsletter,* which later became *Mir,* an all-English magazine dedicated to youth issues and run by the present editor of *Iskra,* Jim Popoff. *Mir* (which in Russian means "commune," "peace," and "world") also functioned as an early place for historical recovery projects. Staff from *Mir* conducted interviews with Doukhobor elders and printed autobiographical excerpts in an effort to learn more about their history and to debate the meaning of Doukhobor identity. *Mir* became a way for younger Doukhobors, who were no longer part of the communal world remembered by their elders, to come to grips with questions of Doukhobor identity and its survival in contemporary Canada. It was an important forum within which autobiographical excerpts, interviews, and other types of autobiographical expressions made it possible for younger Doukhobors to refigure their own identities.

Many of the people who worked on *Mir* or who contributed to it returned to the Kootenays and assumed positions of leadership in the USCC and in affiliated Doukhobor organizations in the 1970s and 1980s, a period during which Doukhobors began to attempt to recover aspects of their heritage and to reinterpret them so that they would be in accord with their present situation. As Doukhobors – particularly Community Doukhobors – assimilated into the larger Canadian cultural milieu, they also initiated ways for Doukhobor living to survive in alternative contexts, including a co-op store, social programs, youth festivals, and educational initiatives. Doukhobors also participated in non-Doukhobor peace movements. In 1980 the USCC contributed to building the National Doukhobor Heritage Village in Saskatchewan, while a communal Doukhobor village is run as a museum at Ootishenie, British Columbia. Doukhobor choirs have toured across Canada and have cut albums. The youth movement now runs workshops on Doukhobor identity each year, while Doukhobor craftspeople, writers, and artists are now trying to preserve and to reinterpret (for Doukhobors and non-Doukhobors) the history and meaning of Doukhoborism as some Doukhobor ways of life disappear. Community Doukhobors have found that more and more of its documentation must be made in English since fewer and fewer Doukhobors speak Russian.[14] For a people who have always transmitted their faith practices in terms of the Russian language, this may mean that Doukhoborism will die when the language is no longer spoken by the majority of its members – a problem discussed constantly in *Iskra*. Migration back to Russia has been posed frequently as a solution to this problem.

It is hard, as John W. Friesen and Michael Verigin observe, to say whether the efforts of Doukhobors in Canada to resist some aspects of dominant culture and language, combined with an acceptance of other aspects, will forestall wholesale assimilation as participation in youth events is low and, in the case of youth festivals, not serious enough to facilitate cultural interaction (Friesen and Verigin 1989, 200-1). At the same time, younger Doukhobors are beginning to produce materials on the Internet concerning Doukhobor history, beliefs, and practices; there are now Doukhobor artists and writers who are exploring their heritage; and there are workshops for younger Doukhobors wanting to work through political and spiritual issues.[15] Only Doukhobors themselves will be able to say whether Doukhoborism will survive in its present form, given the alterations and accommodations Doukhobors have made during their first 100 years' sojourn in Canada. However, the efforts that Doukhobors have made to record autobiographical narratives and to publicize them in Russian and English may contribute to new ways for Doukhobor identity to be figured, perhaps enabling Doukhoborism to survive into the second century dating from its arrival in Canada. It is this effort that I now explore in detail.

3
Vechnaiia Pamit in the Diaspora: Community Meanings of History and Migration

All of us, human beings, have a part of God within us. The earth is
not our permanent homeland. We are merely pilgrims on this earth,
for our real birth place is in Heaven. Our physical, earthly body is
not our real being. Our real being is the soul within our body.

— Psalm 24, the Living Book[1]

In her poem "Of Other Generations," published in 1974 in the Doukhobor
English-language magazine *Mir,* Elaine J. Makortoff connects issues of
memory and her relationship with the early Doukhobor migrants. She
identifies her impulse to remember not as an unambiguous look at her
past but, rather, as a "half-turning" between her present and another generation's discourse:

my head's always half-turned
looking at the backs of things
listening to what dead men said
what the dying are saying.
(Makortoff 1974, 44)

This way to remember does not produce confident memories of migrant
identity or a firm immigrant paradigm, but confused memories about people on the move. In Makortoff's poem, a gap exists between how the
migrants came to Canada and how the migration is to be remembered.
She calls the undecidability of these memories "the collisions in my mind"
and says that these collisions are "refugees/expatriots and exiles/migrant,
outlaws/free agents and farmers" (Makortoff 1974, 44). These collisions
are between the condition of migration and how it is seen. Either migration appears as diasporic – the migrants had to relocate somewhere else
against their will and now hope to return, or the migrants are labourers,
her ancestor-farmers, who make "an endless furrow / that another generation / stalks and consumes" (44).

Makortoff's poem expresses her dual heritage as analogous to her own
process of remembering, figured as a collapse of time between her own
generation and the older one, and confusion about how the earlier generation relates to her own identity. The poem concludes without resolving

this ambiguity about what place means – an ambiguity that even extends to what kind and size of plants the narrator looks at and whether the people in her vision are her farmer ancestors or "strangers" who claim affinity through a different heritage:

> I sit at the axis of a great plain
> or is it the mind's eye —
> there are decades of heaving alfalfa
> or are they the waves in this blade of grass ...
> on the horizon my farmer ancestors
> plow the endless furrow
> or are they a generation of young strangers
> who call to me by name.
> (Makortoff 1974, 44)

Makortoff highlights a slippage between her own place, time, and identity and the identity of a previous Doukhobor generation, between then and now, between what they are doing and what she can see. This is not Homi Bhabha's third space, where hybridity operates as a political strategy to recast the terms of cultural debate or political action in a non-dialectic way,[2] but, rather, an attempt by the poet to *catalogue* the undecidability of hybrid origins by writing them as unresolvable pairs. Diasporic identity can be seen here in the decision to "half-turn" towards origins where even the meaning of origin is "migrating," unclear, open to the writer's interpretation. Who does she see? Who is hailing her, within her own discourse and in her rhetorical "half-turn?" Who or what interpellates her as a Doukhobor subject? How will she respond to the collision of meanings?

In autobiographical writing by Community and Independent Doukhobors, this "half-turn" to the past also surfaces as an attempt to investigate the diasporic origin and migration of Doukhobors from Russia to Canada. It also invests the current meaning of Doukhobor group identity with an understanding of origin and the migration experience that is both sacred and political, mediated by the act of autobiographical writing and speaking. The act of this "half-turn," the attempt to figure origins as both sacred and historic, individual and collective, informs non-traditional forms of autobiographical writing in magazine articles and transcribed interviews by Community and Independent Doukhobors. But it occurs in ways that call into question an understanding of autobiography as a discourse that can only occur in published books as part of a liberal-capitalist economy of identity, where identity is seen as a unique, interiorized selfhood that can be communicated, subverted, and then packaged and sold as a "narrative commodity." Homi Bhabha's comments on the work of daily life and how this becomes part of a national culture can be applied to a different purpose here. According to Bhabha (1994, 145), "the scraps, patches and rags of daily life must be repeatedly turned into the signs of a coherent national culture, while the very act of the narrative performance interpellates a growing circle of national subjects." Bhabha's connection between the incorporation of local forms into a pan-national sign of "the people" can be a way to understand the work performed by Doukhobor short reminiscences, interviews, and excerpts from committee testimony. These "scraps, patches and rags of daily life," written or dictated for Doukhobor magazines, speeches, or committees on Doukhobor identity, work autobiographically – that is, in a way that collects the split geographic experience and split historic experience of a diasporic subject under one singular life sign so as to configure remembered migration and settlement experiences *into writing* within what had been an oral way to remember. Interpellation occurs not necessarily as a recouping of Doukhobor subjectivity as national subjectivity but, rather, as part of a hybrid formation between writing and oral narrative, and between reminiscence and autobiographical discourse.[3]

The autobiographical "half-turn" in Doukhobor writing for periodicals and small publications aimed mostly at Doukhobor readers relates migration experiences in Canada to other oral histories of Doukhobor experience, but it also writes that memory into the idea of a national culture as migration trauma that must be surmounted rather than as happy interpellation into and by the official Canadian discourse of multiculturalism. It also forms an alternative to the pain caused by the heritage of absolute difference and the suspicion of difference perpetuated by discourses of the English-Canadian centre. Doukhobors who have written or spoken autobiographically about this pain tend to talk about the silencing of their identity. As Vi Plotnikoff (1998, 205) writes: "To be a Doukhobor was to hide your background, not flaunt it." Annie Barnes's (1998, 22) description of a group of Doukhobor women who gathered to talk about their identity shows how the activity of speaking about identity issues brought about joy, release, and healing through remembering in a safe environment: "They [the women in the group] were so eager, interrupting each other, laughing, when there could have been tears. They were anxious to share some old hurts in a safe place, with other women who understood, in an atmosphere of love and acceptance. As *Verna (Berukoff) Kidd* writes, 'In a group we still seem to find each other and ask about our ancestors'" (emphasis in original). In autobiographical work by Doukhobors, the act of remembering ancestors and of speaking about ethnic origins also operates as an act of healing the collective pain of dislocation and of otherness by sharing "textual" memories with the readership of Doukhobor magazines.

Autobiographical writing that has appeared mainly in *Iskra*[4] and *Mir* features what Vijay Mishra calls the appearance of "home as a damaged idea"

in diasporic narratives. What Mishra (1995, 7) refers to in the same discussion as the "psychic trauma of forced migration" resolves in these narratives when Doukhobor writers and speakers work through the idea of
"home" and the idea of "suffering" found in Doukhobor psalms and oral
history. They do this within hybrid autobiographical discourses that allow
the Doukhobor speaker to remember *for others* and not just for him or
herself, a use of the trope of community memory that Bakhtin (1981b) discusses – and which I address later on – in "Forms of Time and Chronotope
in the Novel."[5] This activity operates in a field between the visibility
offered by autobiographical discourse in Western terms and the sacred
"language" for memory that connects it (in traditional Doukhobor settings such as funeral services) to the traditional Doukhobor meaning of
the Russian phrase *vechnaiia pamit*,[6] which Doukhobors translate as eternal memory *and* eternal consciousness in the Kingdom of Heaven after
death. Autobiographical discourse, where it is invoked, carries with it non-
Doukhobor ideas about singularity and the ability of one subject to speak
about something unique. But for Doukhobors, to be, and to be eternally,
is to remember and be remembered within a community. The act of memory is not carried out alone for the work of memory is also the work of a
community.

Autobiography occurs in these texts not as a "new" genre but, in Mary
Louise Pratt's (1992, 6-7) terms, a "contact zone" where a number of non-
Doukhobor and Doukhobor narrative strategies appear together or where,
due to non-Doukhobor requests for Doukhobor articulations of identity,
these contending narratives are called into being. The uncertain histories
of diasporic dislocation (sometimes worked through in English, sometimes
in Russian) in autobiographical fragments, speeches, and interviews combine with *vechnaiia pamit* to form sacred ways to remember and recollect
that are already part of Doukhobor oral tradition. This type of writing,
translation, and transcription appears in *Mir* interviews of older Doukhobor migrants or settlers in the 1970s that were meant to bring their
recollections to a young Doukhobor readership whose first language was
usually English. It was also found in the short reminiscences published in
Mir and later in *Iskra* (in both English and Russian) during the late 1970s
as well as in Gregory Soukorev's English language manuscript in *Iskra*,
which was published in a serial format over six issues (the Russian language version had been published in *Iskra* in 1945). This enabled non-
Russian-speaking Doukhobors to learn about their heritage.

Before I begin to look at how autobiography develops in this type of
contact zone of writing by and about Community and Independent
Doukhobors, I examine how the term "diaspora" operates and what role
diasporic identity plays in *vechnaiia pamit* and related ways of remembering origins in Doukhobor psalms, songs, and hymns. The term "diaspora"

has been growing in popularity in the areas of history, literary criticism pertaining to ethnic minority writing, postcolonial theory, and globalization studies, among others. The original meaning of diaspora, a term referring first to Jews not living in Israel and then to the original dispersion of the early Christians from Jerusalem, has been widened to include a number of groups forcibly expelled from their lands of origin (e.g., the Armenians after the Second World War). When Paul Gilroy (1996, 22-23) connected diaspora with "the black Atlantic" in order to negotiate a postmodern homology between migration and subjectivity and an essentialist longing for pure race origins, African Americanists began to use the term to refer to the multiple, syncretic, and hybrid forms of cultures and ideas that form part of black identities and the legacy of the colonial trade systems between Europe, North/South America, Africa, and the Caribbean. This connection between a non-essentialized, and yet strategic, identity linked to more than one cultural form and the memory of more than one place was soon applied to examinations of the transnational movements of other labour forces in response to economic globalization.

The close associations of identity, origin, and forced migrations with a hope of return have proven fertile in a number of migrant contexts, particularly as technological developments such as the telephone, the video tape, and the aeroplane mean that mass migrations and their tie to transnational demands for cheap labour begin to challenge ideas about nationality and its fixed associations with "grounded" citizens rooted in their native soil. As Jenny Sharpe points out, following Appadurai (1996) on transnationalism, diaspora has become related to the "flow of capital": "*Transnationalism* denotes the permeability of national borders in the electronic transmission of capital, labor, technology, and media images. *Diaspora* designates the political and economic refugees, immigrant and exile communities that inhabit advanced industrial and newly industrializing nations and city-states" (Sharpe 1995, 188).

When this kind of recognition of diasporic identity is hooked to the flow of information and capital as potentially destabilizing for nation-states, some theorists link it to postmodernist critiques of the nation-state as an eternal, fixed entity. Diaspora, in the thinking of these theorists, troubles the easy homologies made between nationality and ethnicity.[7] Diasporic identity is understood to be a strategic double-functioning identity developed by migrant groups between the homeland and the host nation. Diaspora has also come to express the cultural forms from the land of origin that a migrant uses as a way of dealing with his or her present position. These cultural forms, particularly when theorists discuss diaspora theory and transnationalism, can include technological developments that work to dissolve previous spatial and temporal barriers between the host country and the land of origin.

When connected to fractured ideas of "home land," the most prevalent use of the term "diaspora" is connected to postmodernist ideas about transnationalism and the representation of homelessness. This is because the idea of diaspora retains traces of cultural practice and memory of the home place, deployed literally or figuratively, in some type of hope for return. As Ien Ang (1994, 5) observes, diaspora is bound up with ideas of home, both "imagined" and physical: "Diaspora is the (imagined) condition of a 'people' dispersed throughout the world, by force or by choice. Diasporas are transnational, spatially and temporally sprawling sociocultural formations of people, creating imagined communities whose blurred and fluctuating boundaries are sustained by real and/or symbolic ties to some original 'homeland.'" While it is tempting to apply diaspora to an idea of permeable borders that challenges the modernist idea of nation, a kind of "aporia" that changes otherness to a "lack" that changes the politics of the centre, it is also wise to heed Sau Ling Cynthia Wong's (1995) caution that the world is not borderless and that international travel requiring passports and visas does not imply a nation-less, class-less world where diasporic migration automatically makes room for political action.

But this critique of dehistoricized diasporic study can also operate as the term's strength. When it is connected with a historicized geographic awareness, as opposed to a rhetorical "third space" or "borderzone," the notion of "diaspora" becomes a way of examining the work that the notion "home" does in the *collective* identity of a migrated group. It can also refer to group identity (rather than to an individual identity) as a group deals with ways to represent past dislocation and present locatedness. Collective identity and locatedness is mentioned throughout work on diaspora, although collectivity is often jettisoned in favour of talking about the subject, as in Ang's (1994, 5) statement that "it is the myth of the (lost or idealized) homeland, the object of both collective memory and of desire and attachment, which is constitutive to diasporas, and which ultimately confines and constrains the nomadism of the diasporic subject." The collective imaginary of a diasporic group and how it decides to deploy its understanding of origins amidst the cultural forms of a host nation not only constrains the nomadism of a given diasporic subject but also provides a way to negotiate, to win, and sometimes to lose what *this* identity means *here* and how it relates to a *there* that must be acknowledged, longed-for, invented, argued about, and remembered by pluralized subjects. Clearly, the Doukhobors constitute this type of diasporic group, particularly since they were forced to migrate to Canada and, for many years, were expected to return to Russia. They have even made numerous attempts either to return to Russia or to migrate from Canada to another country in order to continue the way of life that they had developed in Russia.

An important part of group memory concerning the place of origin and its relationship to the current "placing" of diasporic subjects is what Vijay Mishra (1995, 26) calls the sacred. The sacred, he argues, is a narrative about the place of origin that makes intervention in the current situation possible. This has been left out of contemporary theories of diaspora. What the sacred does is create an alternate idea of home that, in Mishra's formulation, does not have to become part of either a colonizer rhetoric or a set of moves scripted for the host nation's migrant others that seals off migrants from the places from which they came. He explains that "the 'sacred' is a function of narratives that the almost self-contained diasporic communities constructed out of a finite set of memories. They gave permanence to mobility ... by creating a fixed point of origin when none existed ... since its narratives are transhistorical, the absurdity of the move for a disempowered diasporic community is overtaken completely by the illusory power of the act itself, from which the colonizer is excluded. This is true of all religious attitudes in the diaspora" (27). The sacred, then, can operate in diasporic groups where religious discourse is important as a node of resistance to the bipolar confusions of "there" and "here" and the tendency of dominant discourses of nation to equate race/ethnicity with nationality and national belonging. In what Mishra calls the "diasporic imaginary," the sacred becomes a way to heal the wounded ideas of home and homelessness and ground the identity of diasporic subjects in ways that do not reference a national memory or a national culture. Existence, rather than pure resistance, becomes imaginable and possible.

The term *vechnaiia pamit* can provide a way to understand how the Doukhobors, who clearly are a diasporic group, figure the idea of home within a discourse that allows the sacred to function wherever memory operates. In a traditional Doukhobor funerary service, for example, *vechnaiia pamit v Tsarsvii nebyesnom* (everlasting consciousness in the Kingdom of Heaven) is said of the deceased to affirm that the body dies while the soul does not (USCC Kootenay Men's Group 1995, 1), while "biographies" of the deceased are said at the gravesite and, in recent years, printed in *Iskra* as a way to honour the memory of the deceased. This is because to remember is also to perform an act of eternal consciousness (19). The act of memory is an eternal act recited by the whole community and not just by one person, and it is demonstrated in action through the telling of life stories. *Vechnaiia pamit* is a recitation of the community's history in sacred terms, as in Doukhobor psalm 355 from The Living Book, which begins with "eternal memory be to our righteous forefathers who were buried as the true Doukhobors" and which continues with an account of the 1801 migration to Milky Waters. The latter was a sacred act because it was undertaken "for the sake of the truth"; it was a migration to an area referred to as "our Promised Land." In contrast, the region of the Transcaucasus, the

Doukhobors' subsequent place of migration, is referred to as "our Land of Suffering." The listener is finally exhorted to continue the community traditions for "whoever else remains alive and hears of this history, should not desist from continuing these deeds to the end" (The Living Book 1978, 256). *Vechnaiia pamit* is a historical recounting, a sacred interpretation of migration, and an exhortation to keep the faith.

It becomes possible, then, to think of Doukhobor psalms, hymns, and the stories told by elders as a type of *vechnaiia pamit,* or sacred memory of migration experiences that are enacted again and again as part of the "diasporic imaginary" when they are told, recited, or sung. This oral tradition forms the sacred language of migration, resistance, and suffering also found, or referred to, in Doukhobors' written autobiographical productions. The psalms of The Living Book refer to humankind as strangers who wander on the earth, a situation analogous to the multiple migrations Doukhobors have experienced and to their willingness to undergo hardship. Psalm 15 describes how communal living not only functions as an exemplar but also prophesies that the Doukhobors will enter earthly history in an apocalyptic moment: "The commune's virtues, its exemplary life, shall triumph over the world – this earthly materialistic kingdom – whose end is nearing. Then, Doukhobors shall become known to all mankind, and Christ himself shall be the only worthy King. Around Him shall gather all nations. Only this honour shall be preceded by a time of great trials and sorrow" (The Living Book 1978, 56).

In more widely sung hymns and spiritual songs, Doukhobors also remember the persecution undergone by their ancestors after the 1895 Burning of Arms, usually in light of their subsequent migration. Doukhobor identity in all groups depends on the memory of this resistance, in part because it has at times provided the basis for pacifist resistance to government activity in Canada but also because it keeps both the reason for and the fact of migration intact. The stress in many psalms, spiritual songs, and hymns on Doukhobor identity as the identity of those who have migrated keeps migration at the forefront of the diasporic imaginary, particularly in light of Doukhobor leader Lukeri'ia's prophecies that the Doukhobors would eventually return to Russia after a period of wandering and suffering.[8] The diasporic imaginary also supports the identity of Doukhobors as a migrant group from Russia and substantiates actual efforts made by Doukhobors in Canada to maintain connections with their original homeland. For example, the USCC Standing Committee on Migration is the latest in a series of efforts made by various Doukhobor groups to investigate the possibility of a return to Russia. *Iskra* also carries reports on Russia that describe ongoing Doukhobor efforts to maintain connections there. These include: Doukhobor student exchanges with Russia, projects to help Russia (such as the fundraising efforts to help

Chernobyl victims), reports on the activities of Doukhobors who live in Russia, and commentary on Russian affairs generally.

In recently composed songs performed for the Canadian Museum of Civilization's (1998) multimedia Doukhobor exhibit – such as "Toil and Peaceful Life," which begins "We are the people who left home one day, / We were told we could no longer stay," or in the solo "Our Tribute," where the singer cries while he relates the hardships of the young men who were imprisoned in Russia and then sings "And to Canada, we all have migrated" – Doukhobor suffering after the Burning of Arms is closely related to migration. Even a poster from that exhibit stresses resistance and migration as key Doukhobor experiences. The poster features a photograph of Doukhobors on one of the migration ships, a map of their migration path from Russia to Canada, and the two most significant dates for Doukhobors in Canada – the 1895 Burning of Arms and the migration to Canada in 1899. Both activities – resistance to oppression and migration – form the spiritual and material touchstone of Doukhobor identity. They have enabled Doukhobors to see their difficulties in Canada in spiritual terms that were often not immediately comprehensible to Canadian authorities, and they also enabled them to resist significant attempts to assimilate them far longer than did most migrant groups. These representations of homeland, collective oppression, and migration form a language for Doukhobor experience that provides a point of negotiation for Doukhobors' attempts to remember their history along spiritualist rather than empirical lines. They also enable Doukhobors to write themselves into autobiographical texts as individuals who are ultimately responsible to a community and to communal memory.

Smaller English-language autobiographical texts appeared in *Mir* and still appear occasionally in *Iskra,* providing a way for Doukhobor readers to learn about Doukhobor history, identity, and tradition. Many of the smaller pieces that appear in *Iskra* have been transcribed and translated into English by the speakers themselves or by their children in an effort to accommodate the disappearance of intergenerational oral learning and the declining use of the Russian language among Doukhobors. The challenge the writers of these texts face, therefore, is not just a local historical one. Shorter Doukhobor speeches, reminiscences, and explanatory notes work against assimilation by reminding readers of the diasporic position of the Doukhobors as migrants from Russia, while the constant references to migration to Canada and movement within Canada indirectly refer to Doukhobor subjectivity as a migrant subjectivity related to their spiritual mission on earth. These concerns with rootlessness are grounded in one of two ways: either in the writer's exhortation to remember one's origin as a "Spirit Wrestler" who resists injustice or in the evocation of autobiographical discourse itself, which combines with oral Doukhobor discourse to invoke a pedagogical hybrid subject that the younger generation can "learn" about and from.

An example of a narrative that an elder originally told to benefit younger people, and that has been recast into a public format, can be found in a set of recollections by Nikolai Perepelkin. Perepelkin related his experiences to his granddaughter, Hazel Samorodin, who, with Tim Samorodin, wrote the narrative down in Russian, translated it, and published it in *Iskra*. In the narrative, the Samorodins preface Perepelkin's remarks with conventional details about his date and place of birth (Perepelkin 1993, 24). Perepelkin's reminiscence, however, features a plural subjectivity that is found literally in the narrative and is implied in his telling of the story to his granddaughter so that she can retell it to others.

His story focuses on the experiences of Doukhobor men hired to work on the railway. Perepelkin interprets the events in a binary format: the hardworking men are teased by non-Doukhobors who do not understand them. These experiences include moments of prejudice from non-Doukhobors, who cut their tent ropes or put ashes in their food. The Doukhobor men are also refused water during the 300-mile walk home to their families. However, one non-Doukhobor woman does give them milk to drink, and "this gesture of goodwill by this gentle lady stuck in the memories of all of us" (Perepelkin 1993, 24). It is unclear in the narrative who "us" actually is. It is possible that Perepelkin was with the men, but the next sentence seems to indicate that he was not: "Finally, our workers arrived home after a nine-month absence" (24). It does not actually matter where Perepelkin is in the narrative since the subjectivity recounted is plural: the work of the men belongs to the community.

Iskra's decision to translate and print "Grandma Melanya's Story," a short autobiography from a contemporary Russian Doukhobor elder, indicates how Canadian Doukhobors are encouraged to maintain diasporic connections to their "homeland" and their "home identity" by means of short life narratives. Grandma Melanya describes – probably to a Doukhobor interviewer for *Iskra* – her two short years of school and her work as a Russian peasant, which includes weaving, cooking, haying in the fields, and tending cattle. She also describes square dancing, singing or talking "with the girls," and "a shot or two to celebrate" for fun (Melanya 1996, 47). These activities would present a living reminder of agricultural life to Doukhobors who still endorse rural communal living in principle but who do not practise it. But, like Doukhobors in Canada, Grandma Melanya discusses the loss of Doukhobor tradition and the difficulty of passing it on to the community's youth since they have "no songs to sing, no stories to tell, as our ancestors would say" (47). She ends her narrative with a statement of loss – "a lot of things have gone out of the lives of us *Dukhobory*" –

but then invites Doukhobors in Canada to visit her community next year to see the old ways: "come and see us" (47). Here is a life narrative that functions not in terms of nostalgia but, rather, in terms of diasporic connections to communal living, Russian language, and Doukhobor tradition. Grandma Melanya's exhortation to come and see them (rather than to come and see her) makes her life narrative a point of connection between the groups and an invitation to Doukhobors to directly renew their traditions. Autobiography operates here as the point of contact, transcribed and translated, between groups in order to strengthen Doukhobor connections to their traditional culture and their Russian homeland.

The article by Joe and Florence Podovinikoff, written for *Iskra* and entitled "Former Saskatchewan Doukhobors Recall," represents a different type of recollection designed to emphasize Doukhobor identity via a remembered diasporic connection. Unlike Perepelkin's recollection, the Podovinikoffs recall a specific event – their first impressions of Peter Chistiakov upon his arrival in Canada. They do not recall this for the benefit of their grandchildren, as did Perepelkin, but for the benefit of those they call "the younger Doukhobor generation of today" (Podovinikoff and Podovinikoff 1989, 18). Their intent is to advise the younger generation to read the letters and speeches of Peter Chistiakov for guidance. The decision to discuss a personal experience, therefore, is didactic and closely related to the act of resisting assimilation, which they call "the difficult period of spiritual confusion" that they believe Chistiakov foresaw (20). They refer to the "personal experience of our own early years" as their reason for thinking that Peter Chistiakov's writings hold value for younger Doukhobors who want to understand Doukhobor identity issues and challenges. They believe that, "eventually[,] reality leads us back to our own unique historical roots, carrying their own unique ramifications, which the leader understood well" (20).

This remembrance of Peter Chistiakov, therefore, exists as a didactic aid that points to his writings. The function of the personal experience of the Podovinikoffs is to stimulate the desire for "eternal memory," the memory of the sacred, in the younger Doukhobor community and to connect that memory to aspects of Doukhobor religious faith and history that link it to the diasporic imaginary. This is why their memory of Chistiakov focuses first on the impact of his arrival "from the far away 'Rodina' – *Rossiya*." *Rodina* is the Russian word for homeland, and the Russian (rather than the English) word for Russia is used and italicized for emphasis. Peter Chistiakov's arrival is not a matter of personal nostalgia – as the Podovinikoffs say, "we were 14 at the time" and so they would not remember Russia – but, rather, a living connection between the land of origin and the place where the Doukhobors had migrated. Chistiakov, having just migrated himself, symbolizes the Russianness of Doukhobor identity: his clothes, for example, are Russian, and he wears "Cossack boots" – "to us he was truly a phenomenon from another world" (Podovinikoff and Podovinikoff 1989, 18). Indeed, he connects that other world to the current world of the Podovinikoffs. The Podovinikoffs see Peter Chistiakov's arrival as a revival of the diasporic imaginary since he aimed "to make Doukhobors aware of their historic calling [and] to preserve the high principles of their forefathers" and, among other things, asked Doukhobor women to wear traditional, not "foreign," dress (18) so that they would remain "Doukhobor" and not assimilate into Canadian society. Through this recollection of Peter Chistiakov's influence and importance, the diasporic imaginary is filtered through the Podovinikoffs' decision to use a personal narrative format to stress their youthful experience of Peter Chistiakov, their purpose being to enable the younger generation to understand and preserve Doukhobor identity by remembering their Russian roots.

While *Iskra* mainly features autobiographical passages and stories by USCC members, the editors of early issues of *Mir* made an effort to acquire material by Doukhobors from other groups. To this end, *Mir* asked some Doukhobors, whom they considered to be members of the Independent Doukhobor community, to write articles about the history and background of the Independent group. Two of these articles, one by Peter J. Popoff about the Independents and one by Ivan G. Bondoreff about the Named Doukhobors of Canada[9] have short autobiographical prefaces. These serve to introduce the authors, but they also construct an alternative history of Doukhoborism for a readership that could be unfamiliar with this particular type. These narratives, therefore, not only situate individual Doukhobors but also serve to revise the idea of a Doukhobor subject for the benefit of other Doukhobor readers. There are subtle "clues" as to the identity and worldview of the writers, and these serve to inscribe them both as Doukhobor subjects and as Independents.

Peter J. Popoff's "Autobiographical Note," for example, begins his short narrative not with his date of birth but with the actions of his parents which marked them as Independents. He writes that he was born "shortly before my parents applied for an individual homestead and moved onto it, as they chose not to migrate to BC, and the communal lands in the area were already parcelled to individual owners" (Popoff 1974, 13). Like Fred Davidoff and Peter Maloff (see Chapter 5) and the oral narratives in Chapter 4, Popoff's writing expresses his identity in terms of how his parents decided to deal with the locational changes made by the Doukhobors after the Canadian government tried to get them to register for individual homesteads and to swear an oath to the Queen. To be an Independent, therefore, was to decide to react to spatial change by *not* migrating to British Columbia. Identity, land use, and reactions to non-Doukhobor authority are connected here to signify to other Doukhobors what it means to be an Independent Doukhobor.

Popoff identifies himself with the Doukhobor tradition of pacifist resistance and the willingness to be jailed when he describes his participation in a 1932 demonstration to protest the assemblage of global powers for war and the mass arrests of Doukhobors in British Columbia. He also mentions his arrest in 1937 in Grand Forks for not registering as was required by the War Measures Act. These details come before Popoff describes his committee involvement with Doukhobor groups, before he describes his career, and before he discusses his present life in Grand Forks and provides the names of his wife and children. This autobiography, therefore, stresses Popoff's Independent roots and his commitment to political protest, both of which mark him as an Independent who has not compromised Doukhobor ideals. This emphasis prefigures the conclusion of his article, which addresses the usefulness of the Independent movement to Doukhoborism generally: "In addition they [the Independents who did not go to war] had shown that a person does not necessarily renounce his faith in God nor in the Doukhobor teaching merely by not subscribing to either of the formal groups ... [There may be no future for the Independents:] their involvement in the Doukhobor cause may, however, assist others who will rally to the call to fulfil the destiny of the Doukhobors" (Popoff 1974, 42).

Ivan (John) Bondoreff's "Autobiographical Note," like Popoff's, expresses his identity in terms of his family's location, which Doukhobor readers would recognize as a sign of its shifting group affiliation. For example, Bondoreff's (1975, 12) family originally settles at Blaine Lake, Saskatchewan, "living a communal way of life for a few years." This changes when the organization of space changes due to the government survey and the division of the land into homesteads: Bondoreff's most important childhood memory is connected to this event as he is the boy selected to pull the quarter assignments out of a cap: "I remember I didn't even have grown up pants on yet" (12). The life of his family changes drastically after this event since, due to the actions of the federal government, the CCUB asks them, along with the rest of the Blaine Lake community, to move 200 miles to community lands in Saskatchewan (and then to British Columbia).

However, by 1919, after his marriage to Mary Kabatoff, Bondoreff's family signals its Independent affiliation by moving out of the CCUB to a farm at Blaine Lake (although this is not overt in the narrative and the reasons for moving are not detailed). Bondoreff then lists his more significant community activities since that time – activities that mark him as an Independent who will deal with the non-Doukhobor world. He participates in Doukhobor activities, being active in the formation of the Named Doukhobors (an organization with which he works until 1939), but he also contributes to the formation of non-Doukhobor organizations such as the early Labour Party and listens to J.S. Woodsworth talk of forming the CCF. He also mentions that he knew Mackenzie King and Diefenbaker very well, but he prefaces this with his position as the trustee of the Doukhobor Prayer Home at Blaine Lake and includes a separate paragraph about his role in trying to prevent the National War Services Board in Saskatchewan from conscripting young Doukhobor men (Bondoreff 1975, 13). In other words, Bondoreff's autobiographical passage is designed to indicate his twin affiliations as an "independent" Doukhobor (he does not call himself this but affirms his loyalty to the Named Doukhobors of Canada) and as a participant in non-Doukhobor life. His relatively traditional autobiographical structure begins with his birth year and location and contains other non-Doukhobor features, such as the date of his marriage and his public commitments. However, it also contains signs that Doukhobors would read in order to understand the changing affiliations of his family (e.g., its decision to move into the CCUB in Saskatchewan and British Columbia and then to leave the CCUB and move to Blaine Lake in 1919). Clearly, Bondoreff's autobiography demonstrates his twin allegiances.

Although *Iskra* mainly publishes material by and about members of the USCC, an autobiographical testimony by a former Freedomite woman, Luba Poznikoff-Koutny, indicates how autobiographical writing can be used to begin healing in the Doukhobor communities. As part of a feature article on the first Krestova reunion in 1996, Poznikoff-Koutny responds to an article in an earlier issue of *Iskra,* in which Doukhobors in all communities are urged to acknowledge incidents of family abuse, harmful incidents of religious fanaticism, and their difficulties with the authorities. Poznikoff-Koutny (1996), whose parents moved to Krestova because, after being incarcerated at Piers Island, they could not afford to live anywhere else, retells her life story beginning with her birth in 1936 and ending with her early life at Krestova, where she experienced "the terror, confusion and fear" of home burnings and anti-educational sentiments, but where she also experienced close friendships, plentiful home-grown food, and Russian schooling.

Poznikoff-Koutny describes her difficulties with the English language and with her marriage to a dedicated Freedomite after her parents moved away from Krestova when their house was burned, but she resolves her emotional dislocation by organizing the reunion (24-25). As with other short autobiographical narratives, Poznikoff-Koutny's is intended not as something for others to emulate but, rather, as a *confession* that will give others the courage to confess their hurt and, thus, enable them to become healthy individuals and healthy members of the Doukhobor community. Here, autobiography functions as part of a confessional discourse that occurs not as a response to inner compulsion but, rather, as a public narrative written so that others will also write about past familial and communal problems. She asks for a direct response from other members of the community, whom she calls "dear friends." Her narrative operates as a hybrid form, consisting of the non-Doukhobor confessional tradition (which she hopes will ensure "emotionally healthy lives" [Poznikoff-Koutny 1996, 25]) and communal traditions that both inspire confessional rhetoric.[10]

Cecil Maloff's autobiographical speech, originally presented at an event honouring Doukhobors at Cowley, Alberta, in 1984, was not designed to detail shifting allegiances and negotiations between non-Doukhobor and Doukhobor ways of representation and of political activity but, rather, to represent general ideas from Doukhoborism to non-Doukhobors. Interestingly, the editorial note in *Iskra,* which prefaces this speech, mentions that it received "a very positive response and is printed for the benefit of readers, by request of the author" (Maloff 1992, 36). Clearly, Maloff intends his presentation of Doukhobor identity and its origins to function as a "memorial sign."[11] This indicates that the function of *Iskra* as a publication is to negotiate new parameters of Doukhobor identity through printed texts of all types, including those autobiographical texts called into being by non-Doukhobor requests for ethnic minority "visibility."

Maloff's intention to thematize his Doukhobor identity in order to enable non-Doukhobors to gain visibility is evident from his opening paragraph, which emphasizes his heritage as a migrated "Spirit Wrestler" as well as his exact date of birth and his desire to negotiate with, rather than to repudiate, the idea of Canada as a nation: "my heritage was instilled in me from my ancestors, from the day when I was born, August 3, 1917. It is the inheritance of 300 years of existence of a name 'Spirit-Wrestler' – Doukhobor, and its ideas and aspirations, which brought us to this beautiful God-given country and its wonderful people" (Maloff 1992, 36). Maloff continues to combine features of autobiographical narrative not found in other Doukhobor autobiographical writings with features common to other narratives. For example, he stresses his location not in terms of continuous migration, shifting group allegiances, or the government land surveys but, rather, in terms of his attachment to the land itself: "I have yet to see more beautiful scenery than at Cowley, Alberta ... I love this little place on Earth" (36). Non-Doukhobors appear in the narrative not as the surveying government or as people who misunderstand his group but, rather, on an individual level, as friends. Even though they differed from him, "at heart, I still loved them, and miss them still. We parted as friends when they had their duty to do according to their heritage" (36).

This reference to heritage forms the point of negotiation for Maloff between Doukhobor and non-Doukhobor life, and it allows him to remain loyal to Doukhobor traditions of resistance to earthly authority. Although he mentions only that his education is limited "because of domestic circumstances" (these probably refer to Doukhobor parents who kept their children from school in reaction to government pressure), Maloff uses this lack of formal schooling to discuss the advantages of Doukhobor

alternative education rather than to apologize for non-institutional participation or to condemn secular education itself: "Although my formal
schooling was very limited and was only to grade three, because of domestic circumstances, I'm thankful to my ancestors for their inspiration,
enlightenment and enchantment which gave me a soul of understanding.
This is an understanding of life and beauty, of what I live with, and what
makes me tick, which makes me always contented and happy, with love
to all living creatures on this planet Earth" (Maloff 1992, 36). Similarly,
Maloff uses the parting with his friends as an occasion to discuss his own
heritage in terms of his Doukhobor identity: "I also had my duty to do
as a Doukhobor – what I have learned from my ancestors" (36). This probably refers to a decision to resist conscription during the Second World
War. From this point of difference, Maloff can then insert his discourse of
non-violence as originally belonging to Doukhobors, Quakers, and others
– a discourse that is now developing into a world movement for peace that
non-Doukhobors, such as Jonathan Schell (whom Maloff acknowledges)
have begun to use.

Maloff's autobiographical speech operates as a way to insert himself, and
then his beliefs in non-violence, into mainstream non-Doukhobor discourse without abandoning his identity as a Doukhobor. He does this by
minimizing internal Doukhobor differences in areas such as communal
living, vegetarianism, and Russian language use, and by appealing to the
aspect of the diasporic imaginary that is related not to migration and
absolute difference but, rather, to the peace movement and to general
Doukhobor educational alternatives. Maloff's decision to print his speech
for Doukhobors may reflect a more recent tendency in Doukhobor groups
to use life narrative to negotiate between Doukhobor identity and ideas of
Canadian citizenship through the discourses of peace activism. It could
also, if Maloff identifies himself as an Independent Doukhobor (from the
speech it is impossible to tell), represent another way in which Independent Doukhobors like Peter Popoff and Ivan Bondoreff negotiate between
Doukhobor identity positions and public life in Canada.

The early interviews conducted by the staff of *Mir* indicate how autobiographical discourse provided a way for younger Doukhobors who were not
confident Russian speakers to understand and debate the status of the
Doukhobor diasporic imaginary. In addition to articles about Doukhobor
identity and history, interviews with Anna Markova (Peter Chistiakov's
daughter and John J. Verigin's mother) about her life and migration, and
interviews with Nick Arishenkoff and Cecil Koochin about life in the
British Columbia commune, contain significant autobiographical sections
that evoke the discourse of the single, liberal subject who has the ability to
construct a single narrative within a cooperative interview format.

Autobiographical moments are called into being by the interviewer, but the parameters of autobiography are sometimes changed by the speaker to include others in the Doukhobor community, past and present. The result is a record of a hybrid subject that narrates between the discourses of persecution and survival in Russia and the discourses of assimilation and misunderstanding in Canada. This hybrid subject also narrates between collective Doukhobor subjectivity and the individual subjectivity privileged in autobiography by narrating *for* others (in this case, Doukhobor youth) and *with* others (the interviewer and other people speaking). The subject here is not an internal and private self but a public identity produced for the community's benefit at a time when young Doukhobors were trying to deal with mixed feelings of pride in their cultural heritage and the silencing of their ethnic background that occurred when they worked or studied in non-Doukhobor settings.[12]

Jim Popoff's interview with Anna Markova for *Mir* illustrates one way in which this hybrid subject can be represented. This interview was the first for *Mir;* it was conducted in Russian and later translated into English. The preface makes the purpose of the interview clear. Doukhobor history is "one of struggle and persecution for [Doukhobor] beliefs, which tended to vary radically from those of the surrounding society" and are recorded in hymns and folk songs; however, "in recent years ... a progressively widening gap seems to have developed between our self-sacrificing forefathers, and ourselves" (Markova 1974, 3). This gap, which is widening due to assimilation and to the shift from a Russian-language oral psalm culture to an English-language print culture, is addressed by Markova, whose life "provides a living example to inspire our generation" (3).

As the daughter of Peter Chistiakov and the mother of John J. Verigin, Markova was already revered. And, because she did not migrate to Canada until 1960, having spent much of her adult life in Stalinist camps, she was also the single living link between the Doukhobors in the Soviet Union and the Doukhobors in Canada. It is a measure of the respect granted her that the Community Doukhobors did not officially acknowledge the death of Markova's brother Peter Iastrebov (the Hawk) in a camp and proclaim John J. Verigin as the honorary chairman of the USCC until Markova reported in 1960 that he had in fact died in 1942 (although in 1957 the Red Cross had informed the USCC of Iastrebov's death) (Woodcock and Avakumovic 1977, 344). Thus Anna Markova's life story provided an example of two major aspects of the Doukhobor diasporic imaginary: (1) she had suffered for her beliefs and had been spiritually sustained by her faith, and (2) she had lived most of her life in Russia, the Doukhobor country of origin. Anna Markova's story fits into both the Doukhobor oral tradition, which has the elders teaching the young about Doukhobor beliefs, and the English-language print culture, which appeals to

Doukhobors who are no longer comfortable with more traditional forms of communication.

The interview begins with the interviewer asking Markova to provide "a brief biographical outline" for the benefit of the magazine's readership. Markova (1974, 3) agrees, saying: "Very well, I shall do so, only with certain reservations. The biography of my life is a complex one; on the one side it is replete with human interest, on the other it is ... sad. However, in spite of everything I shall attempt to relate what I can recall about myself and even touch upon certain things pertaining to my earlier life in Russia." Although much Doukhobor autobiographical writing has occurred because non-Doukhobors requested this format, here is an example of a Doukhobor requesting that very format as a memorial sign. Markova's response, although it seems reluctant, affirms that the narrative is "replete with human interest" and so can be told for the benefit of others. She then reads or recites a lengthy autobiographical narrative that she had prepared in advance. This narrative follows a classic autobiographical format: Markova relates details she cannot remember, such as her date of birth, where she lived as a child, and how Chistiakov became the leader of one of the Doukhobor groups in Russia. Then, saying "We lived ... (at this point I begin to remember about myself, about my life)" (Markova 1974, 4), she relates details she can remember, such as her first marriage in Orlovka; the Doukhobor migration to the Don region; the death of her husband during the migration; the birth of her son Ivan (John) one month after her husband's death; her father's 1927 move to Canada to head the Doukhobor groups in that country; her second marriage; the birth of her second son, Peter; and then her son Ivan's adoption by Chistiakov before he was taken to Canada without her (5-6). Up to this point the tone of the narrative is strictly factual and is almost without commentary. And then Markova mentions the arrest and imprisonment of her second husband, her brother, and herself in Siberia. Her son Peter is left behind with a family in the village of Veriginka, "left to the mercies of fate" (6).

The narrative becomes agitated as Markova relates how her son's birth date was falsified by the family in which he was staying, with the result that he was called up for the draft during the Second World War. He resisted the draft, was arrested, and then was drafted. He was killed at the front in 1945. Markova refers to the war as "a period of human carnage (as I call it) – a war, which required a lot of cannon fodder," and she refers to her son as a victim of "people who secure their own wellbeing at the price of other people's misfortune" (Markova 1974, 6). Markova sums up her life as being that of someone who suffered because of being a mother (not because of being a wife), because of being the daughter of the Doukhobor leader, and because of holding pacifist principles: "And so, this is how it happened that I lost my two children: one I kissed goodbye at the age of six as he left for Canada, and the other, by the whims of fate, at a few months past eighteen years of age, became the victim of such circumstances as make it very, very hard to talk about" (6).

The next part of Markova's narrative deals with her twelve-year imprisonment, the deaths of her husband and brother in Siberia, and her subsequent life as "a totally displaced person, bereft of home, of belongings, of everything that had meaning in my life" (Markova 1974, 7). She deals with her displacement by trying to learn more about her brother's death when she settles near someone who had lived with him in the camps. She describes her state at the time by referring to a Russian saying: "denuded, despoiled and dispossessed" *(yako nag, yako blag, yako nyet nichevo)*. Fortunately, her conditions gradually improve over the next four years (7). From here, the narrative abruptly moves to a description of her plane landing in Vancouver and the end of her isolation as, after thirty-two years, she is reunited with her second son, John J. Verigin.

Markova's conclusion converts these experiences of dispossession and dislocation into the traditional Doukhobor image of suffering, particularly suffering in prison, as a type of school or university – an image that stresses Doukhobor beliefs in non-institutional learning and in experience as providing its own religious education. Her "biography" becomes a Doukhobor "life sign" that can educate others: "So, now you can see that my biography, though perhaps of little interest to some people, to me was its own kind of school ... a university. I was able to see human life – the lives of people – through the broadest of spectrums. It could be that God sent me these experiences to try me – although I never felt a sense of guilt or blame for any wrong doing on my part. Throughout my 15 years in Siberia, nevertheless, I certainly learned a lot" (Markova 1974, 7). Markova continues this theme with a discussion of how she lost her second husband and her second son. She says that her decision to forgive the Soviet Union and the family who betrayed her son was a response to her "inner voice" (a reference to the Doukhobor belief that the rational inner voice is a manifestation of God) (8).

The interviewer says that he is "left somewhat speechless" and asks for details of Markova's faith in God (Markova 1974, 8) as well as for her opinions on other issues. Markova provides these in the form of an appeal. Based on the construction of her life as a narrative of Doukhobor response to suffering, she says that Doukhobor youth should "not forget their birthright, their purpose, their Doukhobor goal" (Markova 1974, 40), and she advises them to use their education to "study Doukhobor history" while "rely[ing] on their own high intelligence and intuitive wisdom" to determine what Doukhoborism is (41). This appeal becomes the reason for her life narrative, which in turn provides her with the authority to link

younger Doukhobors with the diasporic imaginary of suffering and passive resistance to persecution in Russia. In other words, Markova's narrative exists as a hybrid Doukhobor identity construction that combines (1)
oral narrative and written autobiography, and (2) a single-subject narrative
and a narrative that invokes the tradition of the elders passing on cultural
knowledge to the young. As she concludes: "It makes me very happy to
know that there is something in my life that could serve a useful purpose
for the cause of the young people who are trying to find themselves and
their identity with their own traditions and faith. I wish them every success" (42).

Jim Popoff's interview with Nick Arishenkoff and Cecil Koochin about
communal living in British Columbia before the end of the CCUB[13] contains a different set of assumptions about Doukhobor identity, resistance,
and the value of remembering ancestral sufferings. Unlike the interview
with Anna Markova, this interview was meant to provide information
about what communal living was actually like, but its introduction admits
that the request for autobiographical information from Arishenkoff and
Koochin results in a long outpouring of anger and resentment concerning
the way that the dispersement of CCUB assets after bankruptcy was han-
dled by non-Doukhobors (Arishenkoff and Koochin 1974, 3). Arishenkoff
and Koochin's decision to connect their life stories with the difficulties the
commune experienced as a whole is an example of Doukhobor subjectivity, which refuses to stay singular and to remain within the confines of an
orderly written format. Individual subjectivity here operates in concert
with a plural subjectivity that allows Arishenkoff and Koochin to collapse
communal experience into their own experiences and analyses of Doukhobor identity as migratory and separate from Canadian life, sometimes
to the surprise of the interviewer, who says in the introduction that the
staff of *Mir* was "somewhat overwhelmed at the degree of emotional fervour ... [T]here seemed to be no end to the outpouring of grievances which
were recounted" (3). *Mir* interprets the experiences in the CCUB recounted
in the interview as a life sign for the present Doukhobor generation
because, "at the very least, their effort [i.e., the effort of the interviewees
and everyone else in the CCUB to make communal living work] provides
an example, and a learning experience for the future, and their great dedication and faith ... will provide an inspiration for many generations to
come" (3). The introduction also makes the point that the personal recollections of both men are geared to discussing wider issues rather than simply to providing biographical details as "even now, [they] inadvertently
reveal a need for a confirmation of their ideas, and a degree of recognition
for their individual efforts" (3). It recognizes that, even "inadvertently,"
Koochin and Arishenkoff treat their life narratives as participating in a
larger discourse about community issues and that this can connect these

stories with the concerns of younger Doukhobors due to the hybrid quality – sometimes singular, sometimes collective – of the subjects produced
in the narratives. Thus, the autobiographical discourse asked of Koochin
and Arishenkoff at the beginning of the interview functions as a request
for a life sign that can ground Doukhobor identity. This is similar to the
request made of Anna Markova.

The interview begins with a request for "a brief personal background
about each of you," with Koochin as the first respondent (Arishenkoff and
Koochin 1974, 4). Koochin's narrative begins with his birth year of 1899,
which identifies him as one of the first Doukhobors born in Canada with
no personal memory of Russia. He remembers his childhood in Tambovka,
Saskatchewan, as happy and interprets this almost immediately in terms
of his positive attitude towards communal living, which involved "a firm
belief that this was the best of all possible life styles" (4). The virtue of
communal living becomes the dominant theme in the rest of his narrative
as he goes on to foreground the large financial contributions his village
made to the CCUB. Koochin's recollection of his family's move to the Verigin commune in 1910 also stresses how "all of our worldly possessions,"
including a black stallion, were "submitted to the jurisdiction of the Verigin commune" (4). After his family moved to British Columbia in 1913,
Koochin recounts how Peter Lordly personally gave him tasks and moved
his family between Saskatchewan and Grand Forks to serve the needs of
the communal organization. He then details his positions in the CCUB
after the arrival of Chistiakov. His narrative ends with his resignation from
the CCUB board of directors "when matters became unbearable for me"
due to pressures from the people themselves and from Chistiakov. He
stresses, however, that he paid dues to the CCUB until the very end, and
that he has always paid dues to the USCC. This functions in the narrative
as proof of his loyalty to the communal ideal (5).

In response to the interviewer's request for "a brief summary of your
autobiography," Nick Arishenkoff's narrative begins with a reference to
the suffering of his parents during the persecutions in Russia and with his
parents' subsequent migration on the first ship (Arishenkoff and Koochin
1974, 5). This comment serves to orient his narrative not so much towards
the virtues of communal living as towards the suffering Doukhobors have
undergone both in the past and, as he makes clear, in the present. Migratory dislocation in the host country figures strongly as Arishenkoff states
that he does not remember the earlier years of Doukhobor settlement but
that he remembers the stories the elders told about their arrival: "I do very
clearly remember, however, the accounts of elders about the arrival in
Canada, particularly about the friendly greetings, expressions of sympathy
for the suffering the Doukhobors had endured, and promises of freedom
to pursue their religion and way of life in the new country" (Arishenkoff

and Koochin 1974, 5). This statement fulfills several narrative functions at once. It affirms the Doukhobor oral tradition of learning from elders and passing that knowledge down, and it displays irony for, while the initial greetings of Canadians were friendly and promises were made, they were quickly broken and became the bases for Arishenkoff's subsequent grievances against the Canadian government and non-Doukhobors. Finally, Arishenkoff's personal memory of stories told by other people means that the major focus of his "autobiography" is not the centrality of his own development or even his own life course but, rather, the history of the Doukhobor commune's development and eventual demise. In other words, his account mixes elements of memoir and autobiography, with a stress on a collective Doukhobor subject, while his own subjectivity appears in response to community events. For example, while Arishenkoff recalls where he was when he heard the news of Peter Lordly's sudden death, his description of the emotional impact of this news is collective: "the people were thrown into a state of mourning and despair" (5).

After he describes non-Doukhobor rioting against Doukhobors (which illustrates the undeserved hostility directed against the group) and provides details about the CCUB's debt problems before the arrival of Peter Chistiakov, Arishenkoff returns to a personal description of the labouring jobs he had and then describes his personal sense of loss when the new jam factory was burned down: "Of all the many losses by fire of CCUB property the loss of the Grand Forks jam factory hurt me most in a personal sense. For many years I had worked at heavy jobs. Now I had acquired an easier and more interesting job. I enjoyed my new duties and was very disappointed when I had to sharpen my old seven pound axe and return to the woods" (Arishenkoff and Koochin 1974, 6). This personal moment in the narrative serves to demonstrate the pressures placed on the CCUB as the result of arson, but Arishenkoff assigns blame for the fire to non-Doukhobors rather than to the Sons of Freedom. This is in keeping with the binarisms he develops in the rest of his narrative between the CCUB and the government officials who take control of it and deliberately destroy it. His personal story serves to demonstrate this theme, as, for example, when he discovers that planed lumber from a communal sawmill is being sold off for less than the raw material cost and that a sawmill fire might have been started or approved by the non-Doukhobor receiver in an attempt to impoverish the commune when it went into receivership (7).

Arishenkoff's narrative ends when the interviewer asks to take a picture of Koochin and Arishenkoff because they look very earnest – Arishenkoff says that he is angry – at this point. Arishenkoff then sums up his position by indicting the Canadian government and speaking against the forces of assimilation, and he appeals to the idea of *vechnaiia pamit* as a way of thematizing the events he has discussed. The event he references is the

Burning of Arms and the need to remember it: "We should all think back and remember our forefathers, the pathway which they had to thread for hundreds of years. They withstood every imaginable kind of torture and persecution and that's why we are in such fortunate circumstances today, compared to many people in the world, who have suffered wars, and other disasters. That is why we sing hymns of praise to these people. Hymns such as 'Sleep on, you brave fighting eagles' and 'In the Struggle for Freedom,' giving praise which they justly deserve" (Arishenkoff and Koochin 1974, 7). For Arishenkoff, memory of this event will keep the Doukhobors from assimilating, although he wonders if this will be enough. His life story thus ends on an ambiguous note:

> I often think about my own life (I am nearly 73 years old!) and the accomplishments of my own generation. What have we accomplished for our children, for future generations? Who will sing hymns of praise to us? I remember my mother used to tell me often, how her grandmother was ashamed to bath with others because of the two badly-healed scars on her back where strips of flesh had been torn out as tortures for her beliefs. Yes, she was ashamed of the scars with which she had been earning freedom for me, her great-grandson. (7)

Here then, Arishenkoff touches on his individual life and wonders whether it is a true life sign and whether his whole generation can function as a valid life sign for the next generation of Doukhobors. Collective identity and individual identity become symbiotic as he reflects on his own life and on his own remembered connections to the Burning of Arms events.

The interview with Koochin and Arishenkoff demonstrates how, in a format not usually thought of as autobiographical, autobiographical discourse can combine with traditional oral ways of remembering and enable Doukhobors to interpret events through the touchstones of their diasporic imaginary (e.g., communal living, persecution, and migration). The hybrid form that results allows for a hybrid Doukhobor subjectivity to develop for the public benefit of other Doukhobors. Furthermore, the narratives do not have the autochthonous quality of more traditional autobiography but, rather, are created by the speakers in response to a request for autobiography made by another person. In other words, these narratives are made for others and, to some extent, by others (i.e., if the interviewer's request for autobiography and the function of the narratives as exemplars for other Doukhobors are taken into consideration). The subject produced in them is a mostly collective public subject that exists as a life sign linking the suffering and survival of former generations to the next Doukhobor generation. The work of *vechnaiia pamit* enables the sufferings of the speakers' generation to be converted to the heritage of suffering from those who endured 1895, and this suffering may be understood as spiritual and collective.

Gregory (Grisha) Ivanovich Soukorev's[14] text, entitled "My Renunciation of Military Service" in its initial 1938 publication in English in the *Nelson Daily News*, its 1946 publication in Russian in *Iskra*, and its recent 1996 English-language publication in *Iskra*, forms a central part of the diasporic imaginary of Doukhobors and is centred on the events following the 1895 Burning of Arms. It also indicates how, in the collection and subsequent translation of first-person narratives such as this one,[15] autobiography operates as a way of inscribing an alternate history of Doukhobor identity that connects *vechnaiia pamit* to the narrative of a single subject featured in non-Doukhobor autobiographical writing.

Doukhobors still recall the suffering of their relatives who were tortured in 1895, especially when they recall that they or their relatives still have scars on their backs. These scars are represented as a touchstone of Doukhobor identity in which the body literally becomes a text for remembrance. This trope appears in the absence of other kinds of textual records about the 1895 protests and is important for people whose culture is primarily oral and who believe that the life of the spirit cannot be separated from the body or its everyday labours. Nick Arishenkoff remembers his grandmother's scars during his interview, and Mae Popoff also remembers those who were scarred (Tarasoff and Klymasz 1995, 50). But Soukorev's manuscript is unique. According to William Rozinkin (1992, 28), in his regular historical column for *Iskra*, Soukorev read a written version of this manuscript – presumably in Russian – to other Doukhobors in the 1930s, and "his story brought tears to many listeners in Glade [BC]." This is unusual since few Doukhobors were print literate in Russian or English, particularly those from the generation that had survived tortures in Russia, and there is no other record of a written narrative of this length being read in public settings. Even rarer was Soukorev's desire for non-Doukhobor people to understand his story. According to Rozinkin, Soukorev asked William Sheloff, a Doukhobor man, to translate his story into English. In 1938 Sheloff translated Soukorev's narrative and then went with him to the office of the local newspaper for the area, the *Nelson Daily News,* to ask the non-Doukhobor editor to publish the English-language version. The editor, whom Rozinkin describes as a staunch supporter of the Royal Canadian Legion, did not believe that the story could be true due to the graphic nature of the torture descriptions. And then Soukorev showed him the scars on his back. The shocked editor believed Soukorev and published the narrative in ten instalments (Rozinkin 1992, 28).

I argue that Soukorev did this because he wished to write the Doukhobor narrative into Canadian history not as other but as part of Canada's role in accepting persecuted peoples. Just as Soukorev's readings made

Doukhobor listeners cry when they were asked to bear witness to this story when it was read in their own communities, so the translation and publication of "My Renunciation of Military Service" was intended to make Canadians become witnesses as well – and this is all the more extraordinary because the narrative is pacifist and, in 1938, Canada was preparing to enter the Second World War.[16] The manuscript's republication in *Iskra* in Russian and recently in English shows that this narrative has the symbolic capital that Soukorev wanted it to have: it began as an oral account and has been transmitted into print for subsequent generations to read, including those who no longer speak Russian. Clearly, Soukorev's efforts to publicize the manuscript represent a series of acts of negotiation between written and oral cultures and ways to remember, between young Doukhobors and old, between Russian speakers and English speakers, and between Doukhobors and non-Doukhobors. The subject in the written manuscript operates as a hybrid subject designed by Soukorev to "speak" to both types of interpretive communities. *Iskra's* decision to print the English-language version of the manuscript that Soukorev's grandson, Alex Markin, and his wife, Anne, gave to the editors brings this combination of listening and reading communities full-circle. Originally designed to reach multiple audiences, the manuscript now reaches an audience that combines the characteristics of the separate audiences fifty years later as fewer Doukhobors speak or read Russian and fewer young Doukhobors learn about their cultural traditions by primarily oral means.[17]

Soukorev's narrative begins with a relatively short section about his family life, which includes his position, at the age of sixteen, as the head of his family after the death of his father. But the narrative quickly moves to the clash between Soukorev's principles, which are related to the village resolution not to serve the tsar and to refuse military service, and what he calls "my innate love of all living beings, born of close contact with nature in my adolescent years" (Soukorev 1996a, 60). The rest of the account is what I call a witness narrative – that is, a narrative in which the subject is constructed in terms of witnessing a specific, usually traumatic, event. The subject is not presented as someone who grows and changes in response to events but, rather, is presented as a "pure," unchanging witness who records events.[18] As a witness narrative, Soukorev's account depends on picturing the monstrosity of the guards who represent the authoritarian state and the steadfast refusal of the prisoners to give in. According to Soukorev, "in keeping with my convictions I immediately declared that I would not take part in the drawing of lots" when his time came to be called for military service, and, in a pattern repeated throughout the account, the authorities ignore him and humiliate him (61). Humiliation, however, has no effect on him, and so he is "tested" again with a medical exam, which he also refuses, explaining that he is a Christian and so cannot kill. This the authorities also ignore and take him to prison. On the way there, Soukorev's family and friends meet him and, in keeping with the stark binarism of the text, urge him and his friends "to be brave and strong, and not to stray from the teaching of Jesus Christ, Who died on the Cross in agonizing pain and torment which should always serve as an example for His true followers" (62). As true followers, therefore, Soukorev and his friends begin to turn to the discourse of Christ's sufferings in order to console themselves.

The narrative echoes this parallel with the life of Christ as Soukorev is then imprisoned in a heatless cell for three days and nights (a corollary to Christ's sojourn in the grave for the same length of time), during which he consoles himself with "a mental picture of the anguish of my Lord Jesus Christ" (62). Again, when Soukorev is let out and treated still worse, he asks Jesus Christ to help him "and patiently suffered all condemnations" by remembering Christ's instruction to turn the other cheek (62). This is successful, and Soukorev does not give in, although, when he is transferred to "the disciplinary prison," his fellow Doukhobors report that they are downcast because of the treatment they receive there. They say that "in spirit we are still brave ... but in the future we shall trust in our Almighty Creator, Christ the Saviour," because they are losing strength (64).

The pattern is repeated when Soukorev "categorically refuse[s]" to engage in rifle practice and so is imprisoned for three days and nights. He refuses to drill, and the cycle begins again (Soukorev 1996b, 40). Then the flogging with the thorny rods, the worst torture Soukorev receives, begins. The struggle here is elemental, with the good of an individual placed against the evil of the state. For example, "the guard with his flogging rods stood in readiness, looking at me like a beast at its prey, ready to devour at a moment's notice" (40), while Soukorev, lying prone with his clothes off and soldiers holding him down, is "fully prepared for the inhuman torture of punishment which could only be evaded by abdicating the great truth of the testament of our Lord Jesus Christ" (41), who functions as an example to follow. This part of the narrative catalogues in graphic detail the punishment Soukorev receives, including descriptions of the blood freezing to his underwear so that he cannot move around or remove his pants after the beatings. Soukorev uses this occasion to reflect on his inability to write fully about the experience: "it would require a gifted master of the writing art to describe the agony of mind and body that I endured in my harrowed state during this period. I called on the Lord God for relief and this alone seemed to ease the endless suffering" (41). This occasion, when Soukorev's body reaches the apex of suffering, forms a space in the narrative for reflection on the sufferings of Jesus Christ and a lament that Christ's teachings have not yet been understood by those who beat him. This strengthens Soukorev so that, eventually, he resists beatings, saying to a sergeant-major, "You have the power over my flesh, but you could not possibly force me to betray my spirit" (42). It is at this point in the narrative, when he cannot describe his suffering and when he relinquishes his body completely to the authorities, that Soukorev appears to take on the characteristics of Christ. Here he puts into practice the words of the psalm I quoted at the beginning of Chapter 2, the implication of which is that the place where one is, and where one's physical body is, are not "real." Soukorev's narrative dramatizes this change between the merely "human" and someone who bears the image of God in his body as a sacred change. His body becomes a text where suffering can be read, just as the text about his body can be read. He can now resist temptation, the final test of the singular subject, and then be rejoined to another aspect of the sacred: the community of those who suffer.

For example, after Soukorev's final defiance, three people tempt him: a priest who comes to convince him to serve the emperor and two fellow Doukhobors who come to convince him to give up the struggle. Soukorev replies to the priest, the symbol of religious authority that Doukhobors reject, by quoting scripture about not killing, much as Jesus quoted scripture to dispel the temptations of the devil at the beginning of the Gospels of Matthew 4:7-11 and Mark 4:8-13. The priest, like the devil in the biblical accounts, leaves (Soukorev 1996c, 53). To Vaily Lebedev, the first Doukhobor who tempts him, he says, "'Lebedev, go away from me ... leave me and do not tempt me!" (54), much as Jesus says to Peter, "get behind me Satan" when Peter tells him that he will not suffer and die (Matthew 16:23). Later, when he decides to bear arms for a short time "to give me a chance to strengthen myself" (Soukorev 1996c, 54), he does so as part of a collective decision-making strategy so that all Doukhobors being tortured could survive as part of "an all-out struggle" to the death (55). From this point, Soukorev uses the first-person plural instead of the singular since all Doukhobors will now suffer as a group. As he says, "I am using the word 'we' frequently because, all-in-all, there were over thirty persons in our party" (Soukorev 1996e, 40).

When the surviving prisoners are finally exiled to Siberia, they leave with "an indelible memory, one that would remain with us for the rest of our lives, of the ruthlessness of the servants of the then reigning Romanoff generation, and the 'kindheartedness' of the Russian Orthodox church," but upon leaving "we were happy in the knowledge that we had not betrayed our faith" (Soukorev 1996d, 28). The binary contrast between the Doukhobors and the authorities continues in comparisons between Doukhobor behaviour and the behaviour of their Russian prisoner counterparts, who swear constantly, refuse to work (Soukorev 1996e, 39-40), and complain that the Doukhobor prisoners should not be allowed to work because they are richer than the others. The non-Doukhobor prisoners, unlike the Doukhobors, also drink too much and cause problems. For example, when the prisoners are to pilot a raft downriver to Siberia, drunken prisoners run it aground. The Doukhobors, after assuring their suspicious guards that they will not run away, extricate the raft (Soukorev 1996f, 9-10).

After a brief description of Siberian exile, which, once they are allowed to work for food, is "not too bad," Soukorev describes their migration to Canada in 1905 after they are set free (Soukorev 1996g, 96). He does not describe life in Canada, however, since the purpose of the narrative is to prove how the Doukhobor prisoners survived; instead, his narrative ends with a revisiting of his principles: "I have always kept strictly to all the Doukhobor principles, and I continue to do so until today. I earn my living by my own toil, and live a vegetarian way of life ... Always an opponent of war" (97).

In the version published by the *Nelson Daily News,* Soukorev adds more information about Canada in order to anchor the narrative as part of Canadian history and identity, saying that Canada is "the land of the free, a haven for the oppressed" (Soukorev 1938, 6) for the benefit of his non-Doukhobor audience. He also adds more information about his own body so that non-Doukhobors can understand what Doukhobors already know: that the body and the soul are the same thing and that both can testify. Thus, before the passage about his faithfulness to Doukhobor principles, he says: "My memory is fading as a result of many years, my sight is getting dim, but the ugly scars on my back are still there to tell their story, and nothing could erase or blot them from my sight" (6).

Clearly, Soukorev's manuscript is both a historical document and a reminder. It directly taps the Doukhobor diasporic imaginary of corporeal suffering for pacifist ideals in order to remind Doukhobors to adhere to Doukhobor principles, which involve collective action. Soukorev's narrative privileges his position as an individual subject for much of the account but only so that *his body,* rather than his personality or selfhood, is foregrounded. This is because it is his body's endurance of torture that provides his testimony, both in the narrative itself and for doubters like the newspaper editor. Once his body has performed this function in the narrative, collectivity resumes and the Doukhobors strive together against the cruelties and misunderstandings of non-Doukhobors, thus gaining access to another part of the Doukhobor diasporic imaginary that is played out in Canada. As a witness narrative about events that are commemorated in numerous Doukhobor hymns (e.g., "How Fortunate Were Those People," "Sleep On, You Brave Fighting Eagles"), Soukorev's narrative both personalizes the historic account for the benefit of non-Doukhobors and provides fresh information to fuel the Doukhobor diasporic imaginary for Doukhobors who need to be encouraged to preserve their Russian-based traditions.

Doukhobor autobiography in magazines, as it develops between the traditions of oral and collective *vechnaiia pamit* and the discourse of autobiography as a single written sign, hybridizes its subject in order to negotiate with, and at times even to resist, non-Doukhobor ideas about what a subject is and how it (or often, they) relates to the idea of nationality, origin, and language. This discourse of the subject is constantly remade as the requirements for Doukhobor identity change in response to conditions in Canada and, in Mishra's (1995) sense of the "sacred," foregrounds the religious struggles that prefigured migration in order to heal its pain. To this end, autobiography can occupy the hybrid space between the undecidability of Doukhobor origins as always-migrating and the hallmarks of the Doukhobor diasporic imaginary that are being remembered. Sometimes, in Makortoff's (1974) "half-turn" to the past, which makes memory sacred within the present moment of remembering, the diasporic imaginary can be recast in these narratives as suffering, resistance to oppression, and commitment to peace and thus be seen as part of a Doukhobor identity that is still healing, still being given a hybrid language, and still being worked out.

4
Negotiating Identity: Doukhobor Oral Narratives

> The Doukhobors say: "Record in heart, proclaim in word." They
> add: "It is nothing unusual to write down on paper but it is
> important to penetrate one's heart with truth." Therefore, he
> who pays enough attention to his inner self, he who learns "the
> true spirit of Christ," will not require anything that has been
> written down because in his heart it has been already recorded
> and his mouth will proclaim the truth if he deems it necessary.
>
> — The Living Book

In a 1995 *Iskra* article entitled "The Story of One Psalm," Jim Popoff discusses how Hazel (Mahonin) Sookochoff was able to recall a psalm composed by her father, Vasiliy Ivanovich Mahonin. In 1933 Vasiliy Mahonin taught each of his daughters a speech for a youth meeting. Vera, Hazel's sister, died of cancer during the 1950s; there was no written copy of her speech, and, over the intervening decades, Hazel had forgotten hers. However, just before the 1995 centennial of the Burning of Arms, "seemingly out of nowhere, words and phrases from the long-forgotten speech began coming to [Hazel's] mind" (Popoff 1995, 14) and she was able to piece together the whole speech. However, the speech she had recalled was not hers but that of her sister. She was urged to pass on a written copy of the speech to the USCC Executive Committee, where John J. Verigin recommended that she recite it as a "psalm" at a special *molenie*,[1] which took place forty-one years to the day after her sister's death (14). Jim Popoff subsequently prepared a translation of the "psalm" and printed Russian and English versions of it in his *Iskra* article, along with his description of the circumstances of its making.

In the article, the value attached to the oral composition and remembrance of the song is strong, although Popoff does not directly refer to Hazel Sookochoff's experience as miraculous or even spiritual. What is indicated, however, is the pervasiveness of Doukhobor oral culture (the composing of psalms and passing them on to one's children for public recital) and the links, within oral culture, between memory and spiritual versions of Doukhobor history. The content of the psalm underscores this since its subject is the "eternal remembrance" of the Doukhobors who were tortured in Russia after the 1895 Burning of Arms. The saying of the psalm (since it was recited and not written) makes it, and its speaker, a "living monument" and a part of *vechnaiia pamit,* the eternal life desired for all Doukhobors. As it says:

> Today we shall present a *living monument* to the heroic Doukhobors
>   spiritual warriors of Christ.
> It shall be written not in stone, but in your hearts, and not with ink
>   but with our sacrificed martyr blood!
> (Popoff 1995, 15, emphasis mine)

The rest of the psalm compares the sufferings of the early Christians in Roman arenas with the sufferings of the Doukhobors, and it exhorts all Doukhobors to continue "a legacy of freedom ... so that we would be peacemakers upon this Earth!" (Popoff 1995, 15). The suffering Doukhobors are finally wished "eternal consciousness," which, literally, is *vechnaiia pamit* (eternal memory or eternal consciousness).[2] The psalm thus operates as a commemoration of orality and the power of memory while at the same time imparting a blessing to the martyred Spirit Wrestlers. Oral memory is both the occasion of *vechnaiia pamit* and the means of connecting Doukhobor identity with the descendants of the earlier Doukhobors since it can be enacted each time the psalm is recited or sung. History here is not words on a page or "written ... in stone"; rather, it is written in the hearts of those who recall the event of martyrdom. Orality and memory as found in the rhetoric of *vechnaiia pamit* are key parts of what Peter Chistiakov sometimes referred to as the "Doukhobor University,"[3] a non-institutional way of imparting knowledge about Doukhoborism to each generation through psalms, memorized catechisms, and stories about Doukhobor history that recount its events and combine them with spiritual interpretations. These aspects of Doukhobor epistemology are honoured in the *Iskra* article, even as the orally recalled psalm is reprinted in both Russian and English, an example of the ways in which oral composition, translation, and transcription help to fulfill the call of the psalm to remember Doukhobor identity and purpose.

Intertwined aspects of orality and literacy in the acts of questioning, oral narration, and transcription comprise another aspect of autobiographical writing that provides one of the most compelling reasons to widen the critical understanding of autobiography beyond the traditional understanding of it as a single written text produced by one person. As Carole Boyce Davies (1992, 6) points out, what she calls "lifestory," or oral transcribed narrative, has the potential to call "into question the notion of standard autobiography as extended, linear narrative, and invites instead more complex approaches to text, discourse, author and narrative." The uses of orality and literacy, and the circumstances of the utterance in autobiographical writing and speaking, can involve other narrative interventions as well since oral narratives are addressed *to* someone who, presumably, can hear and immediately respond. Collaboration and dictation are included among these interventions. As Mark Sanders (1994) observes, autobiography critics have given little thought to collaborative texts, despite the inclusion of collaborative or dictated autobiographies such as *Black Elk Speaks, The Autobiography of Malcolm X,* and *I, Rigoberta Menchu* in the autobiography canon as "ethnic texts." This has created a situation "where self-created autobiographies ... have ostensibly defined the field, functioning as both model and sign, [while] the dictated autobiography has remained 'invisible' on one account or another" (445). Since the texts I have just named all feature speakers who do not belong to the dominant racial, ethnic, and cultural groups that the autobiography canon treats as paradigmatic, collaboration should be examined as a key component of life narratives made by people who are excluded from dominant autobiographical discourse. For instance, collaborative narratives should lead us to ask: who requests the life narrative and for what ends? Do "colonized" speakers have a "non-subaltern" voice? Or is that voice co-opted by the collaborator in the interests of "professional" information gathering about the "object" of study? Who "owns" the text that results and how does each collaborator see ownership? And, most important, what subject(s) is (are) produced and who produces collaborative discourse for public consumption?

Collaboration is a dynamic process, particularly when different levels and understandings of orality and literacy motivate the collaborators. These can highlight inequalities in the balance of power relations between speaker and interviewer and/or transcriber. The "text" that results can be the product of an oral dialogue about the terms of identity and memory rather than a hybrid tension, which relies more on a mixture of elements than on conflict: "Thus they [collaborators] engage in a dynamic and often conflictive creation process, one which produces a text that does not necessarily resolve tensions or correct dissimilarities, but instead both imbibes and embodies them, often seeks to mask them, but ultimately relies upon them as essential sources of meaning" (Sanders 1994, 446). Dialogue can occur at the level of the produced subject or subjects, as Carole Boyce Davies (1992, 12-13) points out: the assumed stability of an autobiographical "I" destabilizes in collaborative narratives to a "we" who can be both the teller and recorder. Or, as Roxanne Rimstead (1996, 162) observes, the "we" a teller invokes as a subject-in-relation to others in her or his community refuses to be inscribed as singular. These oral narratives by Doukhobors feature many of these concerns in addition to imagery and themes shared with autobiographical writings. The speakers of these narratives work out identity questions in negotiation with the rhetoric of those who interview them so that orality operates in concert with writing in ways that reframe what autobiography can be. It also recasts how auto-biography can operate in a community that now collects its own life stories in ways that do not deny orality but, rather, treat oral traditions of life narrative and representation with dignity and respect.

Recorded autobiographical narratives by Doukhobors also share similar-ities with other collaborative narratives and, to some extent, with the life histories that Bodianskii and Bonch-Bruevich transcribed (Popov 1908). Since none of the narratives I discuss had been transcribed or translated, the interviewing processes involving subject negotiation between the interviewers and the speakers are quite pronounced. As in the transcribed narratives by Bonch-Bruevich and Bodianskii, the construction of a hybrid subject does not occur in these recordings at the level of the recording process. This brings me to my own role in constructing the texts for this chapter from archived recordings of Doukhobors talking about their life stories to other Doukhobor interviewers.

Transcribing oral Russian narratives into English may seem to remove them from any meaningful context, particularly since I worked with nar-ratives that other people had recorded in the 1960s and 1970s, with scant information about the participants. Because of this, I cannot have the participants check my transcriptions. At the same time, the Russian record-ings are relatively inaccessible because they are archived and because they are in Russian. In order to provide access to them, I transcribed them with the help of a Doukhobor, Jim Kolesnikoff, who sat at his kitchen table for hours and translated the recordings as I wrote down what he said. Like my translator, I, too, have probably altered narratives and made them more "suitable" for public access. In doing this I have lost something: the tim-bre of a speaker's voice, the sound of laughter, perhaps some intricacy of the wording used in the original language. My process of selection also alters how the material will be understood. But the recordings themselves have already sacrificed other things for the sake of access and permanence: the expressions on the faces of the speakers and the look of the room in which the interview took place. Although the speakers are not able to assess whether I, as a non-Doukhobor, should make their words widely available or not, all speakers did agree to have their words recorded. And so Jim Kolesnikoff and I translated and transcribed the recordings as accu-rately as we could, although I realize that my intervention (in particular) changes some of the initial meanings of the original exchange and creates the "third language" of translation (and, I would add, of transcription), what Walter Benjamin (1969, 76) calls the "echo" that only serves to remind the reader/listener of the presence of an original that cannot ever be the translation. However, foregrounding my intervention (and, to a lesser extent, Jim's intervention) in this way makes it possible for me, as an outsider, to assess the politics of inside and outside during the original making of these oral narratives. Our own collaboration, which involved discussing what words meant, how to represent what a speaker discussed, and why I might be interested in what the speaker was saying, reflected that earlier collaboration between speakers and interviewers.

Our re-enactment of transactions of orality also enabled me to see how a recorded orality could produce a dialogue about identity that, due to the recording's unedited qualities, refused to resolve into a "smooth" identity narrative. Thus elder Doukhobor speakers can interact with non-Doukhobors (and younger Doukhobors) in a way that preserves something of oral discourse, which constructs a self-in-relation to others that is not concerned with interiority, while the transcriber makes the narrative more permanent and, in the case of the Joint Doukhobor Research Committee text, more widely available to the Doukhobor community. In recorded and transcribed formats, the elders' teaching can potentially be preserved and assessed as younger Doukhobors seek to recover and reinterpret the events of Doukhobor history and thought. Communal identity does not have to be "anchored" in the written word but, rather, in the recorded and transcribed narratives I examine here, the written word can combine with orality to create ongoing conversations in Doukhobor communities about what it is to be a Doukhobor.

Although the majority of Doukhobors now have at least a high school level of institutionalized education, oral ways to remember and recollect life experience and history are still important to the maintenance and reworking of Doukhobor identity, as Popoff's (1995) "The Story of One Psalm" indicates. While the amount of material published by Doukhobors about their history remains relatively small, Alexander Bodianskii's 1908 collection of Doukhobor narratives about Doukhobor resistance to Russian authorities is a sign of the richness of Doukhobor oral tradition (Novokshyonov 1908). The centrality of oral utterance to Doukhobors themselves can also be seen in the relatively large number of recordings, translations, and (in some cases) transcriptions of recorded material that have been made by younger Doukhobors who wished to preserve and make more public the stories and teachings – in Russian – of older Doukhobors. These teachings are in danger of being lost once that generation dies. The recordings and transcriptions made of Doukhobor women are particularly important because almost no written autobiographical narratives by women survive: as the principal guardians of Doukhobor tradition and the spiritual leaders of a number of revival movements, Doukhobor women often resisted institutional schooling more strenuously than did Doukhobor men and, when working in the outside world, have always had to negotiate the double barriers of xenophobia and sexism.[4] In a different way, the text from the Joint Doukhobor Research Committee (1997) provides a way of seeing how communal orality can work in a group situation. In the symposia proceedings, for example, oral recollections by Doukhobors often serve to educate other Doukhobors about the history and goals of Doukhoborism. They represent another use of autobiography – a form of rhetoric between speech and writing – that contests the usual position of writing as the best way to record and rework history. In the symposia, their testimony about themselves and what they remember becomes part of the public debate regarding how Doukhobor history and identity will be interpreted.

The oral narratives I examine in this chapter have some features in common with the written narratives published in *Iskra* and *Mir*. Like the interviews in Chapter 3, these narratives invoke aspects of the Doukhobor diasporic imaginary of suffering and pacifism in Russia. They feature shifts between singularity and plurality, emphasize community life, and stress migration to Canada and internal migrations in Canada as signs of group difference. And, in the sense that they are transcribed oral narratives, the interviews with Anna Markova and with Cecil Koochin and Nick Arishenkoff do not differ much from these recordings and transcriptions. However, with the significant exception of the *Toil and Peaceful Life* oral history volume by *Sound Heritage*,[5] these narratives were not recorded just so that they could be translated into English. This means that the Doukhobor subjects constructed here do differ from those that appear in other written narratives because, as I have said, the transition from oral to written narrative and from Russian to English does not, in this case, produce hybridized narratives. The rhetorics of refusal, laughter, and non-linear storytelling all appear as ways for the subjects of the interviews and of the symposia debates to engage in dialogue. In these cases, the intent of the utterances is important, whether it is to educate non-Doukhobors about Doukhoborism (as in the early narratives recorded by Bodianskii and Bonch-Bruevich [Popov 1908]), to pass on stories to younger Doukhobors who requested them (as in the recordings made for the Salmo project), or to engage in dialogue about Doukhobor issues (as in Harshenin's [1965] recording and the Joint Doukhobor Research symposia text).

The speakers in the interviews I discuss negotiate with their interviewers, whether they are Doukhobor or non-Doukhobor, concerning what self-narrative and Doukhobor identity will be, far more than they blend elements of Doukhobor and non-Doukhobor representation. They often reframe what they wish to impart to their "insider" interviewers and draw them into a dialogue in which identity is constructed with an awareness of the presence of another speaker.[6] What does combine is the transcribed "text" that was produced after the interview. The text becomes the approximate representation of speech that operates between "oracy" – a term that places orality on par with the idea of literacy – and the printed word. This mixture of orality and literacy could be considered what Bakhtin

(1981a, 358) refers to as "two social languages within the limits of a single utterance, an encounter, within the arena of an utterance, between two different linguistic consciousnesses." Although Bakhtin was discussing novelistic discourse, his assertion that the textual field could operate as a place where utterances could meet each other has parallels to the ways that the discourse of Doukhobor orality meets either non-Doukhobor narrative expectations or Doukhobor narrative expectations, each of which comes from a different context in the textual field of the recorded and transcribed interview. As identity issues manifest themselves at the level of this combined discourse, so Doukhobor identity *representation* becomes a field within these "oral/written" narratives in which identity issues can be worked out.

This type of utterance, which occurs between written and oral ways to remember and recollect, has become part of Doukhobor historic record for other Doukhobors to read in Bodianskii's and Bonch-Bruevich's work, and in oral testimony for the Joint Doukhobor Research Committee. The initial desire of many of the speakers to relate their stories so that younger Doukhobors can understand their traditions is now being fulfilled not in oral transmission but, rather, in written transcription of these narratives that rework oral conventions. The identities produced in these narratives at the time of speaking and in transcription are the result of a collaborative process that stresses the interconnectedness of what Ian Adam has called "oracy" and literacy (Adam 1996, 97), or what Peter Dickinson (1994, 319) refers to as "orality in literacy," which problematizes what has been called the "great divide" between orality and literacy. The "great divide" debate has followed in the wake of Walter J. Ong's (1982) widely influential argument in *Orality and Literacy* that was prefigured by Havelock's (1971) and McLuhan's (1966) work on print culture. Ong argues that orality has a radically different set of practices and grammars than does literacy. The forms of orality and literacy, he argued, affect the cognitive processes of the people who use them, which means that oral thinking and literate thinking differ profoundly. This is why, Ong suggested, orality prefigures literacy. Moreover, oral epistemologies are destined to be superseded by literate epistemologies: "orality needs to produce and is destined to produce writing. Literacy, as will be seen, is absolutely necessary for the development not only of science but also of history, philosophy, explicative understanding of literature and of any art, and indeed for the explication of language (including oral speech) itself" (15). Ong suggests that hermeneutics requires self-reflexivity and that writing, which is a more permanent memory record, is a technology that allows for self-reflexivity. The grammar of orality, by contrast, can only retain and retrieve by resorting to mnemonic rhetorical patterns and the use of repetition (34).

Challenges to Ong's absolute division between orality and literacy, and to his ethnocentric view of epistemology, include Ruth Finnegan's (1988, 161) contention that abstract notions of literacy and orality do not reflect how literacy and orality are actually used in any given culture. She argues that the contexts of the use of both orality and literacy should be studied in any fieldwork situation (180). Ian Adam's (1996, 110-11) critique of Derrida's speech/writing binary leads him to agree that there is no "pure" orality due to the presence of pictography, which represents oral signs, and that to posit one is to romanticize oral culture in order to make writing its "dangerous" but necessary supplement. Meanwhile, Matei Calinescu (1993, 178) asserts that orality is part of reading and, thus, "contaminates" the supposed purity of literacy. Peter Dickinson's (1994, 321) assertion of orality in literacy means that "both orality and literacy become embodied by/in specific processes of speaking, writing and representing that encompass not only the individual text or utterance but also their place within a given discursive formation, including the persons involved in, acting upon, and/or affected by the sound-, word-, or meaning units."

The critique of the great divide theory generally advises that study of a particular group leads to more complex notions of the relationships between orality and literacy and the use to which each is put in the cultural formations of a group. In the case of the Doukhobors, this certainly holds true. Although the Doukhobors generally did not acquire much formal education until the 1950s (and in some cases not until the 1970s), some Doukhobors, particularly those who assisted Peter Lordly and Peter Chistiakov, were Russian-language autodidacts and, at times, self-taught in English as well. Both Lordly and Chistiakov were literate and wrote instructions and speeches for distribution among the Doukhobors. Lordly, in particular, read widely while he was in Siberia in order to develop new practices for his followers. Many older Doukhobors in the Kootenay region of British Columbia recall being sent to "Russian school" when they were children. Vladimir Bonch-Bruevich, the collector of Doukhobor psalms and songs who published a text version of The Living Book in 1909, wrote that Doukhobor elders sometimes wrote psalms out for him (The Living Book 1978, 104) or showed him versions of psalms that were recorded in small notebooks (35). From the nineteenth century on, therefore, literacy has played an important, although not central, role in Doukhobor culture, while orality in combination with literacy, particularly in the form of psalm singing and the collection of life stories, continues to play an important part in maintaining the Doukhobor diasporic imaginary.

An early example of Doukhobor oral autobiography can be found in the narratives transcribed and collected by Bonch-Bruevich, the compiler of The Living Book, and Bodianskii, a Tolstoyan who lived with the Doukhobors during their first years in Canada. Bodianskii and Bonch-Bruevich presumably recorded these stories by elder Doukhobors as a way to publicize events in Russia surrounding the Burning of Arms and the subsequent tortures endured by the Doukhobors before migration. These stories, although they do follow a recognizable outline, also contain traces of oral negotiation, particularly when Bodianskii was the transcriber. The one narrative I include that was recorded by Bonch-Bruevich does not include these traces, but it does share narrative similarities with the others. Therefore, although Bodianskii presumably did reword what the Doukhobor elders told him (as his own responses to questions are not included), the relationship between him and the Doukhobor speakers remains, to some extent, oppositional rather than hybridized as the speakers renegotiate with him what Doukhobor identity and what telling a life story can mean.

Although Bonch-Bruevich and Bodianskii were not "professional" anthropologists, they were doing anthropological fieldwork by collecting what anthropologists call life histories. These are accounts requested by anthropologists that, previously, were thought to be too qualitative to yield hard "data" but that, since the work of Vincent Crapanzano (among many others) over the last twenty years, are now seen as a way of gaining valuable information. Life histories are gathered when the anthropologist and the person interviewed agree to engage in a collaborative effort. But this collaboration should be analyzed as a negotiation over a life narrative, wherein the narrative produced may not be what the anthropologist "requires." As Crapanzano (1984, 955) argues, life histories are "the result of a complex self-constituting negotiation. It is the product (at least, from the subject's point of view) of an arbitrary and peculiar demand from another – the anthropologist. The interplay ... of demand and desire governs much of the content of the life history, and this interplay, the dynamics of the interview, must be taken into consideration in any evaluation of the material collected." And Margaret Blackman (1991, 56) reminds scholars that "most life histories are also shaped by Western conventions of biography. That is, they are presented as retrospective accounts of a cumulative life story, related as continuous narrative ... with a clear beginning and ending, and a developmental, chronological orientation." But she adds that the speakers who are requested to produce this kind of life history may not necessarily produce the intimate, confessional narrative expected within Western traditions (59) and that the motives for sharing life stories, such as the desire to pass traditions on to other group members in a permanent format not accessible to the speakers, may not be the motivation that the person who asked for the narrative expects (61).

This collecting process is further complicated by the political motivations of collectors when they recede into the narrative's background but still clearly shape the conditions for narrative utterance. As Rimstead (1996, 141) asks: "How can transcribing a story from the oral sphere into the privileged realm of written culture constitute political or social coalition, given that it implies power dynamics between the culturally dominated and the culturally dominant?" The narratives transcribed by Bodianskii and Bonch-Bruevich share many similarities with collaborative life history work produced by anthropologists, particularly in the renegotiation of narrative format and group identification, which is the product of a collaborative process. But they also share the characteristics of activist collaborations examined by Rimstead as both Bodianskii and Bonch-Bruevich were activists who assisted the Doukhobors with the transition they were making as new migrants in Canada. Indeed, they thought that Doukhobor beliefs about collective activity were similar to their own and, therefore, worth publicizing. In both cases, collaboration produced narratives that clearly operate in response to the requests of their non-Doukhobor interviewers, but they also resist the implied linearity of written narrative at key points so that the speaker's narrative goals, which do not always match those of the interviewers, can be achieved.

For example, Vanya Novokshyonov's (1908) narrative, entitled "Turning Down the Post of Village Headman,"[7] begins with a deliberate statement in which he agrees to tell a story (presumably in response to Bodianskii), but he reframes the terms of hearing it so that they are in tune with Doukhobor beliefs. He negotiates with Bodianskii, agreeing to tell the story but then changing the conditions of listening to suit his purposes: "I will tell you the story you would like to hear, but you will then make your own judgment. It is easy to tell the story; however, understanding is not given to everyone: one has to be a spiritual person to understand. If you judge by appearances only, much will remain unclear in our cause and experience" (1).[8] Novokshyonov decides to produce a type of autobiographical narrative that, earlier, I referred to as a witness narrative. This narrative is being called into being by Bodianskii, a non-Doukhobor who requires it in order to publicize the Doukhobor cause. Bodianskii, in other words, wants a public Doukhobor subject to be produced in order to retell the circumstances of torture. He wants a reliable witness narrative about what "really" happened. However, Novokshyonov stresses that the importance of the story lies not in his act of telling it but, rather, in that other aspect of orality, the interpretive ability of the listener. Novokshyonov, then, is telling his listener that he needs to hear the story as a sacred story that requires the reader to understand Doukhobor action as spiritual. He asks Bodianskii to respect Doukhobor difference but to understand it in Doukhobor terms within a Doukhobor context. As autobiography, then, Novokshyonov's narrative also asks its readers to read for the Doukhobor subject *in context* in terms of a collective Doukhobor subject and history. Although Novokshyonov does relate his own conflicts with authority, he intends them to be seen in terms of the greater struggle of Doukhobors with Russian authority and with the idea of secular authority itself.

This is why Novokshyonov (1908, 1) explains the sacred interpretation of the events of the Burning of Arms as a way of prefacing his own story:

> Our faith lies at the root of the experience we went through; so you have to look deep under the surface, and in this depth you will trace the beginning of our cause. How shall I put it for you to understand? Everything that has happened to us, happened because we do not believe in a stupid God. Our God is not a fool; our God is an All-Perfect Reason; therefore, one must use one's reason to serve him. And if one's God is a foolish God, foolishness, then, is the way to serve such a one. That is something for you to understand.

This narrative is not to be understood as "mere" history or a retelling of events but, rather, in a spiritual sense. The Burning of Arms, as Novokshyonov says later, is to be seen as part of a spiritual revival experienced by all Doukhobors who decided to follow Verigin's direction (2). Events such as the redistribution of property that occurred before the protest are pointedly referred to as spiritual events that mark Doukhobor difference. They are also potential points of contact between Doukhobors and non-Doukhobors. Novokshyonov emphasizes both aspects of this type of discourse by addressing Bodianskii directly. This oral method of getting attention indicates that Novokshyonov is attempting to control the narrative so that the Doukhobor cause is understood: "You, Aleksasha, are a just man; you should not be surprised by our decision. How can one call himself a Christian, if one lives like a wild beast? Our God is not a fool – I told you that already" (3).

After he relates other details about Doukhobor suffering (such as being whipped by the Cossacks for burning their weapons, deciding not to have children, and leaving home villages before migrating), Novokshyonov concludes this part of the narrative by saying: "that is all that there is to be told about our common cause. If you got it right, that is good; if you did not, it is not my fault" (6). This last sentence solidifies Novokshyonov's narrative control since, as he did at the beginning, he makes the listener responsible for understanding the context of the Doukhobor resistance. Having done this, he can now present himself as a Doukhobor subject within the context of that struggle. As he has instructed his listener to understand Doukhobor events as events with spiritual meanings, Novokshyonov's presentation of himself as a pacifist resister against an angry government illustrates his earlier discussion of Doukhobor pacifist resistance to government authority. He is a "pure" subject who does not change in response to conditions but who endures them as a subject-in-relation to other Doukhobors. This is a sign of the rightness of the Doukhobor cause. As Novokshyonov says, the events that the Doukhobors survive purify them as a group. A pure individual signifies the purity of the group since "it is very important that a man going with a spiritual sword to the sacred struggle should be pure and shining of spirit. As we were going through our spiritual baptism, our souls purified" (2).

When Novokshyonov describes the beginning of his resistance, he discusses it in terms of his own feelings and those of other Doukhobors: "Well, I grew at some point disgusted that I serve as a headman; I felt as if I were working for the government. Serving as headman became disgusting not only for myself, but for other Doukhobors who held the same post" (Novokshyonov 1908, 6). After all of the Doukhobors decided that they should not serve as headmen, Novokshyonov has a confrontation with the district police superintendent when he tries to give up his post. The confrontation quickly becomes polarized, as Novokshyonov refuses to take back his seal, the symbol of his office, and is forced to have an interview with the chief officer, "a man of notorious reputation: a huge man of enormous strength and a very cruel one" (8). Like other Doukhobor witness narratives (such as Soukorev's "My Renunciation of Military Service," which I discussed in Chapter 3), Novokshyonov's body is the means for resistance and testimony. After an argument, the chief officer threatens Novokshyonov with his fist, and Novokshyonov thinks about the beating he will receive. However, the chief officer hits him only once: "You see, I bleed easily; and as he hit me on the nose, the blood jetted out in two fountains almost two meters high" (Novokshyonov 1908, 9). Novokshyonov's subjectivity depends on outright confrontation and resistance, and the survival of violence. His physicality (he bleeds easily) brings victory, while his willingness to bear pain indicates his spiritual strength.

"The Suffering of Vasily Ivanovich Popov for the True Way," a narrative about the Russian persecutions that resulted from the Burning of Arms, and which was transcribed by Bonch-Bruevich, deals with a similar oppositional subjectivity and casts it in terms of the Doukhobor belief that suffering makes pure, steadfast subjects. In this narrative, however, it is not possible to tell what Bonch-Bruevich has requested. Popov's story begins with opposition and emphasizes the plurality of Doukhobor subjectivity as Doukhobors resist authority. This time, the Doukhobors will not provide registration information: "the lieutenant-colonel came to see us about our birth certificates, – we did not agree. I told him that we are all listed in 'The Book of Life'" (Popov 1908, 1). The rest of the narrative consists of stark oppositions between the swearing, angry officials and Popov, or the Doukhobors generally, who steadfastly resist them. As Popov says to one official who threatens to whip him, "the power is yours, but the will is God's," while the official replies, "I will have none of your talking, shut up" (1).

After one of these exchanges, in which Popov says that God is the only tsar, his body also becomes the focus of mute, pacifist resistance. Horsemen beat him until he loses consciousness, and then he is taken to prison. He regains consciousness, notices his injuries, and explains to a Cossack who asks him about the basis for his resistance that the central tenet of Doukhobor resistance is found in the Doukhobor psalms. This is the idea that the body is not as important as the soul, which is why he can endure beatings "for the truth. They can kill the flesh; however, they are unable to touch the soul of a righteous man" (Popov 1908, 3). This narrative is repeated almost word-for-word as the narrative of Popov's son, a story told to Popov by one of the newly arrived prisoners, with the same result. Popov tells this story about his son because it illustrates the common suffering of all Doukhobors. As with Novokshyonov's narrative, Popov's subjectivity is collectivized when he suffers and is tied to the necessity of representing himself as a pure subject as opposed to the corrupt subjects who serve the tsar.

Two narratives by Vanya Bayoff about life in Russia and events surrounding the Burning of Arms, recorded by Bodianskii, also assert the rhetoric of orality for the recorder to hear and understand. Like the Novokshyonov's narrative, Bayoff's stories – "Babushka's Grief" and "Execution" – contain lengthy preambles that constitute one side of a conversation with Bodianskii. And, like Novokshyonov's narrative, Bodianskii has clearly requested that Bayoff tell stories, and he has perhaps talked to her about the value of memory since both preambles deal with issues connected to orality and memory. Here, Bodianskii "appears" as a non-Doukhobor who requires autobiographical recollection to be produced, a situation that Bayoff is either not used to or cannot "produce" as a non-Doukhobor would wish. The stories that he does tell, therefore, are responses to a request for autobiography that, in some ways, refuse the conditions of autobiographical narrative. For example, Bayoff does recall stories his grandmother told him about the forced migration to Milky Waters in "Babushka's Grief," although the beginning of his narrative is about his inability to remember. Bayoff discusses how he did not listen carefully to his grandmother's stories and did not grasp their spiritual meaning. He talks about this by finding some commonality between Bodianskii's thoughts about memory and his own:

> You say, Aleksasha, that to possess the knowledge of the olden times is the same as to live even before one's actual birth in flesh. And you are right here. And you are also right when you say that this knowledge is useful. But I, myself, to tell you the truth, lacked this understanding formerly, and even if I heard some accounts of the times past, I was not listening carefully; I used to listen then to those stories for entertainment only, as one listens to a fairy tale, and that was why I would soon forget all I heard. And today, there is little I can remember to share with you. (Bayoff 1908b, 1)

Bayoff has been asked to provide a memory, but he cannot supply what is being requested. The resulting narrative, therefore, is about how he did *not* pay attention to the stories of his *nyanka*[9] and about how her own story was not possible to understand because "she used to tell her stories in a manner that was totally incomprehensible for small children: she used to cry and lament and just repeat the same things over and over again" because her grief robbed her of the ability to express herself clearly (Bayoff 1908b, 1-2).

Bayoff describes this grief as a story of sacrifice for Doukhobor ideals since *nyanka* grieved because she had left her husband and children in order to be with the strongly believing Doukhobors at Milky Waters (Bayoff 1908b, 4). The lament Bayoff repeats for Bodianskii is a type of life-narrative. In it Bayoff's *nyanka* relives her sacrifice of years before, going to grieve in a cluster of willow bushes near a river and singing "I was taking leave, and away I went / To my God, my Lord I surrendered my life / My young children, small kids, were like berries red / On my branch, but now all my berries are gone" and wondering if her husband is well, "you, the proud one, unforgettable, / you, my dear husband, Gavrilo Ivanovich" (9-10). By retelling this story, Bayoff can now spiritualize it as a sacred narrative since he recalls that, as a child, he could not understand what his grandmother was singing about, although he now sees her grief as noble and spiritual as it was shared by "the God-created birds and small animals [that] quivered from her grief" and by another, older, woman who had experienced tragedy and would grieve with her. In other words, Bayoff's story recasts what can be remembered so that it has spiritual meaning for latter-day Doukhobors enduring persecution in Russia.

The beginning of Bayoff's longer narrative, "Execution,"[10] also negotiates with Bodianskii's request for autobiographical narrative. Bayoff begins with what appears to be a reply to Bodianskii's "request," but he does not tell his life story in terms of his birth, childhood, and adulthood, which he clearly understands is what has been asked of him. He tells Bodianskii: "All right, if you wish, I will tell you about my life; only you are not going to enjoy the story or think much of it. How was it when I was a small boy? What is there to tell? I was growing up exactly as our little boys are growing up now. We, Doukhobors, live according to notions that are different from those of the Russians" (Bayoff 1992, 1). Here is an example of a narrative in which the speaker decides not to conform to the expectations of his non-Doukhobor questioner. He reframes the narrative structure so that he can tell his stories thematically rather than chronologically. Bayoff will tell his story, but it will not be the story of an individual subject's growth and maturity – the story Bodianskii has asked for. Instead, Bayoff discusses the differences between the violence of "Russian" (meaning Orthodox Russian) child-rearing as opposed to the child-rearing practices of

Doukhobor parents, who do not beat their children or abuse them in other ways. He does this by telling two stories of how he personally witnessed the beating of children (1-2). Bayoff directly addresses Bodianskii as part of his analysis of this problem and even calls him "grandfather," presumably to indicate that he considers him an elder who has wisdom and understanding. He concludes, and asks Bodianskii to conclude, that the Russians beat their children because they have not rejected priests and religious rites: "Grandfather, what do you think: where does this cruelty in them come from, why is there no God for them? I think, Grandfather, that this happens because they have wasted their God on prayers and priests, and on all sorts of piety" (3).

Bayoff moves from this discussion to general comments about Doukhobor families (Bayoff 1992, 4). He makes these comments as a way of introducing his major theme: his eventual separation from his father. Bayoff mentions that his father, although he is a Doukhobor, is a heavy drinker who did not become a follower of Peter Lordly and who did not adopt the stricter dietary practices that Lordly advocated. Bayoff says that his father and mother told him to get married even though he himself did not see the point (5). This early rift develops further when Bayoff, after describing the beginning of Peter Lordly's leadership and the opposition from the Small Party of the Gubanovs, describes how his father wanted to retain the old ways, "but I, Grandfather, when we started talking about Christian life and values, was absorbing these words like a dry soil absorbs the wetness of rain. I felt so much joy in those talks that I used to go by foot for many versts to our meetings to listen. And my parent [father] was irritated by this. This was how the discord started in our family too" (7). When Bayoff's father finally embraces Bayoff's wife, Tanya, in jest while he is drunk and using profanities, both Bayoff and Tanya leave Bayoff's family home and begin to belong formally to the Large Party that followed Peter Lordly. This separation, and Bayoff's decision to cease smoking, eating meat, and drinking alcohol, meant that "the distance between my parent and myself was growing, and we became strangers" (9).

At this point in the narrative, Bayoff talks about the Burning of Arms, but in order to do this he focuses on his own spiritual growth and the growth of Verigin's group, which was fostered by meetings about the upcoming protest. This allows him to collapse two temporally distinct events into a single theme: that of Doukhobor approaches to education. For this reason, he departs from his description of the meetings to a discussion of literacy and the understanding of outsiders in Canada. This discussion serves to underscore the virtues of collective group decision making and its superiority to institutionalized learning. Bayoff begins by saying, "we did not have any schooling; you know that even literate people are scarce among us, but I will tell you one story" (Bayoff 1992, 10).

This story concerns a non-Doukhobor doctor who came to a newly established Doukhobor community to treat the ill and to discuss Doukhobor faith with some of the elders. The doctor has the conversation with the elders, whom he presumed to be educated, and then asked to speak to some uneducated people.

His Doukhobor translator laughs when he hears this and says to them, "which of you is a university graduate? Tell us the truth! Well, which one at least can read and write?" Bayoff continues: "And who was literate among us? I am illiterate, Nikolasha is illiterate too; Aldosha has some knowledge of the alphabet, he can read, but his writing is very poor, he can hardly draw the letters; Efimushka and Alyosha are illiterate too ... well, I do not know how to explain it to you why this doctor thought that we were educated people, because we did not talk about anything else but human life, land, power, authorities, and morals" (Bayoff 1992, 10). In what is clearly an ironic moment, Bayoff pokes fun at people who think that Doukhobors without formal education do not have alternative ways of learning and cannot discuss abstract issues. It also provides Bayoff with a gloss that explains how his spiritual development deepened the rift between he and his parents: "Now then, I told you about this just to show that we now have understanding and notions; well, I can make comparisons using my own example. What were my ideas and notions when I lived at my parent's, and what are the ideas and notions that I got later?" (11). Bayoff identifies this difference as the reason for his contentment since "after all that has happened to me, I am calm and content; and I am calm and content only because the new notions and ideas helped me to accept life" (11).

Bayoff then returns to discussing the events of the Burning of Arms and the attempts made by Cossacks to round up Doukhobors. Before he describes his own experience, which forms the title of his narrative, however, he decides to digress. He discusses his fear that he will fight back when he sees others beaten, and then breaks off to say: "Listen, Grandfather, do you know what I think about the human soul and human life? I will digress here from my story to explain all this to you, because it is more important for me than anything else" (Bayoff 1992, 12). Bayoff's direct address to Bodianskii and his decision to digress indicate that he has decided not to tell what he refers to as "my story." "My story" by this time is not a retelling of the Burning of Arms, his own experience of punishment, or even a chronological account of his development from childhood (presumably this is what Bodianskii meant when he asked him to tell the "story" of his life) but, rather, a narrative about a number of different topics important to Doukhobors (such as the nature of education, families, and pacifist behaviour), which he links together thematically. Bayoff has so much narrative control that he can "digress" even from his own reworking of "my story" because, like Novokshyonov, he views his narrative primarily as an education for the non-Doukhobor listener who has requested it. His life story is not to be understood merely as the narrative of someone who has survived Cossack torture but, rather, as the outcome of the Doukhobor spiritualization of suffering. As Bayoff explains, "if our flesh acts, it does not act by itself; it is driven by the spirit embodied in the flesh" (12). This involves an understanding of suffering that, Bayoff realizes, his listener may not understand, for he says "it is hard for me to express my opinion, Grandfather" and several times attempts to clarify his statements (12). Bayoff states that a person can embody either a good or an evil spirit that was originally disembodied and that purity is necessary for spiritual development "because ... unworthy deeds leave an impure trace in one's life, and there is no way to redeem them" (14).

This explanation is important for understanding the rest of Bayoff's narrative since his main point is that he "has been always afraid to succumb to the impure, to commit an unworthy deed, to tell a lie, to be crafty, to hurt someone, and to get enraged" (Bayoff 1992, 14). He says that his greatest test in this area involved enduring punishment after the Burning of Arms. His narrative then elaborates upon a series of tests both of his body and, in a parallel typology, of his spiritual purity. First, a mounted Cossack tries to trample him, but he resists this by banding together with other Doukhobors. Then he endures a whipping that could "drive a powerful spirit of malice and resentment into a man; but – save me, God – I resisted the impulse," and he refuses what he refers to as the "lawlessness," rather than pain, being beaten into him (15).

In the last part of his narrative Bayoff relates the details of his own torture, which he refers to as an "execution."[11] Here, his earlier story of his father's estrangement resurfaces as his father leads the Cossacks (who are to beat Bayoff and his wife) to their house, presumably to take revenge for his son's decision to follow the Large Party (Bayoff 1992, 16). Bayoff then relates how he and Tanya are captured and how he loses consciousness but then regains it only to see Tanya naked after her beating: "even now, I can see this picture clearly, I just close my eyes and I see all this clearly in front of me" (17). He then describes in detail the effects of his own beating, which almost killed him (18). His father, he recalls, watched as his wife and mother helped him pull up his pants while the Cossacks laughed at him (18).

The importance of this event for Bayoff is that his body did not betray him and so his spirit stayed pure. He endures. This makes the beating and humiliation ordered by his own father bearable, and, although he migrated to Canada, he looks forward to his own death: "As I understand, everything that could have been taken from me, was taken; through my trials and tribulations so much malice and resentment was used up and disappeared from the earth that it is not possible to require anything else from me. As I understand it, I managed to resist all the malice that was pursuing me; I did not let it penetrate my soul, and it is now completely wasted. I am calm and content now about my whole life, and I will die a reconciled man" (Bayoff 1992, 19). The point of Bayoff's narrative is the transmission of Doukhobor beliefs about the spirit and the body, which explain how he was able to endure both family separation, humiliation, and physical punishment. His narrative ends with his belief that he is prepared for death: his successful migration to Canada means little to him. In fact, the last line of Bayoff's narrative is about the failure of his family to migrate since "my parent did not go to Canada and did not let nyanka go, and my brother was exiled to Siberia" (19). Bayoff's subjectivity depends upon his resistance to the malice in his own family and to the cruelty of the authorities as well as upon his belief in group decision making. His decision to link his life events thematically in terms of Doukhobor differences from non-Doukhobor Russians and non-Doukhobors in Canada means that he responded to Bodianskii's request that he "produce" his life with an alternative set of stories – one that brings spiritual context to the events he witnessed. Autobiography, in Bayoff's narrative, is a negotiation between the narrative Bodianskii asks for and the one that Bayoff ultimately makes. As Bayoff's calling Bodianskii "Grandfather" at key points shows, he decided to address his interviewer directly when he reframed his narrative in terms of what he believed to be important.

The work of the late Alex Harshenin, a linguist of Doukhobor background who made recordings while researching Doukhobor dialect, provides a valuable resource for the study of oral Doukhobor autobiography, even though he did not intend to record narratives for anything other than linguistic purposes.[12] Harshenin's interviews clearly indicate how, during the interview process, he and the people he interviewed engaged in a set of exchanges about Doukhobor identity and the importance of memory. In his interview with Fred (Fedya) Zhikarov and an unknown speaker, Harshenin (1965) attempts to direct the discussion, perhaps in the hope of yielding Doukhobor dialect words. Zhikarov, however, immediately decides to reframe the discussion in terms of what is important to him, which is his rejection of Verigin's leadership:

> HARSHENIN. Let's start our interview. Let's deal with the earliest recollections you have, going back to your youth, what kind of work you did.
> ZHIKAROV. I'll start from when I decided to leave the community.[13]

Harshenin asks Zhikarov why he left, and Zhikarov repeats what he'd said about his confrontation with Peter Lordly, even when Harshenin asks him if others left. In other words, Zhikarov presents himself as a free-thinking Doukhobor who is able to confront Lordly:

> ZHIKAROV. I just got fed up, tired. Simple as that. So I came to Lordly and
>   told him I want to leave. He said, "Why do you want to do that?" I want
>   to live on my own.
> HARSHENIN. You had the courage to say all that?
> ZHIKAROV. Yeah.
> HARSHENIN. Did others do this at the same time?
> ZHIKAROV. Yes, others did it. He said "It's up to you. You have the right,
>   I permit you." I thanked him and that was it. So I packed up my belong-
>   ings and left.

At another point in the interview, Zhikarov challenges Harshenin's role as the interviewer – the person who determines what information will be exchanged. When Harshenin asks Zhikarov where he moved after he left the Community, Zhikarov refuses to provide this information:

> H. Where was this place [where you moved]?
> Z. There is a shack out there. It was just off the boundary of the commu-
>   nal lands.
> H. Was this Oobezhishche[14] in Grand Forks?
> Z. I think you know the place, it's not far from here.

This is an example of what Rimstead (1996, 144) refers to as the refusal of some speakers to go along with the conventional roles of interviewee and interviewer. Zhikarov does this by playing the role of an "outside" researcher conducting the interview, with Harshenin cast in the role as a Doukhobor "insider" who does not need to be told things for the record, and who knows (although non-Doukhobors probably would not) where "here" is.

Harshenin's role as interviewer changes again when an unknown speaker joins Zhikarov and begins to discuss in detail how bricks were made at the CCUB brick factory (where they both worked). This conversation occurs in English, despite Harshenin's efforts to have both speakers return to Russian and to historical context by asking, in Russian, when the factory was burned (presumably in a Freedomite arson attack). But both speakers ignore Harshenin and continue to argue about how bricks were baked, although they do switch into Russian for the rest of the conversation.

At another point during this discussion, Harshenin becomes an "insider" and talks about whether a non-Doukhobor had the right to with-hold the water supply from neighbouring Doukhobors. Although Harsh-enin attempts to discuss the issue in terms of the abstract concept of justice and claims solidarity with his speakers by exclaiming "Justice, justice, we need justice," Zhikarov and the other speaker do not agree. They point out that "justice is on the hands of the first taker [of the rights]" and that the non-Doukhobor farmer had been there before the Community. This discussion leads Zhikarov and the unknown speaker to talk about how, until after the Second World War, the Doukhobors were considered to be of lesser status than were the English-speaking settlers of British origin. Zhikarov and the unknown speaker have, by the end of the interview, complete control over what is represented in the conversation. They can now ask questions of Harshenin as an "insider" on their terms, and the interview ends with Zhikarov's words:

UNKNOWN. The Sons of Freedom settled in certain areas not paying a cent in taxes. The grandfather Kazakoff, is he related to you?

HARSHENIN. He's got that nice little beard. What's his name, Koozia?

ZHIKAROV. Well, he doesn't live there.

In this interview, Harshenin's initial attempt to create a narrative agenda that would develop according to a life story pattern is altered by Zhikarov and the unknown speaker, who turn the discussion to a common Doukhobor theme (their work) and contemporary political events in the Doukhobor communities. Zhikarov uses the interview format to present himself in a way that highlights the parts of his life that he thinks are meaningful (leaving the community, working in the brick factory). In doing this, he changes Harshenin's role to that of another Doukhobor conversing with him from that of a researcher who is not involved with the workings of the Doukhobor communities. Zhikarov changes how his subjectivity is constructed in the narrative – from that of an interviewed subject to that of a participant in a conversation. He constructs his subject *in relation* to the others who speak.

Like Harshenin's interview with Zhikarov, the interviews conducted with Doukhobor elders as part of the 1977 Salmo, British Columbia, recording project indicate a dialogue not only with the topics of discussion but also with the type of subject produced.[15] In most cases, the interviewers ask generic questions designed to highlight Doukhobor difference (e.g., questions about marriage practices, clothing, and housing). While the speakers often comply, there are points in the interviews when they revise the request or decide not to respond. Bill (Vasily) Bondareff's (1977) interview, for example, starts with what he calls an autobiographical section that he constructs in response to his interviewer's request that he describe his birth and his youth. His "autobiography" shifts between the first-person and second-person plural when he discusses communal living or the refusal to swear the oath of allegiance. Bondareff's use of the plural supports his endorsement of communal living in British Columbia before the death of Peter Lordly, when individualism was not thought to be an ideal state of being and labour for the community was highly valued: "Life was very attractive and everyone enjoyed life. Of course I must emphasize that all these enterprises were the result of difficult labour. At this time it was simply pleasure and happiness to live in the community. Everyone was happy. We used to go to a 'big bay' for swimming where a lot of young people would gather, girls and boys. Very beautiful. This good life lasted until 1924." Bondareff's support for communal living is similar to that of other Doukhobors. His descriptions of it in the first-person plural, then, represent Doukhobor identity in what he considers to be its ideal form: communal living under the leadership of Lordly. Lordly's direction to younger Doukhobors not to work outside the community is interpreted positively by Bondareff, since it preserves "pure" Doukhobor identity: "He [Lordly] didn't want us to become 'bums.' He wanted us to be modest, of course intelligent and educated in the spirit of the Doukhobors."

Like Cecil Koochin (Arishenkoff and Koochin 1974) in his interview with *Mir*, Bondareff represents his identity as a Doukhobor in terms of communal living. Although he mentions that, after Lordly's death, one of the elders in his family went back to Blaine Lake, Saskatchewan, he stresses that his family lived in the CCUB until its demise in 1935 and that his family (with other families) bought land during the repossession: "but we continued the Doukhobor way of life." In other words, they continued to live and work communally. Bondareff ends this part of the interview by affirming that communal living is as central to Doukhobor identity now as it was in the past. He links the act of communal living to a type of spiritual testimony that the interviewer should be able to see and understand. This "challenge" to the interviewer is similar to Novokshyonov's (1908) challenge to his interviewer to interpret physical events in a spiritual way. According to Bondareff (1977), "we continued to live our Doukhobor way of life right up to today. Today you can see what we have among us. Well, you can make your own deductions just from looking at us as we are and thank you for coming and looking at us."

At some points in the interview, Bondareff, like Zhikarov, decides either not to respond to questions or to reframe them in terms of his own ideas about representation. When he is asked about his formal education, he affirms Doukhobor principles, saying that "our parents told us that we had to first of all go through the school of God, meaning the life we lead. The emphasis was on the school of living and not on any formal education. The emphasis was on toil and peaceful life." When he is asked about his ability to speak English, he says that he can get by but that is all, and then he immediately asks if there are other questions (presumably because he does not wish to discuss this). At the end of the interview, when he is asked about retaining Doukhobor ways of living, Bondareff answers first in English, and then switches to Russian to abruptly end the interview:

INTERVIEWER. Do you still maintain your Doukhobor culture?
BONDAREFF. Oh yes [in English]. For me it's not a problem, I think I'll retain our Doukhobor culture until I die. It's our life. If you think that's enough, I'm ready to go.

The interview with a Freedomite woman from Krestova who is referred to only as Mrs. Bojey[16] is similar to Bondareff's in that it stresses communal living rather than individual subjectivity (Bojey 1977). An exception occurs in her description of psalm-singing, although she ties it directly to working on the farm as a young girl: "We didn't have to go far [to prayer meeting]. I liked prayer meeting so I used to go often. I read [recited] psalms; my parents taught me how to cook at home." Like Bondareff, Bojey sees communal living as a state of equality – a state in which "everyone looked alike[,] [e]veryone had the same food." She said that her family always tried to live together communally. When she mentions her marriage, she stresses the importance of its communal nature: "later on of course when I got married and lived in Alberta, we lived together with the Wishlow family for three years or so. That's not too important but we still worked together communally."

Bojey reframes the narrative structure in terms of her own interests. When she is asked directly, "Do you still hang onto Doukhobor culture," she replies, "Of course I support it." When she is asked about what kind of clothing she wore as a child, she replies "Doukhobor clothing" and offers no details. However, a question about whether she ate fish or meat prompts her to tell a story about her family and its devotion to Freedomite Doukhobor principles (vegetarianism is a sacred practice for devout Doukhobors): "We never even ate fish. We still don't eat meat and I taught my children not to eat meat. My daughter didn't, my son [didn't]. At that time we had no support from the government in terms of parental aid. When my husband died, my son Fred was sixteen." This detail leads Bojey to describe how she supported her grandmother while the children worked outside the community for money until the family joined the trek to support the Freedomite prisoners at Agassiz. However, she recollects this trek in terms of loss and illness rather than in terms of Freedomite ideals:

Then we went on this trek. All the Sons of Freedom in our area went on this trek and so did we. Whatever money we had in savings we gave away to other people. We had given our money away; we had spent our money and we had nothing to pay taxes and we lost our property; we lost everything. My son died and everything was lost. [At this point the tone of the

speaker sounds very sad; many pauses.] Whatever remained in the building was stolen and broken. We came back to bury my son. That's when I
saw what happened to my house. When we came back, everything was
broken; there was nothing salvageable. We lived in Agassiz maybe eight
months, then we moved to Vancouver. My husband had two operations
in Vancouver.

Despite the pathos of this story, the interviewer does not comment on
it and continues to ask direct rather than indirect questions. He asks
repeatedly whether Bojey remembers "any interesting happenings." Bojey
responds to this either by saying that she has forgotten events or that she
did not (like others) keep a scrapbook about what happened to the Freedomites. She finally ends this line of inquiry by saying, "maybe we tape
too much unnecessary information," and she refocuses the discussion on
central Doukhobor ideas symbolized by the bread, salt, and water on the
table over which the interview is taking place. Bojey uses these symbols of
Doukhoborism to affirm central Doukhobor practices (such as the rejection of clerical and government authority) and to draw attention to why
communal living ended: "On the table, that's bread and salt and water.
That's our oath of allegiance. It's our Christian rules. When people got
married we always have bread, salt and water on the table which means we
don't need any clergy. But of course although [we follow the rules of]
bread, salt and water the government still forced us to follow their rules.
Of course people have stopped living the communal way. In the days of
the community we lived together." Thus Bojey displays her Doukhobor
principles by discussing her life events either in terms of tactile symbols
(such as bread, salt, and water) or in terms of Doukhobor practices (such
as vegetarianism and communal living). Her refusal to discuss events that
the interviewer considers "interesting" reflects her desire to be seen as a
Doukhobor subject anchored in Doukhobor living practices.

Helen Popoff (1977), another Freedomite woman from Krestova, uses
the interview format to discuss spiritual issues in the tradition of Doukhobor female elders, who undertook most of the spiritual instruction and formation in Doukhobor homes.[17] She also talks about Freedomite protest,
her status as a healer, and the hostility of the non-Doukhobor world, but
she discusses these things on her own terms. She begins the interview, for
instance, by treating a question about Doukhobor living as spiritual rather
than material and as about cooperation rather than competition: "We
lived, we respected each other, brothers and sisters. God helped us and we
relied on God more. When one forgets about God, everything seems to
change. God helps us do good things. The whole world is in a huge race.
This is because we have forgotten about God. This is not God's work."
When she is subsequently asked about whether she supports Doukhobor

culture, like Bojey, Popoff replies that she does but that she does so in terms of her adherence to vegetarianism. When the interviewer asks her a traditional autobiographical question – her birth place and date – Popoff answers but immediately corrects herself and highlights her lack of formal education, saying, "I am not too well educated, I don't remember." Although she ostensibly does this because she has trouble remembering the date of her birth, her decision to say that she is not well educated indicates that birth dates represent a non-Doukhobor way of measuring time and events, which she links to non-Doukhobor, institutionalized learning. Her haziness about giving this information parallels her non-participation in the institution that creates the discourses that assume the importance of dates.

A similar refusal and reframing occurs when the interviewer asks Popoff if she knows any funny stories. Laughing, Popoff says, "I used to know a lot but now I don't remember them. My parents would tell me interesting things in Russia but here there is nothing interesting." Popoff's laughter cuts off this line of inquiry. Although Popoff initially answered her interviewer with the joke that nothing interesting happens in Canada, she reframes the question as one about the problems with materialism encountered by Doukhobors on the Prairies. This thematization of Doukhobor migration as a flight from materialism allows her to begin another story, which is related to the migration of her family to British Columbia and the parsimony of her rich relatives:

> The following day, we stopped at Drumheller, we thought we would get rest with relatives/friends – [they] wouldn't feed us! The lady said she had not baked any bread, I haven't got anything. Finally she made some eggs and gave us some milk. So we left our relatives and slept in the car. Because it was so cold, March, all five of us are sleeping in the car and we had all these peed-on diapers! We had nowhere to wash them so we hung them outside and dried them and used them over – better than nothing [laughs].

Again, when Popoff mentions in an aside that she went to Piers Island and is asked why, she gives reasons but mentions a nude protest (an area of great interest to non-Doukhobors) almost as an afterthought: "People stopped paying dues, [and they] were thrown out onto the street [literally, highway]. We sat on this highway for awhile and then we were thrown in jail. There was no work anywhere. We sat on the highway, oh yeah, we did take our clothes off. We just took our clothes off, everyone. Then we ended up in jail. Your mother was only ten months old. We got three years." Popoff becomes agitated when she describes how her father was beaten and placed in solitary confinement at Piers Island. This agitation carries over into a question that she is asked about marriage, which causes her to return to the subject of family upheaval during the Piers Island imprisonment. Popoff asks for the tape to be turned off, a sign that she wishes to regain emotional (and narrative) control: "I went to school for four months when I was eight years old. It was an English school ... I did go to Russian school too. Things didn't seem to go into my head at that time. I was upset about domestic arrangements at that time. When you are frightened, you are upset. I can't remember so much about school. Are you taping this? [tape turns off]."

When the tape is turned back on, Popoff decides to discuss home remedies, which she connects with what she interprets as both negative and positive aspects of Doukhobor non-cooperation with authority. Here, Popoff does not thematize or even explain the conflicting interpretations of the medical profession that she enumerates; instead, she tells two stories that indicate how she is able to use common sense to give "proper" medical advice. In a story about her mother, Popoff links home remedies unfavourably to a lack of formal education. Her mother, whose name was Dunia, had cataracts. She was told to put honey on her eyes and look at the sun. But, as Popoff explains, this home remedy did not work:

> That's what she did. Honey, she put some honey on her eyes and then all the bees and wasps surrounded her. But I told her[,] Dunia, don't put that silly stuff on your eyes, eat it, it will help you. Finally Dunia went to the doctor and had her cataracts removed and then she could see. See the kind of fools we were? We had no education. If she'd had just a little bit of brains she'd eat that honey and it would do her some good. Flies flying, using the rag to ward off flies! [laughing].

However, Popoff goes on to tell a story about effective home remedies. She links this story to features of Doukhobor identity by associating good health with a vegetarian diet and by connecting her knowledge of home remedies to her own sense of independence from non-Doukhobor authority, represented here by doctors:

> And you know something? I never went to a doctor and I attribute that to the food we ate. The only time I went to the doctor I got my tonsils out, that was when we were in prison. Our diet was all screwed up. But since that jail time, I am my own doctor. Do you understand that? I can actually cure people. My grandfather had a stroke. He didn't go to the doctor and I cured him on my own. Well, you have to be a doctor to do that.

Helen Popoff's stories, like those of Mrs. Bojey, Bill Bondareff, and Fred Zhikarov, show how, within an interview format, Doukhobor subjects can reframe the interview (which is structured so as to construct identity as an essentialization of Doukhobor difference) to accommodate complex formulations of identity as something that can be negotiated, accepted, or rejected in the respondent's terms. Due to the oral construction of the interview, which allows for dialogue, all the speakers can draw on long-standing traditions of Doukhobor oral history and narrative in order to tell their stories. The tendency of most speakers to discuss collective history and to construct their lives in terms of their activities within communities shows that they are able to view the interviewers' questions as an extension of those conversations that occur in communal, rather than in individual, subject formations. The speakers treat the interviewers not as authorities to whom they must defer but, rather, as others who assist them in constructing their subjectivity in relation to communal identity.

Testimonials by male and female elders, and by Sons of Freedom members in the Joint Doukhobor Research Committee Symposia, indicate how unwritten life stories have been used in Doukhobor communities to discuss Doukhobor cultures, histories, and beliefs within dialogue situations that are similar to those found in recorded interviews. The symposia, which ran from 1974 to 1982 and were well attended by Doukhobors from all major groups, represented a unique effort to work out what Doukhoborism had been and what it would be in the future. This was believed to be necessary because Doukhoborism had been "so poorly transmitted to our younger generation [that] many have ceased to value it at all" (Joint Doukhobor Research Committee 1997, 6). In addition, Eli Popoff's transcription, translation, and collation of symposia testimony represents a unique attempt to bridge the gap between the centrality of oral recollection in Russian found in Doukhobor tradition and the emerging stress on the use of written English to work out many of these same issues amongst younger Doukhobors. Thus the symposia summary records and facilitates a type of "orality in literacy" by respecting oral traditions and by recording them in a more durable format.

As the 1974 invitation to participate indicates, one of the principle aims of the symposia was to encourage elders to discuss their knowledge of Doukhobor history and beliefs: "those who are acknowledged among our people as having knowledge of our history and beliefs, or who have held administrative positions within the various Doukhobor organizations, are urged to share their experiences and knowledge with others by taking active part in the meetings" (Joint Doukhobor Research Committee 1997, 3). Elders were encouraged to discuss their memories of migration and early pioneering days in Canada so that other Doukhobors could understand aspects of Doukhobor history, such as the circumstances of the Burning of Arms, the operation of the CCUB, or memories of the Doukhobor leaders Peter Lordly and Peter Chistiakov. Elders were encouraged to do this because, in Doukhobor communities, beliefs, history, and traditions had always been passed down orally from respected elders. In this way, life narrative becomes related to the idea of testimony and recollections that are not a product of someone constructing a subjectivity in isolation but, rather, a product of community activity. They are constructed for others rather than for oneself.

Elders who came forward and offered recollections often linked them to primary symbolic moments in Doukhobor history. Mike Chernoff does this when he begins his account of his origins by asserting that his grandfathers were both martyrs in Russia for the Doukhobor faith, while his parents had lived in the Community all their lives (Joint Doukhobor Research Committee 1997, 177). But his recital also serves to guarantee his credibility as a narrator who can talk about the history of the Freedomites since the actions of his grandfathers and parents serve to demonstrate that he is a "real" Doukhobor who has not forgotten his origins and his sense of purpose. This is why he introduces this link between his origin and the Doukhobor diasporic imaginary as a way of "guaranteeing" that what he says is reputable. As he says, "being a descendant of this lineage, I have direct knowledge of the suffering for their faith that my grandfathers went through, I feel that their life's accomplishments were very great, even though they were illiterate peasants" (177). This "apology" for illiteracy actually becomes a source of the narrator's pride in Doukhoborism for, as he says, they owe their success to their having chosen "a right pathway of life" (177). He uses the choice of his ancestors as a way of describing his own upbringing in the Community and his subsequent experiences as Peter Chistiakov's secretary. Mike Chernoff's story of his grandparents' and parents' faithfulness establishes his own faithfulness as a community worker and as a narrator.

William Ogloff's autobiographical speech establishes his narrative position in terms of another important sign of Doukhobor identity: belief in the sanctity of communal living. In a passage entitled "My Recollections of Life in the Christian Community of Universal Brotherhood," he gives his birth year and birth location and mentions that he was born "to devout Doukhobor parents, Timothy and Matryona Ogloff" (Joint Doukhobor Research Committee 1997, 197). This mention of the devoutness of his parents signals to his audience that Ogloff is a reliable Doukhobor narrator. After describing the migration of his family to British Columbia, a move that tells his Doukhobor audience that his family endorsed communal living and followed Peter Lordly's directives, he tells a story about how, as a youth, he ate some oats that were meant for a baby. This story becomes a way of indicating that, in a community, one should serve others and not simply please oneself. He calls the whipping he received for doing this "well deserved" (197). When he subsequently describes working for the Community when his family moved back to Alberta, Ogloff develops his endorsement of communal living as a hallmark of Doukhobor identity and spiritual formation: "I developed the skills needed [to herd cattle on horseback] and really got to feel a sense of satisfaction that I was doing my bit in this large Doukhobor undertaking set up for the good of all those that were part of this commune" (199). Ogloff ends his story with a short description of his six-month stint in an English school and his first job. The occasion of this job also marks his passage into adulthood, which he identifies with becoming a dues-paying member of the Community: "I was very satisfied with myself that I was a full-fledged, responsible adult person" (200). For Ogloff, membership in the CCUB is the primary link to Doukhobor identity, and it both marks his passage into adulthood and ends his narrative.

Lucy Maloff, the wife of Peter N. Maloff, who had been an early Freedomite leader in the 1930s,[18] does not tell her life story for the Joint Doukhobor Research Committee but, instead, provides an account of Peter Chistiakov's visit to her home. She does this because the committee had asked people to come forward with stories about Peter Chistiakov (Joint Doukhobor Research Committee 1997, 364, 451). Thus Maloff's narrative serves two purposes: it relates details she remembers about Peter Chistiakov and also indicates her own commitment to Doukhoborism. Maloff's account stresses the strengths of Chistiakov's leadership and his endorsement of Freedomite protests against militarism in the late 1920s. It also records her husband's commitment to Freedomite ideals, which was strengthened by Peter Chistiakov's visit. Chistiakov's actions and his speech to the assembled people convinced Maloff to let her husband join a Freedomite protest despite the hardships that her family would endure because of his absence (365-66). Maloff's story fits into Doukhobor ideas about suffering for true causes and adhering to one's ideals while, at the same time, describing Chistiakov's connections to the Freedomites.

The narrative begins with a short section about Maloff's husband, who became a friend of Chistiakov after his arrival in Canada, and then moves on to her preparations for Chistiakov's visit in 1928. The preparations become the test-case for her strong faith, which is manifested in her decision to make borscht for Chistiakov's lunch. This detail is important because it indicates the family's dedication to Sons of Freedom ideals and practices and emphasizes Lucy Maloff's own work:

> at this time our family was on a totally vegan-vegetarian diet. We did not use any milk or egg products whatsoever. We did not even wear leather boots or shoes. This strict vegetarianism was one of the things that my husband respected in the life-concept of the original Sons of Freedom. At this time there were many Sons of Freedom who did not even use cooked

> food but lived mainly on raw vegetables, fruits and grains. Most used
> footwear of sewed cloth, but the more devout all walked around in "lapti,"
> a sort of sandal knitted out of wool-yarn. There was absolutely nothing
> used that would hint of lavishness. During this winter I had knitted 17
> pairs of "lapti" from self-spun wool yarn. (Joint Doukhobor Research
> Committee 1997, 365)

When Maloff's mother and sisters try to have her make borscht in the
manner of non-vegan Doukhobor families, Maloff's refusal indicates the
strength of her convictions, which are strengthened through receiving
the consensus of her own family (365). Although Maloff says that "at first
I was very nervous and kind of worried about my decisions to serve our
vegan-vegetarian meal" (365), Chistiakov approves of the borscht, which
brings her relief because her choice is "correct" (366). This moment also
illustrates Chistiakov's approval of the Sons of Freedom as, after the meal,
he remarks that the young Freedomites in the room are "our real highest
Doukhobor University output." However, he later strikes and sharply criticizes a young Freedomite man who criticizes the materialist basis of the
CCUB (366). Maloff's account indicates the gendering of her religious convictions through food preparation and the making of lapti. It also implies
that true Doukhobors should endure difficult domestic arrangements as
part of suffering for what they believe.

Although the initial goal of the Joint Doukhobor Research Committee
was to enquire into Doukhobor history and beliefs, comments by and
about Freedomite depredations (arsons and bombings) dominated the proceedings for much of the symposia. Freedomite testimony for the symposia ranges from recollections about the initial 1902 trek (which began
the Freedomite movement), to the mass imprisonment of Freedomites at
Piers Island during the 1930s, to Freedomite testimony about the Sons
of Freedom, to angry exchanges between Community Doukhobors (who
were targets of depredation activity), to Freedomite radicals discussing
their own version of events. The Freedomite life narratives tend to indicate
how, in oral narratives, autobiographical subject representation can be
used to recover past history and to open it to question. This becomes critical in Freedomite testimony because other Doukhobors did not always
understand either the history of the Freedomites or what motivated radical Freedomites to commit depredations (Joint Doukhobor Research Committee 1997, 449-50). They did not always know about Freedomite history
and beliefs because non-Freedomite Doukhobors were not encouraged to
socialize with Freedomites (Plotnikoff 1998, 209).

For example, Nikolai Koozmitch Novokshyonoff's discussion of the
1902 trek begins with his assertion that he knows about it because of his
family background. His explanation begins with his autobiography, in

which he explains that he was orphaned and was adopted by his grand-mother, a Freedomite who, for three years, took him with her on Free-domite marches and protests (Joint Doukhobor Research Committee 1997, 107-8). This discussion guarantees his authority when he begins to talk about the Sons of Freedom more generally (108). In a similar guar-antee of authenticity, Vasily P. Podmoryov's account, entitled "A Recol-lection by Vasiliy Petrovitch Podmoryov," begins with an explanation of narrative process, which includes his full name and the reason that one may accept his story's veracity. He is a witness, and he learned about these events by means of oral tradition: "My name is Vasiliy Petrovitch Pod-moryov and I am a live witness to all the inside recollections of the trek of 1902. In our family, these recollections were repeated probably more than a hundred times" (122). In this text, therefore, Podmoryov appeals both to past oral tradition (learning from elders) and to his own status as a rep-utable elder in Doukhobor communities (I am a live witness). Podmoryov uses "autobiographical" details about his family and origin, much as do Chernoff and Ogloff, in combination with oral tradition to guarantee his audience's attention. Here, autobiographical conventions play a rhetorical role (rather than focusing on "plot," which is what drives an identity nar-rative) in that they combine with such oral traditions as direct address, singing or reciting psalms, and describing the "question" that the narra-tive is supposed to answer (none of which are usually part of autobiogra-phies produced by members of dominant discourses).

Other presentations by Freedomite radicals followed a testimonial pat-tern not seen in other narratives. These presentations were usually made not only as recollections for purely historic purposes but also as a way of narrating Freedomite concerns that would be shared by all Doukhobors. For example, Peter Swetlishoff's public repentance for his burning and bombing activity adheres to some of the conventions of confessional dis-course. He refuses to discuss why he committed depredations and instead offers a type of life story that centres on his concerns with Doukhobor materialist tendencies. Swetlishoff openly treats his own story as a discur-sive opportunity to address, or "answer," other Doukhobors: "I am answer-ing in the following printed lines, in which I am briefly going to explain about my former understanding of certain occurrences that I had lived through. In particular, what I was guided by and what it was that brought me to this idea of the whip that awakens like a loud sounding bell calling forth for spiritual re-birth" (Joint Doukhobor Research Committee 1997, 603). Swetlishoff's description of his "awakening" into Freedomite activity stresses his research into Doukhobor history and his rejection of materi-alism and private property rather than any enthusiast activity. In this way, his non-Freedomite listeners can find common ground so that they can respond to his call for spiritual renewal as well as to his decision to renounce violence. Swetlishoff, however, emphasizes his self-education as central to his life story in order to retain Freedomite beliefs in the enthusiast reading of Doukhobor history as spiritual typology.[19] The Doukhobors who heard Swetlishoff's statement received it very positively (661). This indicates how aspects of written autobiographical narrative can be used discursively within an oral environment (Swetlishoff read from a document and also spoke impromptu during his confession). Here, autobiography operates as a rhetorical device that enables the speaker to defend his Freedomite beliefs as he traces their origins and then calls on the whole community to change its direction. Swetlishoff's "confession" is not an assurance of his identity or a sharing of his life as a memorial sign for others to imitate; rather, it is the means for speech. His portrayal of his life as an educational experience means that his recantation of bombing and burning is a product of his desire to learn and change.

Taken together, the short autobiographical statements and testimonials that I have examined here combine aspects of autobiographical discourse (e.g. about origins, birth, childhood and parentage) with other aspects of witness narrative and, in Swetlishoff's case, confession discourse. They also combine written conventions with oral ones as the story of each speaker works to guarantee the authority of the person speaking, to commemorate an event, or to make general statements about Doukhoborism. The work of autobiography here is not the work of a narrative that commemorates the life of one person; rather, it forms part of a larger discursive project in which groups of Doukhobors use traditional oral debating and questioning techniques developed in *sobranie* in order to determine what collective Doukhobor history and identity might mean. It is narration undertaken for others, with collective purpose. The Doukhobor saying, which Bonch-Bruevich translates as "record in heart, proclaim in word," affirms the importance, even in recent years, of orality in Doukhobor communities and of constructing a communal subjectivity that asserts the key position that the spoken word, spoken for others, has in ongoing debates between Doukhobors about the future of Doukhoborism and its connection to life narratives.

5
Witness, Negotiation, Performance: Freedomite Autobiography

It would seem unlikely that members of the Sons of Freedom would produce any autobiographical work at all since most of them did not, at least until the 1970s, subscribe to discourses of the autonomous, individual self and the assumption of a place in national culture (which autobiographical discourse has privileged). Of the three major Doukhobor groups, the Freedomites, also known as the Sons of Freedom,[1] have most strenuously rejected the marks of Canadian citizenship, including the payment of taxes; private ownership of property; military service (especially in times of war); registration of births, marriages, and deaths; and public education in English for their children. In their more radical periods Freedomite Doukhobors have also refused identity conventions that have proved highly threatening to non-Doukhobor Canadians and their institutional representatives. Such refusals first occurred in 1902, when more than 1,000 Sons of God[2] marched south across the Saskatchewan prairie, hoping to reach a land "nearer the sun," while throwing away their money and any goods made from animal skins to emphasize their rejection of what they described as Canadian materialism; their refusal to exploit animal labour; and their belief, supported by numerous Doukhobor psalms, that Doukhobor identity is related to wandering, exile, and spiritual pilgrimage.[3]

Until the end of large-scale resistance in the late 1960s, Freedomites used forms of protest (such as stripping, burning farm equipment, and marching) that the earlier Sons of God group had also employed. During times of radical activity from the 1920s onward, some Freedomites burned private property. By the 1960s, as a protest against materialism, radical Freedomites had begun to burn buildings owned mostly by non-Freedomite Doukhobors. Some radicals also bombed symbols of government authority (such as the courthouse in Nelson, British Columbia) or signs of non-Doukhobor material progress (such as CPR tracks or hydroelectric pylons). At that time many Freedomites rejected ideas concerning individual adherence to a secular state, and the separation of religion and the actions of the citizenry, in favour of identities grounded in group affiliation and a belief, based on Doukhobor prophecies of a century before, that they would return to Russia after suffering at the hands of the authorities. This last belief, often misunderstood by non-Doukhobor people, meant that the measures intended to curb their behaviour – imprisonment and removal of any privileges of citizenship – actually encouraged mystic identification with the sufferings of their forefathers and foremothers after the Burning of Arms in 1895. They willingly entered the prisons built for them at Piers Island and Agassiz in order to suffer and eventually – they thought – to migrate.

But, to the authorities and to the Canadian public, Freedomite depredations represented more than vandalism. At least so it would seem judging from the long prison sentences Freedomites received for nudity and arson (from three to twelve years) as well as from the fact that, in 1962, the RCMP charged the fifty-two members of the Freedomite Fraternal Council with "intimidating the Parliament of Canada" (Woodcock and Avakumovic 1977, 352). Freedomites who had committed other types of arson and who had set bombs received sentences as long as twelve years. The long sentences and thorough investigations indicate that Freedomite agitation posed a deeper threat than merely that of destroying selected properties or parading in the nude. Freedomite depredations appeared to strike at cherished ideas of civic pride, the ownership and care of property, and state-sanctioned control of the nude body as a private, rather than a public and politicized, entity.

Popular media labelled Freedomite activity as terrorist and treasonous, and assumed that all Doukhobors harboured similar impulses. Commentators in British Columbia refused to entertain any Doukhobor demands for exile or migration, characterizing their behaviour as irrational, bizarre, even sick, and proof that no Doukhobors "belonged" in British Columbia. A strong public outcry arose against all Doukhobors, whether they had committed depredations or not, and whether they were members of the Sons of Freedom or not. It might be hard for non-Doukhobors to imagine how strong this anti-Doukhobor sentiment was at this time. The publicity that surrounded this outcry was so intense that, today, most non-Doukhobors do not realize that the activities of the Sons of Freedom do not represent Doukhobor activities as a whole.

Anti-Doukhobor sentiment ran so high by the 1950s that the public applauded the BC provincial government's bid to assimilate Freedomite children by rounding them up in a series of night raids (beginning in 1953) and teaching them in English, for up to six years, at the fenced-in New Denver dormitory. This last measure was intended to turn Freedomite children into solid Canadian citizens. For the benefit of the Canadian public, some children at New Denver were photographed with hockey sticks in their hands (see Figure 2) or walking happily through the snow, the implication, presumably, being that institutionalization had made them more "Canadian" (Holt 1964, n.p.).

However, as another photograph shows (Figure 3), institutionalization was not a positive experience for most Freedomite children. After the first few years, parents were allowed to visit only once every two weeks and had to see their children through a chain-link fence, while police and other authorities told them that these measures would continue until they agreed to send their children to provincially run schools that offered conventional curricula. In 1959 the mothers of the children at New Denver finally agreed to do this. The public press was split on the issue, although public opinion across British Columbia generally supported the measures (McLaren 1999, 27-31). Simma Holt's virulent anti-Doukhobor newspaper articles for the *Vancouver Sun* and her book about the Sons of Freedom referred approvingly to these assimilation attempts and recommended that the practice continue until no rebellious Freedomites were left. Others must have agreed with her since John Friesen and Michael Verigin report that 35,000 copies of her book, *Terror in the Name of God*, published by McClelland & Stewart, were sold in its first printing alone (Friesen and Verigin 1989, xi). The widespread public approval of the government's

Figure 2 Freedomite boys at the New Denver reformatory (c. 1953) with Robert Ross, supervisor from 1953 to 1956. Simma Holt wrote in *Terror in the Name of God* that Doukhobor children were introduced to Canadian customs while they were at New Denver. *Department of Archives and Special Collections, University of Manitoba*

actions at the time helped to make the situation even more traumatic for many who were kept at New Denver. Some of the children who were there, or who were affected by the experience, approached the BC ombudsman in 1999 to see if there were grounds for asking for compensation. The ombudsman agreed that the children should never have been confined and that they are "entitled to an apology, an explanation and compensation for their confinement" from the British Columbia government (Ombudsman 1999, 1).

Figure 3   Freedomite children looking through the fence on visiting day at the New Denver reformatory (c. 1956). The fence was built in 1956 to cut down on the number of visitors each child had, according to Principal John Clarkson in a 1956 report to his superiors. Relatives of the children could visit only once every two weeks. The regulations effectively prevented relatives from getting inside, and so relatives would throw food packages over the fence and would have prayers with the children with the fence between them. *British Columbia Archives,* C-01739

Reactions like these indicate that the activities of extremist Freedomites were highly threatening to Canadians on a symbolic level that was out of all proportion to the number of depredations actually committed against non-Doukhobor properties. This was particularly true because Canadian citizenship, as the popular press widely promoted it, consisted of the separation of religious and state activities and a respect for the property of others, which reflected the importance of individual ownership. "Decency" also demanded that people stay clothed in public; this was connected to deportment in national affairs. Not only did Freedomites protest, but they criticized such institutions as schools, courts, prisons, and the military, and to be Canadian meant that all of these institutions were, essentially, beyond criticism. The Freedomites, and then all Doukhobors, were considered by the Canadian public to be "not Canadian" (all Doukhobors had their federal voting rights taken from them in 1931, and their provincial voting rights were taken from them in 1919, 1931, and from 1934 to 1956), other (they were "dirty Douks" as opposed to physically and morally "pure" Canadians), and irrational (they did not recognize the basis of the secular body politic). But in fact Freedomites used their bodies in political ways in order to disrupt ideas about the place of minority people in the rather prefabricated, cramped spaces of the Canadian mosaic.

Given the history of Freedomite protest against what they saw as Western ideas, and given the government acrimony and public anger that greeted this protest, it would indeed seem likely that the Sons of Freedom, of all the Doukhobor groups, would want to reject the Western institution of autobiography and the selves that this form privileges – just as they rejected other Canadian institutional forms. They had no tradition of written autobiographical selves based on Western canonized models,[4] which depend on discourses of identity involving a unique, pre-existing self marked off from all others (or at least on a critique of that self by a writer who knows the discourse). As a communally oriented group with an oral mystical and historic tradition, the Freedomites' constructions of identity did not depend on the Western and liberal-capitalist split between self and life. This split is mirrored by the subject/object split as well. The subject/object split guarantees self-reflexivity, and this reflexivity allows the narrated self to be regrounded in ways that allow it, within an autobiography, to be packaged and "sold" to a reading public. If nothing else, the orality of Freedomite culture, where information can come through dreams, conversations with elders, psalm-singing and memorization, the speeches of leaders, and enthusiast experiences as well as books, combined with the relatively low English literacy levels of many of its members (at least until the 1960s), should have precluded an interest in autobiographical writing.

But these barriers did not prevent autobiographical writing. In fact, the highest number of relatively "traditional" Doukhobor autobiographical works (in the form of prison diaries and writings that are actually entitled "diary" or "autobiography") come from members of the Sons of Freedom or from former members of its groups. To date, I have found two Freedomite prison diaries: one by Alex Efanow[5] from the 1930s or 1940s and the privately published Agassiz diary by Mike Chernenkoff and friends concerning the 1960s protests. I have also found the autobiography of Peter N. Maloff, a former Freedomite leader, which was produced as part of his request for a 1952 commission concerning Freedomite activity, and two autobiographies – one appearing in Holt's *Terror in the Name of God* and one unpublished – that former Freedomite extremist Fred N. Davidoff wrote in the 1960s and 1970s.[6]

Why did Freedomite writers produce this much autobiographical writing? The answers lie in the performative aspects of autobiographical discourse. Some Freedomite writers, already accustomed to pamphlet writing and other forms of public awareness-raising, were starting to use autobiography in this way so that their identities could be performed in public spaces. However recognizable these performances are, though, appropriation of some but not all diary forms enabled Freedomite authors to avoid Western subjectivity's dependence on a dialectics of a singular self and other within a discourse of interiority (upon which Judith Butler's and Sidonie Smith's readings of performativity depend).[7] In this sense, they engaged in a type of *public, exterior* identity performance, which alters the trope of performativity as it makes use of it.

Mikhail Bakhtin (1981b) describes such a situation, in what he terms the original chronotope of autobiography, as a set of ritual praises in the Athenian public square. For Bakhtin, the act of the funeral oration consisted of remembering the face and deeds of the dead person, which later became the custom of telling one's life story in public meetings. These life narratives, Bakhtin writes, took place as a dialogic activity between the speaker and the listeners, which constituted consciousness. As a form of rhetoric, auto/biography was never "auto" since consciousness had to be recognized and inflected by other members of the community, and consciousness itself was not abstracted into "self" but, rather, into a face, or a memory of a face, that was conjured up by the orator. To Bakhtin, biography and autobiography in the Athenian square were the same thing. This "individual" consciousness, in turn, became part of the public consciousness only when it was spoken: the time of the life narrative was superseded by the space in which it occurred. The negotiation of self/other had not yet begun: "Here [in the square] the individual is open on all sides, he is all surface, there is in him nothing that exists 'for his sake alone,' nothing that could not be subject to public or state control and evaluation. Everything here, down to the last detail, is entirely public ... there was as yet no internal man, no 'man for himself' (I for myself), nor any individualized approach to one's own self ... Man was completely *on the surface,* in the most literal sense of the word" (Bakhtin 1981b, 132-33).

An individual was spoken into being and indexed into the history and life of the community because someone had spoken him and others had heard him. Instead of the Lacanian mirror, where the child *sees* himself or herself and recognizes the "I" at the moment s/he sees her or his reflection as "not I," the orator reflects the oration of a citizen's life into the *ears* of the community members, who hear and respond to this life as text with affirmation (Bakhtin 1981b, 133). To praise oneself was to praise the community and to return that praise to the community whole (since Bakhtin holds that there was no inside to hold any part of "bio" away from "graphe"): "to be exterior meant to be for others, for the collective, for one's own people" (135). Before the self/other split, then, there is no dialogic contestation between others but, rather, a meeting-ground of others, where self belongs to the community and does not struggle to permeate or monologize discourses of the other.

Bakhtin's image of simultaneous praise evokes an external type of performativity that does not rely on absolute self/other constructions. Significantly, he comments later that this image of identity formed in the public square disappeared when Plutarch observed that self-reflection could include silent meditation that was not known to others. Plutarch's introduction of interiority into reflection spelled the end of exteriority and of communal identity construction (in which everything can be known and words can permeate each other).

Thus Freedomite performativity could be used to serve purposes other than identity commemoration and circulation. Although, at various times, they renounced most contact with the non-Doukhobor world, Freedomite protest activities took on the character of performances. This was because the earlier members of this sect had learned, during the trek of 1902, that public nudity – which they discovered could shock Canadians – could be used as a protest strategy as well as a sign to other Doukhobors that all Doukhobors should renounce materialism. Later members of the Sons of Freedom remembered these earlier strategies, which involved nude protest, marches, and setting farm equipment on fire, and developed them. By the 1960s Sons of Freedom organizations such as the Brotherhood of Reformed Doukhobors wrote English-language pamphlets to communicate their concerns to the non-Doukhobor world, sent out media press releases, and went on protest parades, including the 1962 march to Vancouver and then to the Freedomite prison in Agassiz, partially in order to get media visibility for their causes. Writing in English became part of a strategy of engagement with Canadian authorities and, via the media, the

Canadian public also, while other aspects of Freedomite religious activity (such as nudity and singing) took on the character of performances designed to heighten public awareness. In this way aspects of Freedomite identity entered a non-Doukhobor public sphere in sets of hybrid combinations that became part of strategies of visibility.

As may be seen in the two examples I discuss, when combined with discourses of testimony in court-room settings Freedomite autobiographical forms hybridize: they become part of Freedomite strategies for visibility while, at the same time, occupying a space between Freedomite Doukhobor traditions of history and communal subjectivity. They also have roots in the collective *sobranie* decision-making process used by Doukhobors generally,[8] and they make some reference to forms of truth-production that Canadian people, specifically the Canadian authorities, understand to be traditional. In this sense, autobiographical documents by Freedomites become testimonials, part of other performative documents required by authorities that exceed what they require of the performances.

The two examples of Freedomite prison diaries I now discuss illustrate how some Freedomite authors have used the trope of exterior performativity within a hybridized autobiographical discourse that blends the private form of the diary with the public form of what, in Chapter 3, I refer to as a witness narrative. A witness narrative has a particular event – usually traumatic and often politicized – as its main focus. The author's identity as a witness to the event becomes more important than his or her identity apart from the event. The first example of a Freedomite witness narrative is entitled *Prison Diary: Events and Experiences in Mountain Prison, Agassiz, BC 1962-1969* and is written by Mike E. Chernenkoff and friends (Chernenkoff i drugie 1993).[9] The second is Alexander Efanow's (1930) unpublished diary entitled "Journal from Agassiz."[10] Efanow's diary includes discussions about the first imprisonment of Freedomites in Agassiz and their subsequent imprisonment at the Piers Island prison farm.

Prison Diary contains many of the features of a diary as day-to-day witness record, with its flexible use of subject positions that change over time and with its dated entries that refer to the weather and to daily events in prison life. Critical discourse usually assumes that Western diaries are by a single author who writes down his or her "private" thoughts; however, the author name on the front page of *Prison Diary* is not Mike Chernenkoff but "Mike Chernenkoff and Friends." The assumption, originally discussed by Felicity Nussbaum (1988b, 132), that diary discourse is private and singular, and that it is produced by a private and singular subject, does not apply here; instead, the preface of the diary and subsequent "entries" combine the diary form's features of immediacy and location with aspects of memoir and witness narratives in order to make hidden events public.

Because it is a witness narrative with multiple authors, this diary contains material not usually found in diary form. In addition to diary entries, *Prison Diary* has historical passages, copied letters, photographs of prisoners and their families, lists of prisoners' names, a recipe for borscht (made by the prisoners), psalms and poems composed in prison by various people, and a variety of narratives, sometimes by other people and sometimes simply attributed to "Dormitory 4," "Dormitory 2," or "Dormitory 3." These narratives describe key problems, such as the force-feeding of vegetarian prisoners with boiling meat broth while they are on a hunger strike, what happened at Agassiz when prison authorities placed Chernenkoff in solitary confinement in another prison, and the death of Paul Podmoroff from pneumonia (brought on by force-feeding during a Freedomite fast). Chernenkoff did not personally witness this last event because he was in another dormitory, so he had another person record it and then tell him about it.[11]

One example of collective authorship occurs when an anonymous author from Dormitory 4 says that *his* diary – it is not clear whether he means Chernenkoff's manuscript or another one – has been seized by the authorities and that he (or others) pieced the narrative together later. He writes, "For me to continue further in connection with this will be more difficulty [sic], but all the same, I will try to do everything I can" (Chernenkoff i drugie 1993, 49). Constructing the narrative at other points becomes a collective enterprise as the first-person singular of Chernenkoff is sometimes replaced by the first-person plural of collective arrangers who say, for instance, that "we are placing here" (50) an account from other prisoners that functions as a witness narrative. However, at a key point in the narrative, when force-feeding begins, Chernenkoff asserts an individuated identity that sounds like a legal testimonial. In order to stop the guard "Jovans"[12] from pushing a bloodied feeding tube down a prisoner's throat, Chernenkoff turns himself into an individual actor: "so I, Mikhail Chernenkoff, walked over and overturned the box which held the tubes and the dish" (19). This moment is vital because it leads to Chernenkoff's subsequent solitary confinement and beating. Chernenkoff's decision to use his full name and the echo of legal terminology – "I do solemnly swear to tell whole truth" – involves the appropriation of a singular subject from a discourse of individuated public truth-telling – namely, that of the trial and the court room. In other words, Chernenkoff's rhetorical individuation appropriates a non-Doukhobor discourse of subjectivity and inserts it into a non-legal setting so that "the whole truth" is told. Since the context, but not the form, of this utterance has been altered to serve these different ends, this serves as an example of a hybridized confession form.

As part diary, part witness narrative, and even as a "biography of Mountain Prison," which is what Chernenkoff called the book in a personal letter to me, this prison narrative operates as a hybrid text that straddles several life narrative forms while producing a hybrid subject that, at different points, is singular and plural, depending on the requirements of its message as a witness document. Thus Freedomite subjectivity appears fluid in this diary, operating much as does autobiographical identity formation in autobiographies of ethnic working-class women, which Anne Goldman (1996, xxiv) describes as a continuum along the trajectories of "I" and "we" rather than as a synecdoche of a culture in the first-person singular or a metonym for a collective in the third-person plural.

This diary's plurality can be read as a strategy that, at times, stresses the collectivity of the imprisoned Freedomites as they experience hardship occurring under the sign (and power) of one name. The witness narrative form of the diary links together the identity and stories of individual prisoners or anonymous inhabitants of dormitories as displaced people who must suffer within the space of the prison. This situation links them symbolically to their nineteenth-century imprisoned forbears in Russia. For example, although, ultimately, the narrative is collected under Chernenkoff's name and a large photograph of Chernenkoff appears as the frontispiece, the preface, which was written by Joe Ogloff rather than Chernenkoff, presents the diary as a public manifesto about a collective conflict. This conflict is linked to a 1,000-year struggle against the evils of the institutions of church and state. Here the diary is intended to be both a witness narrative that encapsulates the whole Freedomite struggle and a collective testament gathered under the sign of one person's proper name. Thus the text's collective purpose overshadows the author's writing of it. At first, authors are not even mentioned:

So this diary was written with the intention that if [it] got safely to the world, and if sometime in the future or the present people are led by fate to read it, they then will be able to appreciate fully the great trouble of the Doukhobor "Sons of Freedom" in Canada, what they were striving for, and for what they struggled and died – they didn't spare their own acquired property, their families, children, nor themselves, in sacrificing everything for the ideal of the Brotherhood and Love of Christ – fighting against all injustices in the only way they could. (Chernenkoff i drugie 1993, i)

In this passage, Ogloff appears to be writing about Freedomite history. But, in a moment that indicates his awareness of the power of a diary to record and witness events, he goes on to introduce Chernenkoff as the diary's author. Ogloff first mentions Chernenkoff as an autodidact who lacks formal education, saying that he "did not go to Russian school and he taught himself Russian reading and writing" (Chernenkoff i drugie 1993, ii). He switches to a discussion of the location and purpose of Mountain Prison at Agassiz, where the diary was written, and concludes with an apology for his own and others' illiteracy while, at the same time, indicating that the diary was a collective effort and had a material existence:

> As for me, I also must say that I am self-taught. And although I helped a lot to improve this diary so the reader could understand it, however, there are many shortcomings, for which I earlier asked the reader to divorce himself from our inexperience. This diary covers the time period from 1962-1972 and it was written on paper taken from jars of canned goods and on yellow paper in which they wrap things bought in stores. (ii)

Here, Ogloff discusses the "unworthiness" of the Freedomites to enter a discourse closely connected to literacy, but he recognizes that, in the diary form, in the assumption of literacy, there is visibility. He gains access to the power of recognition inherent in the Western diary discourse even in his discussion of different credentials because he appeals to the reader to forget what he causes the reader to remember: Freedomite inexperience and illiteracy, which is bracketed by the scene of writing (literally, the prison) and the materiality of writing under duress. In this way, the Freedomite writers of this diary can construct their versions of events within the parameters of a discourse of recognition while asking for the reader to "divorce himself" – that is, recognize Freedomite difference – in order to inscribe their position as writing subjects.

Chernenkoff's dedication features a similar "apology" for difference in his reference to literacy level. This apology validates a narrative style that moves from a singular to a collective version of Freedomite history. It can do this because it is not "professionally" produced. Chernenkoff's dedication, for example, moves from dedicating the diary to his own family and other Freedomites to telling the story of the sufferings of his wife, Lukeriya, while he was in prison. It turns to an account of Paul Podmoroff's death by force-feeding, a topic that occupies much of the diary. Then Chernenkoff apologizes for illiteracy on behalf of the group: "who would have thought the diary would come out in book form," he writes, "for we were all so uneducated, illiterate" (Chernenkoff i drugie 1993, iv). The first sentence of the first paragraph of the diary itself begins with his sense of his own literacy level, combined with an awareness of collectivity and mission: "I am fully aware and conscious of my own lack of ability and illiteracy [sic] to do this business, to describe the events surrounding our experience in a prison specially built for one goal, to keep Doukhobors" (1).

The Agassiz prison diary, then, is not only a collection of historic materials commemorating a sojourn in prison but also a *performance field* where the diary's principal and secondary authors can negotiate collective and individual identities as Freedomite Doukhobors for others to read. In this sense, they engage in a type of identity performance that alters the trope of performativity as it makes use of it. Performativity here is not a trope of radical interiority of the subject where the object is language but, rather, a trope signifying *exterior* identity negotiation with others.

Alexander Efanow's diary, written about thirty years before Chernenkoff's, contains many similar elements that blend diary form, witness narrative, and historic document. Like Chernenkoff's diary, Efanow's includes copied letters from Peter Chistiakov, speeches by Peter Lordly, psalms written by himself and other people, "classic" Doukhobor psalms (such as "What Is a Doukhobor"), and accounts of important events, such as the coming of Michael the Archangel to Krestova, a brief history of Freedomite protest, and general Doukhobor history.

Near the beginning of his diary Efanow includes a dream or vision of Freedomite origins that places Freedomite history on an allegorical level.[13] He characterizes this vision as a prophecy, which, in Doukhobor culture at the time, was thought to contain practical information (just as would a book): "my imagination, given free reins, created by itself mental pictures of our future communal life" (Efanow 1930, 1). The vision is about the waning identity of the Doukhobors, who leave Peter Lordly and join the Anti-Christ (most likely a symbol of compromise with materialist, non-communal living), presented here as a person standing outside a house where Peter Lordly resides. Efanow presents this moment, when he turns from seeing the Anti-Christ to listening to the words of Peter Lordly, as the reason for diary writing. Lordly says to Efanow: "The revelation you are experiencing now is sent to you by God, so that you know what will happen in the near future ... remember everything you saw and put it down to paper; let our people read it and understand. He who has understanding, will understand ... If you failed to understand what you have seen, I will explain this to you" (2). The instruction to write down "everything you saw" could refer simply to the vision, but since the vision continues with Efanow as an actor who separates the "righteous" and those who decide to follow the Anti-Christ, the occurrences in the "near future" probably refer to the formation of the Freedomite group and the mystic beginnings of their protest against their situation in Canada. Here, the injunction to remember and write comes from Lordly, who divinely sanctions both Efanow's role as a writer and the Doukhobors who will later read what he writes. Reading and writing will be part of remembering both the origins and the "mission" of the Freedomites as those who will stay closest to conservative Doukhobor ideals (3-4). The move, "ordered" by God in the style of the biblical Book of Revelation to move from oral memory and prophecy to recorded memory and interpretation, will take place within the diary form but also as a witness narrative that will have spiritual connotations. These Lordly will "explain" – and Efanow's task will be to remember and explain events accordingly.

Other sections of Efanow's narrative recreate that injunction in order to remember, record, and interpret the Oakalla imprisonment of the 1930s. During a discussion of the trial, for example, Efanow (1930, 2) writes that the courthouse scene is a "live picture ... engraved on the sacred tables of our cherished memories," a possible reference to the sacred nature of *vechnaiia pamit* or to a Doukhobor belief that one of the members of the Trinity is signified by "memory." But his personal reaction to the subsequent train journey, when the prisoners were able to convince their train guards that they were not criminals, has, for these Freedomites, already stressed the links between religion, print culture, and political action: "Being Dukhobors, we believe ourselves to be the salt of the earth and light to the world. Therefore, we could not conceal ourselves from the people, and we took steps in accordance with Christ's words: we had proclaimed our convictions to the whole world, in writings, appeals, and newspapers; and after that, we, ourselves, took action" (1). Here, as in the diary by Chernenkoff and his friends, personal experience is collapsed into collective identity, publicity, and witness rhetoric. To be a Doukhobor, for Efanow, is to exist in the plural and in the public sphere, to not be "concealed" from others, and to enter the world of print and then of action as "we, ourselves" (i.e., as plural selves).

Later in the diary, Efanow (1930, 1) writes that, "in order not to forget how we spent those days [in Oakalla prison] in late October, I will recollect them and put my recollections down on paper." At this point, Efanow describes life in Oakalla much as do Chernenkoff and his friends: as continuous, day-to-day conflict with the authorities, which features multiple authors telling stories about similar events. Efanow's role is that of collector and transmitter of these stories. He stresses this role when he describes how he records a poem by another author: "We began spending more time alone quietly in our cells. Once, I left my cell and went along the corridor to cell #7. I see, Kaminoff writes something. I ask him, 'What are you writing?' He produces a whole pile of some notes; these were some newly composed and recorded on paper poems. We began to look them through and read; some of them proved to be very funny and they were put aside to be further worked on. But I selected some to copy for myself. The following is one of those poems" (3). Efanow includes a poem about the death of Peter Lordly, in which the Sons of Freedom are portrayed as wanderers true to his teachings against materialism. Here, Efanow has the role of collector, who includes the writing of others for the public record.

Like Chernenkoff, Efanow also employs the accounts of other authors within the diary form to illustrate the daily (and often successful) struggle against the prison authorities, an affirmation of Freedomite identity as a resistance to all authority. In one case, he does this in order to describe how the men in one cell found out how to receive written messages from the women incarcerated in a cell next to them, and then he quotes what one of them wrote about the Freedomite women's successful refusal to wear prison dresses. Later, he quotes what he refers to as a humorous note from an anonymous author concerning how the Freedomite women humiliated one prison supervisor. This story, like others in the diary, indicates how Freedomite women successfully resist authority by using a mechanism of protest that empowers them and makes authority figures (and their ideas) look ridiculous. Efanow's repetition of their message in diary form also gives them a type of visibility that Efanow has already interpreted as a divinely sanctioned act of empowerment and remembrance. This reaffirms their identity as Freedomite resisters who act, remember, and write. Efanow's quotation constantly stresses that these events were witnessed and written about:

> "Our female supervisor invited us," one sister writes, "and ordered us to play songs for her; we began to play, and she starts dancing. We ask her, "Why are you dancing?" Says she, "Today is my birthday, but I do not mark it." – "We tell her," writes the sister further, "This is not the way to celebrate one's birthday; let us show you how one should go about it." Two of our sisters promptly threw off their clothes, jumped forward naked and started to dance. That is how one should observe the birthday: being completely naked, because naked you were when your mother gave you birth. The supervisor did not like the observance; she went away from us and did not come back for a long time.
>
> There were many other messages in which they wrote how their supervisor did not give them any bread. (Efanow 1930, 3)

In a passage in which he describes a visit from his father from another cell, Efanow underscores not only the interdependency and orality of Doukhobor Freedomite memory but also collapses the history of the current Freedomite struggle into that of the struggle of the imprisoned Doukhobor martyrs of the nineteenth century. In this narrative Efanow's father operates as a living instance of *vechnaiia pamit,* reminding Efanow of the resistance to authority that forms the core of Doukhobor identity. To be a Doukhobor, in this formulation, is to successfully resist at all costs and to remember previous resistance. As Efanow writes:

> then he [my father] started telling me stories about the lives of our forefathers, who had renounced the false church teachings and the priests, exactly as we were rejecting them in our days. He told me how they threw icons from their houses ... he also told me how, after that, they were all arrested in one day and sent to exile ... he told me these stories, as I thought, to raise my spirits. I had always listened to him with great attention. I was

fortified and morally supported by him, rather than by his stories, because he stood in front of me like an angel hovering in the air, and he sent down so much love for me, that love of which Christ had said, "Pray in secret." (Efanow 1930, 302-4)

Like the quoted letters from imprisoned Freedomite women, the inclusion of Efanow's father in this story as the transmitter and interpreter of tradition not only validates Efanow's own experience but also links his own struggle to the struggle of all Doukhobors. Although this passage stays in the first person, the oral catechism Efanow repeats to his father is in the first-person plural, thus linking his own experience with others and evoking divine validation via the sufferings of Jesus Christ:

And my father was standing in front of me many times, so that I would not forget my forefathers and Jesus Christ who had been led to Golgotha. I said, "No, we did not forget our forefathers who had made it known the way for us. They are resurrected in our heroic martyrdom, in what we suffer today. You, my father, are here in prison; you are 72-years-old, and you were beaten and thrown to prison. What do you think of this?" He answered, "This is how it should be." I used to go away from him in joy and high spirits. (Efanow 1930, 304)

This passage indicates how Efanow, like Chernenkoff and his friends, uses the diary form's immediacy and accuracy in order to bear witness to events while, at the same time, the identity performed here is exterior and closely related to earlier conflicts with authority. In this sense Efanow enacts Bakhtin's image of the orator who perpetuates and interprets community memory via the *ears* of its members, where identity is only transacted through a response to what has been said. Here, Efanow records what amounts to a living catechism, where his father interprets prison experience and he responds with the "right" answer, which he will not forget. He, in turn, asks his father a question and also receives the "right" answer – an identity performance that, since Efanow's father had been beaten and imprisoned, is related to activism.

The two autobiographies of Fred Davidoff contain elements found in the Agassiz diary and Efanow's diary, but the circumstances of the manuscripts' production, Davidoff's decision to call both of them "autobiography," and the differences between each version make his writings unique documents. In 1962, while he was serving time in the Nelson jail, Davidoff wrote what is the only formally published autobiography by a Doukhobor in existence: a narrative that Simma Holt (1964) entitles "The Autobiography of a Fanatic" and that forms Chapter 6 of *Terror in the Name of God*. In 1966, Davidoff wrote a second, much more detailed, autobiography based on the Holt chapter. The second autobiography also included his decision to break from the Sons of Freedom and to repudiate his past activities. This manuscript was written or copied into six ten-cent scribblers while Davidoff was in prison at Oakalla. It was never published, although it may have been used as part of Davidoff's successful application for parole in 1967. The contrast between Davidoff's first and second autobiographies raises issues about how this Freedomite identity production can be both a response to a non-Doukhobor request for a traditional Western autobiographical form and a refusal to comply with many of the terms of visibility assumed by widely read forms of autobiography.

For Davidoff, the discourse of resisting or circumventing what a non-Freedomite readership "wants" from him is the discourse of the courtroom confessional and the rhetoric of identity production produced there. Although the discourse of the court confessional is also institutional and non-Freedomite, Davidoff appropriates aspects of its rhetoric in order to have his narrative circulate in the public sphere and, later, to adjust and write against that narrative.

Davidoff's first autobiographical narrative appears under considerable non-Doukhobor rhetorical pressure and duress. As I mentioned, Simma Holt entitled it "Autobiography of a Fanatic," a move that immediately makes Davidoff's story that of the uncontrollable, unpredictable, and exotic other who must be recuperated into a discourse of the Canadian, law-abiding centre. She introduces this narrative as something produced *for her,* which grants her the rhetorical power to interpret it for the Canadian public. Although she mentions that she had disagreed with Davidoff about schooling when she first met him: "Four years later, in his dimly-lit cell in the Nelson jail, Davidoff sat down to write the story of his life, to explain 'the work of the Doukhobors' to me and to the world. When he had finished, he asked to see me and gave me the unique document" (Holt 1964, 217). Holt does not mention why Davidoff would decide to communicate with her; however, it is clear that he knew Holt would print his autobiography in some form and that this would be a way to publicize the radical Freedomite cause. But Holt takes control of the narrative so that Davidoff's story will remain other. For example, in Chapter 14, "The Day of the Black Babushkas," which comes before Davidoff's narrative in Chapter 15, Holt reproduces Davidoff's court transcript, in which he accuses the non-Doukhobor world of conspiring to kill Peter Lordly. In this chapter, she describes Davidoff as overweight, with a face that could sometimes be ugly and sometimes "child-like." She also observes it could manifest "hysteria" (207). After Davidoff's narrative, Holt reproduces a heavily edited series of questions that she wrote to Davidoff, along with his answers. The questions are not meant to elicit information since, in most of them, Holt accuses Davidoff of irrational behaviour;[14] rather, they and other passages about Davidoff and Holt's introduction turn his narrative from a confession of the motivations for Freedomite activity into an object lesson proving the danger of Freedomite thinking. Davidoff's autobiography, which Holt says she presents with only minor cutting and editing (217), tells the story that Holt asks for, although it exceeds the term "fanatic," which she had applied to it.

Davidoff begins with the words "I, Fred N. Davidoff, was born on December 14, 1923, on a farm near Pincher Creek, Alberta" (Davidoff 1964, 217). This is the language of legal testimony, a discourse of truth-production that he shares with non-Doukhobor readers. This rhetorical move validates his discourse as "sworn-in" and, therefore, true. Davidoff then describes his origins as transnational and shifting: his grandparents left the Community Doukhobors, went to Oregon in 1914, and returned to Pincher Creek in 1918. In the United States his uncles escaped the draft and joined the early Sons of Freedom movement in British Columbia. Next, Davidoff interprets as pivotal his grandfather's words to him before his death in 1947 concerning the importance of not buying land. It is also a pivotal moment in the text for his grandfather connects Doukhobor identity to a spiritual understanding of place, migration, and the refusal to "own" a place by buying land:

> [My grandfather said:] "It is my religious belief that we Doukhobors came to Canada only for a time, to fulfil our mission, and the day will soon be at hand when we will leave Canada. I did not accept a homestead because I could not swear an oath of allegiance to no king or queen.
>
> We left Russia proclaiming ourselves citizens of the universe, recognizing Jesus Christ as the only King and his law as the only Law. All other laws are from the devil; throne and government are of the devil."
>
> I can never forget these words. I teach my children man-made laws are not for them. But since they came back from school, my children look at me when I tell them these things like I am a child and they are the adult. (Davidoff 1964, 218)

In a passage that sounds like Efanow's description of his meeting with his father, the words of Davidoff's grandfather comprise Davidoff's education as a Doukhobor while, at the same time, connecting his position as a Doukhobor subject who resists all authority (apart from that of elders) to an understanding of migration as an eternal, spiritual state. But Davidoff's statement that he cannot forget this teaching is placed in opposition to institutional teaching at the New Denver school. His children not only have forgotten their "place"; they cannot learn and so return to the "natural" Doukhobor order of parents and children. An institution – the school – has disrupted Davidoff's past and his present, Doukhobor life and non-Doukhobor life.

The rest of the narrative functions in concert with this set of absolute binarisms, which Davidoff describes as a migratory dysfunction. When his parents move back to Canada and live at an English person's farm,[15] Davidoff equates the contrast between life on this farm and life on the Doukhobor commune in British Columbia with the contrast between Doukhoborism and Canadian living (exemplified by the difference between his words to his children and his grandfather's words to him, and between material values and memories of spiritual life). This conflict is played out in spatial terms: "Thus my life began with conflict between the two different ways: the Doukhobor and the English. I was often a visitor at the home of my grandparents, attending meetings of our own people, many of whom were Sons of Freedom. But I lived on a farm among English-speaking people. The closest Doukhobors were twenty miles away" (Davidoff 1964, 219). Davidoff describes his "true" identity as connected to place (British Columbia), but in the home of his parents his identity is literally "misplaced": with his (originally) Freedomite mother, he wants to move to British Columbia, but his more Orthodox father will not leave his prosperous farm in Alberta or the protection of Community orthodoxy. Davidoff has to speak English at school and Russian at home, and when he is at school he is beaten because he is a pacifist. He refers to his experiences at school and on the non-Doukhobor farm in spatial terms – he was a "prisoner in no-man's land" (219) – and transfers the locational conflict he feels to an inner sense of conflict related to his mother's sense of dislocation due to being a Freedomite: "Within me started to build up a spirit of resentment. My mother felt also as a prisoner on the farm. We had no social contact with the English people because our faith was different. My mother longed as I did to be amongst the Doukhobors of B.C. Her religion was so strong that at the time the Sons of Freedom were sent to jail in 1932 she was also tearing to go, only she had too big a family to leave. So she would undress and go nude in the garden" (219).

In this narrative Davidoff resolves this conflict by choosing one polarity and refusing another, a rhetorical "turn" found in conversion narratives when, as Peter Dorsey (1993, 5) observes, one "sees one's life as text." He does this by equating his rejection of schooling to a rejection of all Canadian institutions, and he presents this as a destination he chooses: "when I was fourteen I had to decide which way I was going. The question for me was whether to continue or quit school." Here school is figured as a place where he enjoys learning but where, nonetheless, the "game" of imperialism is literally sung as the schoolyard patriotic song: "Play up, play up, play up the game" (220). Davidoff recognizes that the "game" of imperialism is about patriotic duty and military service, and he quits school.

At this point in the narrative Doukhobor identity becomes something that Davidoff can choose rather than something inevitable, a religion to which he converts rather than a set of ethnic markings: "I chose my own road in life – to remain a Doukhobor. To me, not to be a Doukhobor is not to live." He believes that if he had stayed in school he "could have obtained any degree of education [he] desired. But [he] would never have remained a Doukhobor" (Davidoff 1964, 220). Later in the narrative, after some spiritual "wandering" (during which he lives in town, attends Orthodox meetings, and has a racist neighbour who does not know that he is a Doukhobor and refers to Doukhobors as "black people"), this conversion to Doukhoborism becomes the lynch-pin of the narrative. It works as a conversion to and within text, improbably occurring at a Pentecostal revival meeting where, Davidoff writes, "I was reborn spiritually ... I had an experience of my inner voice, God speaking within me, saying to read and through this I would find the true road and Truth, which I am seeking" (224). This experience causes Davidoff to join the Sons of Freedom and to move to Krestova. Davidoff has a final "conversion" in jail, where he has the chance to learn Doukhobor songs and hymns from elders. He characterizes this experience as another birth: "Here in jail, I must say were born spiritually forty-four Doukhobors to remain Doukhobors for the rest of their lives" (225).

But by the end of the narrative, Doukhobor identity becomes less a religious choice than part of Davidoff's destiny. This shift occurs when Davidoff discusses migration as the only option for the future of Doukhobor people and intimates that burnings and bombings occur to ensure migration and Doukhobor survival. These activities occur because Doukhobors cannot change their reading of the future, and so the Freedomites are compelled to exist outside Canadian national life and to commit depredations until they are allowed to leave. Here, Davidoff's personal story becomes part of the general Freedomite struggle: "At present I can only show my personal past history. It is a story which coincides with others who are amongst us" (Davidoff 1964, 228). Davidoff concludes with a sense of the inevitability of Freedomite resistance, which becomes both religious and ethnic: "So ends another chapter of our struggles in Canada. A Jew will always remain a Jew; a Catholic a Catholic; a Protestant a Protestant. This goes the same with us Doukhobors, once born a Doukhobor always a Doukhobor, for I am afraid it is in our blood and our faith is destined before we were born ... We bombed and burned because through these acts we believe we will be exiled from Canada" (229-30). While this view of identity remains religious, Davidoff's analogy to Judaism indicates that he sees identity not only as a "faith" but also as something that is in one's blood before one is born. This is an understanding of identity as ethnic and as rooted in the past rather than as something that is chosen. Davidoff's decision to shuttle his identity between these poles, as he moved between Independent, Orthodox, and Freedomite interpretations of Doukhoborism, becomes a mixture that produces Doukhobor identity both as a religion he can choose and as an ethnicity he cannot escape. At the end of this narrative, Davidoff's clear choice, then, becomes his motivation for protest and depredation: his affirmation of his identity personifies and underwrites his resistance.

As I have mentioned, the material circumstances of Davidoff's second autobiographical production are different from those of the first since it is an unpublished manuscript hand-written in six ten-cent scribblers. However, in its production, this manuscript contains the same awareness of non-Doukhobor influences as did the first one. Again, Davidoff uses aspects of autobiographical discourse that are recognizable to non-Doukhobors while altering the form to suit his own ends. He uses the scene of autobiographical utterance as a way to re-narrate his identity *as a performance* in order to correct an earlier version of his life, which he felt had been produced under duress and, probably, to win parole. Here again, autobiographical performativity is external rather than internal and marks not a self-dialogue but, rather, a dialogue between different languages (e.g., the language of confession, the language of legal testimony, and the language of conversion). The opening paragraph, in the form of a hand-written note on the inside cover of the first volume, indicates these multiple purposes and audiences: "Basis taken from 'Terror in the Name of God' by Simma Holt. Increased and Explained as Story Permits. Inter woven with parts of letter to National Parole Board, Mr. Cemetic [sic], Vancouver, B.C. February 18th, 1966" (Davidoff 1966). Davidoff goes on to list the highlights of the manuscript in the form of seven headings, including classic autobiographical "chapters" such as "My Childhood" or "Married Life" and other, less classic, headings such as "My father-in-Law John Perepelkin" and "My Accident of 1952."

Unlike the first autobiography, which was heavily circumscribed by Holt's interventions, this manuscript tells a different story about how the first manuscript was produced. While Holt had mentioned that Davidoff told his story specifically for her, according to him he did so under the orders of John Lebedoff, a leader of one of the Freedomite factions. As he says in a 1969 letter to the publisher of *Terror in the Name of God,* in which he asks the editors to withdraw the chapters of his autobiography from the book, that particular autobiography was a performative gesture only, meant solely to publicize Freedomite grievances. It "was performed by me as a command of duty ... therefore, I was acting as a good salesman, constructed the so-called, or supposed, autobiography of myself, one sided, and I only revealed certain parts of my life. I was fighting by means of the artistic use of the pen. As a soldier uses a sword."[16] In his second autobiography, Davidoff elaborates on the circumstances of the first autobiography's production. On unnumbered loose sheets inserted at the end of Volume 6, Davidoff states that Lebedoff reacted to Holt's request for autobiographies:

> I volunteered to give upon the recommendation of John L. Lebedoff. He John L. Lebedoff said that Simma Holt would help in the solution of our Doukhobor Problems and migration to Russia. Simma Holt ask[ed] a number of individuals to give their autobiographies with John L. Lebedoff encouraging all to do so but no one agreed except, something within compelled me to do so. Although I thought that maybe it was my strong belief and devotion she would use some place in a newspaper and [help?] migration. When she took the story and read it, I met her on Friday March 23rd, 1962, in the Nelson Court House while acting as a Crown Witness at the trial of the seven men who were tried for the burnings ... of the old Community Homes of Oteshenia [sic] and Pass Creek. (Davidoff 1966)

Davidoff's statements indicate how the discourse of selfhood and truth-telling found in autobiography can be requested by a member of the dominant interpretative community yet, at the same time, enable the marginal writer to perform as part of that discourse and still achieve other ends (such as public recognition).

The circumstances of Davidoff's production are already confessional since he wrote the autobiography at the Nelson courthouse where he – as he later claimed, at the request of the Fraternal Council – was to testify against other Freedomites. Davidoff's autobiography, according to the 1969 letter, is analogous to Freedomite court testimony, which occurred under duress but which also became, during the mass trials of Sons of Freedom radicals in the late 1950s and early 1960s, a performance space. Freedomite spectators in court used this space to disrobe in protest, knowing that their activities would be photographed and reported in the media. In the same way, accused Freedomites or Freedomite witnesses turned the confessional discourses of legal proceedings to their own ends in order to call for migration, air grievances against other Freedomite factions, or make demands of the authorities (as Davidoff did at the Nelson courthouse). In the space of the courtroom, where all activities, including discourses of truth and confession, occur symbolically as the manifestation of state authority, Freedomites such as Davidoff developed ways of testifying that responded to non-Doukhobor ideas about truth and confession while generating excess meanings not required, intended, or even desired by the discourses that demanded them. As Davidoff's description of his initial autobiographical production makes clear, for him the act of writing was not separated, in intent, from the act of testifying as both were bidden by the authorities (and, in this case, Holt is also seen as an authority), and both were opportunities for Freedomite concerns to reach a non-Freedomite public in ways that the authorities did not anticipate.

Most of the rest of Davidoff's manuscript serves to problematize the polarized version of Doukhobor identity he discussed in his earlier autobiography. Instead of representing his Doukhobor identity as a choice of faith, for example, Davidoff (1966, 2) begins the narrative by representing it as part of the Doukhobor diasporic imaginary of heroic suffering against authority as he discusses the torture and imprisonment of his ancestors in Russia, the life of his parents at Kars in the Caucasus, and his "Popoff blood." He adds that, due to his upbringing (which was not lax, as he had said in his earlier narrative, but strict), he has not forgotten his grandfather's words. As he says, "my parents raised me from very infancy in a very strict religious Doukhobor culture ... such up bringing [sic] made me not forget the above words of my grandfather, believing that man-made laws are not for them" (5).

This passage is followed by what becomes a familiar commentary on his past as Davidoff indicates that he now believes that the Freedomites were wrong to reject laws and education, and should not have committed depredations. His autobiography becomes a record not only of every circumstance involving the Fraternal Council and every name of those who ordered or did "the black work" but also of how he attempts to record, and repudiate, his struggles between Doukhobor factions by making them appear equivalent to inner struggles over his identity and his purpose in life. These struggles put pressures on the narrative itself. For example, his own account of the Freedomite refusal to work at Agassiz ends with the words "that was the end of the greatest foolishness I have ever lived through" (Davidoff 1966, 117) and mentions that, in prison, he heard about arson and bombing, which he refers to as "the greatest of evil which in later years lead [sic] me to greatest sins and evil involvements" (130). However, at the same time, Davidoff retains the belief that his time in prison was a time of great spiritual growth as he and other prisoners wrote Doukhobor psalms and songs on toilet paper and on the walls of the prison so that they could memorize and discuss them (122-23), thus developing one of the most important spiritual aspects of Doukhobor spiritual life: memory (126). Through memorization, he develops what he calls "a third I. The I of my Soul," which can sense spiritual truths (127-28). However, he maintains that he did not understand what this truly meant and that he was led astray, taking on the identity of a terrorist with spiritual motives.

Davidoff records his release but indicates that he was still tormented by spiritual division. The narrative does not resolve this tension. His eldest children are taken to New Denver, and he and his wife can visit them only every other week. He describes his anguish as that of divided loyalties: "I was free but my children tore my heart apart, I could hear them suffer. Yet, I was a prisoner within my self, following the group and not living as I felt was right ... I developed the worst kind of inner strifes and conflicts, ever inflicted upon a man ... I wanted my children to attain education, which I like and never had anything against basic education, except for the spirit of militarism, yet I was clinging to the group and allowing my children to suffer" (Davidoff 1966, 141-45). Later in the narrative Davidoff writes that he begins to drift between the Freedomite factions of Stephan Sorokin, John Lebedoff, and Mary Malakoff. This drift becomes part of his own inner drift, which causes him to believe that, in order to resolve the conflict, everyone secretly "serves" everyone else. For example, he mentions that Sorokin is both a divinely inspired leader and an angel of heaven who tried to tempt him and his wife to register their marriages with the government (190). He hits Lebedoff and is commended by Sorokin, but feels guilty and begins to serve Lebedoff more openly, saying that he is in turmoil between the two groups. He resolves this tension by thinking that Lebedoff is secretly serving Sorokin, just as he serves Sorokin as a chauffeur and is a member of Sorokin's Fraternal Council while setting off bombs on secret orders coming from Lebedoff's group (199-200). At the same time, he gravitated to Mary Malakoff's group and its extensive use of public nudity, ecstatic prayer, and protest: "I came to debate within myself that these women were very religious and can't be that they are making a mistake" (204).

At this point, Davidoff's subjectivity splits to accommodate these divisions. When he comes to guard Sorokin against Lebedoff's followers, he mentions that Sorokin's greatest danger came from the "fanatics, within the midst of the Sons of Freedom Doukhobors, who didn't know what they were seeking or what they really wanted? I was a fanatic myself" (Davidoff 1966, 207). Davidoff becomes both the threat and the guardian against the threat, while his narrating "I" says that both positions were incorrect. These multiple positions allow Davidoff to interpret Community Doukhobor leader John J. Verigin's commands to cease bombing USCC property as a call to increase bombing activity. Finally, Davidoff's split subject positions end when he denounces the Canadian government during the Nelson trials, then denounces the Fraternal Council while the other jailed Freedomites turn against him (presumably for switching allegiance, although the text is not clear on this point).

Davidoff (1966, 310) ends this autobiography by affirming his citizenship as Canadian and by quoting a Doukhobor prophecy that: "the Doukhobors came to Canada for the founding of a new great nation and it [Canada] is to be their homeland forever and ever. Amen." This becomes the end of his testimony: his reunification as an independent Doukhobor subject depends on letting go of the radical Doukhobor belief in migration as a hallmark of Doukhobor identity and of confessing all his past "sins" to the authorities. This last passage indicates that Davidoff used this auto-biography as a testimony not only to the complexity of his identity for-mation but also to his desire to present a "Canadianized" Doukhobor gloss in order to explain his actions. In so doing, he hoped that, in the form and rhetoric of an autobiographical confession, the authorities would see from both a reply to Davidoff's earlier, unrepentant confession and an attempt to domesticate his unruly subject positions. Thus Davidoff's first and second autobiographies represent negotiations for visibility with non-Doukhobor authorities by means of the confessional form. "Confessions" such as these do not, as Leigh Gilmore (1994b, 54) suggests, so much reveal identity and "the truth" as produce both in response to discursive requirements: "In that discursive setting [of the confessional], where truth is known at least partially through its proximity to risk, identity emerges not as a thing in itself patiently awaiting the moment of revelation but as the space from which confession issues."

Peter Maloff's autobiographical testimony[17] represents a different set of negotiations with authorities, although it too depends on a response to the discourse of testimony's requirements for a truth-telling subject. Like David-off's autobiographies, Maloff's autobiographical section of his report to Colonel F.J. Mead's 1950 commission to study the "Doukhobor Problem"[18] occurs in response to a non-Doukhobor summons to produce testimony. As Maloff states in the preface to a collection of all three of his reports, Mead asked him to appear before the commission because he had been associated with all three Doukhobor movements. For a number of reasons, Maloff (1957, 1) declined and wrote a series of reports for the commission. Maloff's report, then, produces his identity as a location on a border: he is a Doukhobor insider who also understands the non-Doukhobor "outside" and who can tell the truth as a Doukhobor understands it while also responding to the legitimating discursive regimes about truth required by the commission. In order to do this, Maloff tells his life story so that he can be understood as a credible witness. In his report, autobiography is a way for Maloff to write himself into a discourse that would normally exclude him and his testimony while, at the same time, he attempts to unite this discourse of the truthful subject with Doukhobor ideas about universal truth and suffering.

Maloff (1957, 2) introduces the autobiographical section of his report with an "apology" for its inclusion, which might recall the series of "apologies" for illiteracy that occur in the Agassiz diary:

> But before we go into the problem itself, permit me to make an apology for this introduction of myself. My reasons for thus trespassing on your patience will, I believe, seem the more justifiable as I proceed with this

brief account of the experiences that have gone towards forming my character as a man, and as a student of history; my love of truth regardless of the consequences. But of that I will say no more, since, I take it that the nature of your Commission itself is to find the truth and speak it without fear or favour.

Maloff introduces the discussion of his identity as a trespass that, potentially, could be unjustifiable. While his reasons for this apology are in part practical as British Columbia Doukhobors did not have some citizenship rights (such as the right to vote) in Canada at the time. This means that any Doukhobor called to testify *as a Doukhobor* before a commission, rather than as a transgressive subject before a judge, would be participating in discourses of citizenship and democracy that contained no predetermined identity-position for her or him to occupy. Therefore, Maloff enacts his autobiography as a strategy both of visibility and of translation: he will use commonly understood ideas about character formation found in traditional autobiography and combine them with Doukhobor ideas about truth and knowledge, which he states should be those of the commission itself.

In this way Maloff can construct a shared language that is still considered transgressive as Doukhobor identity was never produced under these circumstances. Thus while elements of his autobiography are "familiar" to a non-Doukhobor readership, the circumstances of its production are not: autobiographies in the West are not usually produced as testimonials for a government commission, with the commission expected to understand both the speaker's legitimacy and the (normally unwritten) discourses of the interpretative community from which her/his identity emerges. This is why Maloff presents himself as a speaking subject whose qualifications rest on his occupying a space between inside and outside rather than being an early leader of the Sons of Freedom and one of Chistiakov's trusted advisors in the CCUB: "I will speak in the capacity of an individual representing no one[,] neither defending or accusing anyone, but as an outsider with an inside view, I will present the Doukhobor problem in its true and natural setting" (Maloff 1957, 2).

Maloff's narrative thematizes this sense of identity as a border occupation that can shift as circumstances require. At its beginning, Maloff positions himself as a Doukhobor by offering a discussion of his parents' suffering in Russia as "sincere Doukhobors," their migration to Canada and (like Davidoff's parents) a sojourn in Oregon, and their decision to leave the Community for a time to become Independent Doukhobors so that their children could receive English schooling (Maloff 1957, 3). Maloff is therefore able to act as an expert on these aspects of Doukhobor experience while also describing meeting, in California, "many outstanding men of letters, art, philosophy and religion" (3) who validate his position as an outsider. He expresses this position in terms of his identity: "Perhaps I was born an idealist, because from the very earliest days of my conscious life I knew that I had inherited a highly sensitive nature. All 49 years of my life I have been a strict vegetarian and teetotaler [sic]. This sensitive nature continuously drove me to seek, to study and to solve my very own self towards higher levels of moral development" (3). This passage marks Maloff's identity as hybrid: he provides psychological information about his sensitive nature (which non-Doukhobors would expect in an autobiography) and, at the same time, he describes his sensitivity in terms of his Doukhobor practices. Maloff also combines the non-Doukhobor understanding of "nature" as an essential psychological state with the Doukhobor belief that all people should seek to morally perfect themselves. He expresses the combination of these ideas with the unusual phrase "to solve my very own self," which poses his identity as a problem requiring a solution as he moves between the non-Doukhobor and Doukhobor worlds.

In the narrative Maloff temporarily "solves" this identity drift by joining the Sons of Freedom movement in 1928. His solution involves referring to the revivalist ideas of the movement as coming from "my own people" because he finds a match between outside movements for world peace and harmony and Freedomite beliefs (Maloff 1957, 3-4). But here the narrative changes. Due to what he calls "two big surprises, disappointments, and terrific stunning blows" the Doukhobor faith becomes "their strange faith" rather than his own (4) – a reaffirmation of Maloff's outsider status that structures the rest of the narrative. However, he maintains his insider status by affirming that he has thoroughly researched Doukhobor history and thought and is, therefore, qualified to testify to Doukhobor moral decay (as indicated by traditional signals of Doukhobor backsliding such as eating meat, smoking, drinking alcohol, and manifesting materialist values) (4). He also maintains solidarity with Doukhoborism's mistrust of secular authorities when he mentions that his other "stunning blow" – the fact that "British Law" placed him in an insane asylum when, as a conscientious objector, he refused to comply with the National Registration Act (5).

Maloff's subsequent report comes from his credentials as a migrant (he moves from one Doukhobor group to another), as activist and historian, as idealist and cynic rather than from his credentials as a former Community and Freedomite leader. This enables him to analyze the Doukhobor migration to Canada as a continuation of the struggle against Russian authorities and to present the Sons of Freedom as a movement that is part of the identity struggles of Doukhobors who encountered non-Doukhobor values rather than as a criminalized conspiracy movement (Maloff 1957, 7-8). After suggesting what each Doukhobor faction could do to end the misunderstandings between Doukhobors and Canadian authorities, Maloff apologizes in advance for blaming the government of Canada for not understanding what sort of immigrants the Doukhobors were and for trying to assimilate them. He then takes a Doukhobor position in stating that a United Nations declaration protects the Doukhobor anti-national stance: "if Doukhobors wish to remain free citizens of the world owing allegiance to no earthly government, it is their indefeasible right to do so" (11). By the end of the report, then, Maloff asks for Doukhobors to return to their spiritual roots and for Canada to reorient its moral values "to fit the true humanitarian solution" to the Doukhobor Problem by ceasing to engage in patriotism, a larger penal system, and "narrow nationalist interests" (12). Like Davidoff, Maloff delineates a Doukhobor identity that cannot be hyphenated (it is not possible to be both Doukhobor and Canadian); however, for him the relationship could be a symbiotic one involving practising Doukhobors who are able to participate in national life and a less nationalist government. He views this as a choice: "Whatever path we choose we must realize at once that there is no middle path, and there can be no spiritual half-breeds, which is to be neither a true Doukhobor, nor a good Canadian, one who makes not the slightest pretense [sic] to the original Doukhobor faith" (12). In order to validate himself as one who can recommend such symbiosis, Maloff writes himself into the discourse of testimony in a hybrid form. He is both a Doukhobor who can "translate" his spiritual traditions for a non-Doukhobor audience and an outside "expert" who can validate his position through non-Doukhobor constructions of knowledge (such as historical research and a knowledge of international law). Maloff constructs a rhetorical space in which, in order to call for change, he can arbitrate not only his own story but also Doukhobor history and identity.

Although there are substantial differences between these four Freedomite narratives, it is clear that each of them represents an alternative way to produce autobiography and autobiographical subjects. Because none of these writers was involved in the dominant discourses that construct subjectivity and, in most cases, actively resisted them, their decisions to use autobiographical forms were strategic. They were either tactical manoeuvres designed to gain visibility inside dominant discourses (e.g., Davidoff's autobiographies and Maloff's autobiographical section) or they were hybrid combinations of identities and genres that resulted in externalized, plural performatives (e.g., the Agassiz diary and Efanow's diary). These discourses were all produced in response to dominant non-Doukhobor institutional situations (e.g., incarceration, a request for confessions, or a request for an expert witness). As such, all of these documents represent attempted negotiations with *the scenes* of non-Doukhobor rhetorics. These set certain conditions for identity, with the place of utterance producing one type of autobiographical identity at one point and not at another. These documents do not represent the hopeful resistance to an all-encompassing hegemony (desired by so many liberal critics of minority writing) but, rather, sets of small negotiations, acceptances, resistances, and combinations of myriad forms and rationales for self-presentation and self-production that differ from narrative to narrative and even from utterance to utterance. Freedomite identities in these diaries and autobiographies function as a flexible set of external performatives for readerships that, rather than seeing Freedomite identities as other and as unknowable, could begin to see them as another way to name, another way to know, another grammar of identity.

Conclusion: Negotiating the "I" and "We" in Autobiography

> There are other modes of life story telling, both oral and written,
> to be recognized, other genealogies of life story telling to be
> chronicled, other explorations of traditions, current and past, to
> be factored into the making and unmaking of autobiography
> subjects in a global environment.
>
> — Smith and Watson, *De/Colonizing the Subject*

Sidonie Smith's and Julia Watson's statement in the introduction to
De/Colonizing the Subject: the Politics of Gender in Women's Autobiography
remains valid (Smith and Watson 1992). As the study of autobiographical
work moves away from an exclusive examination of works created with
sole reference to dominant Western traditions and models of subjectivity,
it has become increasingly clear that the parameters of genre that so many
autobiography scholars have tried to set have been called into question at
every level of "auto," "bio," and "graphe." For instance, when Germaine
Brée (1986, 223) announced that "autobiography in the first person plural
is the next to come," she was referring to what she saw as the next topic
of inquiry in the area of women's autobiography. Brée's statement, however, has turned out to be prophetic in the field of autobiography in ways
that she did not anticipate. Recent criticism of autobiographical writing
and speech, which hold that these discourses refer to sujectivities that are
not exclusive to the Western, bourgeois, white, male selfhood outlined by
Smith and Watson, has turned to considerations of alternate ways of
understanding subjectivity. These have altered the "auto" of autobiography even as the writers and speakers appropriate some aspects of that discourse of self.

One of the results of this appropriation has been a blurring of autobiographical forms, which highlights autobiography's position as a discourse
in which resistance to prevailing ways of identifying a writer, a speaker, or
an entire group can take place. This study of Doukhobor autobiography
forms part of this critique of autobiography criticism as the exclusive examination of a commodified liberal selfhood that can be bought and sold.
At the same time, the wholesale challenge Doukhobor subjects make to the
ideas of liberal selfhood does not refuse autobiographical discourse altogether but, rather, harnesses its power to refer and to make issues visible

for writers and speakers who have not previously had access to this type of discourse. This is the essence of what I mean by "negotiation" of memory and identity as Doukhobors have not always resisted, or been able to resist, what dominant discourses have said about them and about their history in Canada. Doukhobors have used autobiographical discourse as an "everyday practice" in de Certeau's (1984, 34) sense, as one of the tactics that enabled Doukhobor ways to understand history and what it is to be human to come, however briefly, into the purview of people who do not know what Doukhobors have thought about these things, or even that Doukhobors can have something to say that might change what "Canada" has been understood to be.

Doukhobor use of autobiographical discourse is similar to the hybridizing of autobiographical forms explored in recent American studies of alternative autobiographical forms and subjects produced in autobiography. To my knowledge, this book is one of the first that treats autobiography produced in Canada as a set of identity technologies used by those who normally would not resort to such forms, who would usually say "we" instead of the autobiographical "I" (and all that that "I" implies). However, the high quality of Shirley Neuman's (1996) collection of autobiography scholarship for *Essays on Canadian Writing* actually serves to highlight the fact that, in the fields of Canadian literature and Canadian studies (in English, French, and other languages), studies of alternative autobiographical forms and subjects are still rare. Emerging postcolonial criticism that links theories about Canadian identity and the development of Canada as a nation-state to literature by migrants in Canada can and should politicize studies of autobiography produced by other people in Canada who were either unable or unwilling to become docile subjects of the British Empire.

Studies of alternate autobiographical production in Canada could also call into question the homology between place and ontology that has been formulated from Northrop Frye's (1957) famous contention that "where is here?" is the fundamental question to be asked about the nature of Canadian national identity. Feminist work on autobiography and collaboration could also be joined to interdisciplinary work on autobiography and oral cultures. This could lead to autobiographical discourse providing new ways of reading class, religion, sexuality, language, and race (but in ways that avoid the "flattening" discourse of ethnicity that we see in Canadian multiculturalism). Readings that take this cultural terrain of autobiography into account can also "cross-read" or listen into the similar debates about autobiography by Aboriginal peoples in Canada, particularly in the areas of narrative appropriation, connections between citizenship and land-use, collectivity, collaboration, and the position of oral representation in (and against) cultures that privilege written autobiographical forms.

I would like to conclude with the words of Betty Bergland (1994, 130), whose call for a radicalization of the autobiographical subject does not sacrifice the web of discourses that inflect how that subject produces and is produced: "it becomes imperative to develop a theory of autobiography that acknowledges the importance of marginalized voices, but avoids the essentializing of individuals and groups, that takes into account complex relationships between cultures and discourses that produce the speaking subject, but avoids viewing language as a transparent representation of the imagined real." Bergland's comments ask that we make a connection between the production of autobiographical rhetoric and the production of the subject. In Doukhobor autobiographical discourse, writers and speakers make this connection, and they make it in ways that do not essentialize difference but, rather, make difference a point of negotiation, critique, acceptance, and refusal. As part of the rhetoric of *plakun trava*, the Russian plant that thrives by growing against the current, autobiographical discourse by Doukhobor writers and speakers indicates how this discourse becomes part of an ongoing negotiation between Canadian identity and Doukhobor identity. These identities, in autobiography, can be collective and yet singular, and they can combine without ever creating a hyphen that would link them yet keep them separate forever.

Notes

Introduction

1 My use of Fred Davidoff's material in no way means that I advocate his beliefs about Doukhoborism. I use this material for rhetorical analysis only. I am not a Doukhobor and cannot unequivocally say whether or not Davidoff was a true Doukhobor or whether or not his autobiographical observations are historically accurate.

Chapter 1: Beyond Auto-Bio-Graphe

1 Caren Kaplan (1992, 209-14) enumerates alternative terms to autobiography that she refers to as "resistance literature," including "testimonio," "ethnography," and "bio-mythography." Smith (1993, 154-88) suggests the term "autobiographical manifestos" for autobiographical writing that leads to political empowerment. Marlene Kadar (1992) has argued for the term "life writing" to accommodate women's letters, commonplace books, and other writing that is not part of autobiographical writing. Francoise Lionnet (1989) and Deborah Danahay-Reed (1997) have separately proposed "auto/ethnography" as a way to describe ethnographic writing by people who are from the group "studied" and who reflect on their insider/outsider status. I admit that I have added "witness narrative" to the mix of terms (Rak 2001, 226-27). This does not include terms for autobiography that are used in disciplines such as history, anthropology, and psychology.

2 To qualify this in a way that still makes my point, the longest discussion of identity in Smith's book occurs in a discussion about Gertrude Stein's view of identity as a "contingent phenomenon" connected to self-consciousness and how this relates to what Smith describes as her sexual identity "difficulties" (Smith 1993, 71-72). What is interesting here is that Smith assumes that identity is associated with identification and with self-consciousness without discussing in detail how this is related to her extensive discussion of subjectivity.

3 Judith Butler's (1997b, 4) question about Althusser's idea of "hailing" – "What or who is said to turn, and what is the object of such a turn?" – is central to this approach to the problem of identity and agency in post-Marxist theory that has been influenced by deconstruction. Donna Haraway's (1995, xiii-xiv) figure of the cyborg subject combines material analysis with multiple identifications within posthuman analyses as a way to figure multiple agencies working against global capitalism.

4 I discuss Althusser's use of this term more fully in the preface.

5 At the beginning of a special issue of *Biography*, focusing on material from the recent international conference "Autobiography and Changing Identities," Susanna Egan and Gabriele Helms (2001, xiii) mention that autobiography may have a mostly Western focus because "the wealth of material produced on new and yet common grounds has overwhelmed alternative options." This could also explain why so much recent criticism on autobiography has an American or Americanist focus.

6 Here I revise Hutcheon's term "ex-centric" to mean those who have been excluded from the centre of a discourse but who still use pieces of that discourse as a way of critiquing

or negotiating it. In *The Canadian Postmodern* "ex-centric" signifies any writers who occupy a margin but who also participate in the centralities of Canadian national life *because* they critique the centre (Hutcheon 1988, 3).

7 Sidonie Smith (1987, 4) has mentioned that William Spengemann (1980) traces the rising interest in autobiography to 1970 with the publication of Francis R. Hart's essay on the subject. However, her subsequent discussion of the New Model theorists accepts Olney's interpretation of the field's development.

8 Here I refer to Candace Lang's (1982, 4) rather acidic summary of Romantic subjectivity as unique, precultural, prelinguistic, communicated, and preserved by feinting into artistic language.

9 In "Discourse and the Novel" Bakhtin (1981a, 361) enumerates different types of novelistic hybrids. His category of the intentional double-voiced and internally dialogized hybrid would seem to fit autobiographical utterances that fall outside mainstream autobiographical discourse: "in it, within the boundaries of a single utterance, two potential utterances are fused, two responses are, as it were, harnessed in a potential dialogue."

Chapter 2: Doukhobor Beliefs and Historical Moments

1 Vladimir Bonch-Bruevich relates this anecdote in *The Book of Life of the Doukhobors* (1978).

2 My account of Doukhobor history is necessarily brief. For a more complete introduction to Doukhobor history, see Woodcock and Avakumovic (1977); Tarasoff (1982); and Janzen (1990). See Yerbury (1984) for information about the Sons of Freedom.

3 Doukhobors call Peter V. Verigin *Gospodii* (Lordly) or, sometimes, Peter the Lordly. I refer to him as Peter Lordly.

4 When Peter Lordly became a leader, the Doukhobors split into two factions. Peter Lordly's faction was called the "Large Party." Most of the Large Party followers migrated to Canada, leaving the members of the Small Party, who supported elders that had worked for Luchechka, in Russia. The descendants of the Small Party followers are still living in Russian Doukhobor communities. See Woodcock and Avakumovic (1977, 81 ff.).

5 A full account of the Burning of Arms and the resistance of the Doukhobor conscripts can be found in Tarasoff (1982, 21-26).

6 In English, the psalm, from the translation in *A Celebration of Peace*, page 73, reads as follows:

Sleep on you brave fighting eagles,
Sleep in the arms of the Lord;
You have received from your Master
Peace and the promised reward.

Now on this hard earned pathway,
Easy for us 'tis to tread;
You paid the price they exacted,
So we could journey ahead.

Many and cruel were the tortures,
You took in Siberian plains;
In Tundrian regions you suffered,
Dreadful and sad were your days.

Today, as we think of your suffering,
And of the hardships you passed,
We pray to abide by your message,
And join the great common task.

Sleep on you brave fighting eagles,
Sleep in the arms of the Lord;
We shall o'ercome all temptation,
And follow Christ and His Word.

7 In his diary *To America with the Doukhobors,* which has been translated into English, the Tolstoyan Leopold Sulerzhitsky provides an eyewitness account of the voyage of the *Lake Huron* and the early settlement.

8 Aylmer Maude, on the basis of his involvement in the initial negotiations with Canada, said that there was an understanding that Doukhobors would make individual land entries for homesteads but would be allowed to cultivate land in common. However, there is no formal record of this agreement, and it is doubtful that the Doukhobors themselves were aware of it (Janzen 1990, 38).

9 "Anglo" in this context refers to settlers who were from Britain or Britain's colonies. These settlers were thought to possess the cultural background that immigration officials thought all other settlers should acquire. See the preface of this book for details about this. Settlers from this background often complained about "other" types of settlers (Janzen 1990, 41-42).

10 All references to the Community and the Commune refer to the CCUB.

11 This is an anecdote that a Doukhobor shared with me in the Kootenays, October 1996.

12 Community Doukhobors and some Freedomites have referred to Peter Petrovich Verigin as Chistiakov, although use of this name seems to be decreasing in favour of Peter P. Verigin. I refer to Peter Petrovich as Peter Chistiakov in order to avoid confusing him with Peter Lordly.

13 The CCUB owed $168,283.14 to the National Trust Company and an additional $192,297.51 to Sun Life Assurance, for a total of $360,580.64. CCUB assets at this time were worth between three and four million dollars. Both companies foreclosed on the CCUB and proceeded to evict the Doukhobors from their own land in 1939. The British Columbia government did nothing to help the CCUB during the time of crisis. However, after foreclosure it bought the Doukhobor land in the Kootenays for $296,500 and allowed Doukhobors to continue to live on it and pay rent.

14 Two examples of this are telling: the publication of a book of Doukhobor funerary practices in Russian and English called *Vechnaya Pamyat* (Eternal Memory) indicates that these customs are being forgotten. The 700-page *Summarized Report of the Joint Doukhobor Research Committee,* a document "dedicated to all future generations, both of Doukhobor descent, and those who in their evolutionary process choose to dedicate their lives to the search for Eternal Truth" (Joint Doukhobor Research Committee 1997, 2) has been translated entirely into English.

15 See Ryan Androsoff's (2003) *Doukhobor Home Page,* a large USCC-supported site devoted to Doukhobor issues <http://www.doukhobor-homepage.com/>, and Jonathan Kalmakoff's (2003) *Doukhobor Genealogy* Web site <http://users.accesscomm.ca/doukhobor.genealogy/>. Sharon McGowan (1998) – who is of Doukhobor descent – has produced *Soul Communion,* a video about selected Doukhobor writers and visual artists. The seventh Doukhobor youth workshop for 2001 is sponsored by the Doukhobor Unity Group.

Chapter 3: *Vechnaiia Pamit* in the Diaspora

1 Bonch-Bruevich's *Zhivotnaia Kniga Dukhobortsev* [*The Living Book of the Doukhobors*] has been translated as *The Book of Life of the Doukhobors.* However, The Living Book is truly the oral psalms, hymns, and songs sung by Doukhobors themselves; the written version is only a guide. It is not a finished "book" but, rather, a book that is always in the process of being constructed as it is sung. Since I must use the printed version here, I use the term The Living Book to stress the ongoing process that goes into singing and interpreting it.

2 In his interview with Jonathan Rutherford, Homi Bhabha (1990, 213) says that "it is only by losing the sovereignty of the self that you can gain the freedom of a politics that is open to the non-assimilationist claims of cultural difference ... it [politics] doesn't need to totalise in order to legitimate political action or cultural practice." Bhabha's comments indicate that hybridity, which he names in the same interview as the "third space" (211), enables other positions to emerge because of its ability to contain the trace elements of earlier histories while setting up new structures of authority. When taken with his statements in *The Location of Culture* (Bhaba 1994) about undecidability, Bhabha's hybrid third space represents an in-betweenness between fundamentalist and multicultural identity

positions, where the "self" disappears and is replaced by identifications and affiliations open to continuous change and flux. This flux, this refusal to take one consistent position, can be thought as a strategy against more fixed, hegemonic cultural formations that seek to locate ethnic identity as always "other" and always powerless.

3 This reading of hybridity can be found in other criticism. For instance, Peter Dickinson argues that Sally Morgan's autobiography *My Place* is a hybrid narrative because she embeds Aboriginal oral stories/narratives that she has tape-recorded into her written text. This narrative technique creates a "double-voice" situation and multiple histories (Dickinson 1994, 327-28).

4 See note 7 and Chapter 2 for background information about the Union of Spiritual Communities of Christ (USCC). *Iskra* is the bilingual (Russian-English) magazine sponsored by the USCC.

5 In Chapter 5 I use Bakhtin's discussion of chronotopic autobiography as a way to rethink performativity.

6 In Doukhobor Russian, the phrase is pronounced *vechnaiia pamit*. I would like to thank Jan Kabatoff for pointing this out to me.

7 See Lavie and Swedenburg's (1996) introduction to the disruption of the "Eurocentre" by marginal workforces that produce hybridized cultural practices (8-9) as well as their discussion of diasporic "double" memory (14).

8 In a recent letter to *Iskra* concerning the question of intermarriage, Marie Maloff mentions how Doukhobors in previous generations thought of themselves as exiled diasporic people and as wanderers. She describes a traditional way of learning about and understanding the role of migration in the construction of Doukhobor identity:

> I remember things that the older people used to talk about, and the expectations that they had. They used to repeat, "we're not immigrants, we are exiles in a foreign land. We will go on to another country some day." Some said "back to Russia"; some sayings referred to Israel (because we are a spiritual Israel) ... many other people who are old and who lived in religious homes must have heard and remembered these things.
> My dad used to often sing *(Krai moi krai rodnoi)* [Land, my homeland]. Throughout all of our years in Canada most people expected to move away – there was a longing in their hearts, and ours. They used to say Lushechka prophesied this and that, and what was said, the people believed, and expected it to come to pass.
> They also believed in a 40 year stay in Canada and then an exile to somewhere else. It did not work out that way, but some people are still expecting something. It is good to have hope, expecting something good. (Maloff 1997, 27)

9 The Named Doukhobors of Canada was an organization formed by Peter Chistiakov in 1928 in an effort to unite the Independent, Community, and Freedomite Doukhobor factions into one group. Chistiakov dissolved this organization before his death in 1939 and, at the same time, also dissolved the CCUB and formed the USCC. Some CCUB members did not recognize the USCC and continued to remain under the Named Doukhobor title.

10 To date, there have been at least two responses in *Iskra* to Poznikoff-Koutny's article, both by Doukhobor women.

11 I use this term as it appears in Susan Hagen's work on autobiography and medieval allegory. According to Hagen (1990, 5), the narrator in a text becomes a memorial sign when the hermeneutic burden of remembrance shifts from the narrative's figuring of memory to the interpretive community's "memory" of other, similar patterns that are not part of the narrative.

12 Vi Plotnikoff (1998, 205) expresses this difficulty: "to be Doukhobor was to be a young adult working in Vancouver yet concealing your roots – the same roots you were so proud of when you stood on the stage of the cultural centre, singing the hymns and psalms your parents, and your grandparents before them, had sung." Elaine J. Makortoff's poem, which I discussed at the beginning of this chapter, contains similar feelings of ambiguity.

13 This was the public name Peter Lordly gave to the communal organization of Doukhobors

in 1896 (Woodcock and Avakumovic 1977, 96-97). Peter Chistiakov dissolved the CCUB before his death in 1938 and created the Union of Spiritual Communities of Christ (USCC) to replace it (307). The USCC remains the official organization representing the Community Doukhobor group.

14 In English, Soukorev's name is spelled "Soukorev" in the *Iskra* issues and in the 1938 *Nelson Daily News* version of "My Renunciation of Military Service." However, in Rozinkin (1992) it is spelled "Soukoreff" and, in *Iskra* 1820, his son's name is also spelled "Soukoreff." For clarity's sake, I have used the spelling that appears in "My Renunciation of Military Service."

15 Two other narratives about the Burning of Arms have been translated and published in *Iskra*. These are Vanya Bayoff's (1992) account entitled "The Execution," appearing in issue 1743 and originally transcribed by Bodianskii, and Vanya Makhortoff's (1987) account of his imprisonment, transcribed by his grandson Mike G. Jmieff for *Iskra*, issue 1648.

16 I discovered no recorded reaction to this narrative in the *Nelson Daily News*. The impact of the serialized article on the readership is unknown.

17 *Iskra* states that the translation is believed to have been prepared by William A. Soukoreff and that it has not been published before. However, Rozinkin's comments do indicate that the translator was probably William Petrovich Sheloff.

18 For the purposes of this discussion, I refer to the 1996 *Iskra* translation by instalment and page number. When I refer to the version in the *Nelson Daily News*, I will indicate as much in the text.

Chapter 4: Negotiating Identity

1 For a discussion of *molenie* and *sobranie* as examples of communal worship and decision making, see the "Spirit Wrestlers" section of Chapter 2.

2 For a more detailed look at *vechnaiia pamit,* see Chapter 3.

3 See, for example, Lucy Maloff's story about Peter Chistiakov (Joint Doukhobor Research Committee 1997, 366). Peter Chistiakov often stressed that it was important for Doukhobors to research and teach about their origins and spiritual concepts. He referred to these activities as the "Doukhobor University," which stressed a non-institutional form of acquiring knowledge.

4 Annie Barnes's (1998, 13-39) article, "Doukhobor Women in the Twentieth Century," written for *Spirit-Wrestlers' Voices,* represents the first published attempt by a Doukhobor woman to work through the complexities of gender discrimination, in addition to other challenges, that Doukhobor women have had to face.

5 *Toil and Peaceful Life* is a collection of fourteen oral narratives by Doukhobor elders that was transcribed and translated by Marjorie Malloff (1977). Possibly because they were recorded for a British Columbia archival series, these narratives appear heavily edited and homogenized for publication. Although with more information about the production process they could be analyzed in their own right, the narratives of *Toil and Peaceful Life* fall outside the scope of this study.

6 I would like to clarify that this is *not* an example of dialogism, which refers to utterances that are always produced with the awareness of another's "word."

7 Novokshyonov relates events that occurred before the Burning of Arms, when Doukhobors decided not to cooperate with tsarist officials. One way that the Doukhobors resisted was to refuse to serve as village headmen. "Village headman" was an official post that, presumably, enabled the one who occupied it to exercise authority in a village on behalf of the local governing officials and to represent the concerns of the village to those officials.

8 All of the quotations from Bodianskii's collection are from an unpublished translation. Page numbering refers to the page numbers in the translation.

9 In "Execution," Bayoff explains that Doukhobors do not call their parents and grandparents by their usual names because this is thought to be hierarchical. He refers to his mother as his "birth-giver" and to his maternal grandmother as his *nyanka,* or "care-giver," rather than calling her by the common term, *babushka.* He also refers to his father as "the parent" (Bayoff 1908a, 4).

10 Besides Soukorev's "My Renunciation of Military Service," this is the only other long narrative by a Doukhobor who survived the persecutions following the Burning of Arms that was printed in Russian in *Iskra* and then translated into English. This makes Bayoff's narrative another important part of maintaining the Doukhobor diasporic imaginary connected to suffering and resistance, although I will not focus on this aspect of the narrative in this chapter.

11 A note in the English-language translation of "The Execution" for *Iskra* states that the word refers to a tsarist executive order for corporal punishment (such as flogging) (Bayoff 1992, 16).

12 During the 1960s Harshenin made more than fifty reel-to-reel taped interviews with Doukhobors. Since his objective was to get Doukhobors to speak in dialect for later analysis, in order to get them talking he asked questions about their lives, which inadvertently produced many autobiographical testimonies. Harshenin's research is valuable because he taped interviews with Doukhobors from the three major groups and because his tapes were made earlier (and are of better quality) than those of other interviews. His status as a Doukhobor meant that the people he interviewed were willing to candidly discuss many issues. Harshenin died of a heart attack before he could publish more than two of his monographs on Doukhobor word choice.

The translation of the interview and the Salmo interviews that follow are approximate. However, the translator and transcriber attempted to approximate Doukhobor dialect with colloquial English wherever possible in order to impart some of the tone of the original recording.

13 All quotations from the recordings of Fred Zhikarov, Bill Bondareff, Mrs. Bojey, and Helen Popoff are from an unpublished translation. No page numbers are used. Readers are asked to refer to the recordings themselves for source information.

14 The name of an old Doukhobor village near Grand Forks, British Columbia. The English spelling of the name could vary.

15 Little is known about the Salmo recording project since information about it is confined to what is written on the labels of the cassettes deposited in Special Collections at the University of British Columbia Main Library. Since the interviews themselves are in Doukhobor dialect, the interviewers sound young, and some of the comments/questions refer to their parents, it is reasonable to assume that the project was conducted by secondary school students of Doukhobor origin. Given the set of questions most speakers were asked, the interviewers may have been researching a project on their elders' cultural origins.

16 The interview tape does not provide a first name. "Mrs. Bojey" could be Mary Bojey of Krestova, but I have been unable to confirm this.

17 The spiritual authority of elder Doukhobor women can be seen in three Doukhobor commemorations of the lives of their grandmothers (see Tarasoff and Klymasz 1995).

18 Peter N. Maloff produced a response to a commission studying Freedomite agitation, which contains an autobiographical section. A discussion of Maloff's work appears in Chapter 5.

19 For example, Swetlishoff refers to the past history of the Doukhobors and their present ownership of land in spiritual terms: "At one time, we Doukhobors were a light for all of the world, the salt of the earth. And now, it is not sin to say that we have become the useless litter of the earth. We have looked back like Lot's wife of biblical times. She looked back and was turned to stone, no longer to be a live entity on earth. If we do not take hold of ourselves, the same thing can happen to us" (Joint Doukhobor Research Committee 1997, 605).

Chapter 5: Witness, Negotiation, Performance

1 This group is interchangeably called the *svobodniki* (Freedomites) or the *syny svobody* (Sons of Freedom), which was a name possibly given to them by Peter Chistiakov when he invented the saying "Sons of Freedom cannot be slaves of corruption" soon after his arrival in Canada. Despite the non–gender-inclusive sound of the latter name in English, the Sons of Freedom groups have had many female members, and have at times had women lead them or play important leadership roles. The names are used interchangeably, although "Sons of Freedom" appears in English more often than "Freedomites."

2 The Sons of God are considered by many Freedomites to be an earlier version of the Sons of Freedom movement (Joint Doukhobor Research Committee 1997, 114-15), although the two movements were not continuous and did not share the same leadership.

3 See, for example, Psalm 5 (The Living Book 1978, 1940). This formula is found in many psalms:

> Q. Why are you a Doukhobor?
> A. To glorify the Lord's name; the Lord's gentleness is together with us.
> Q. What does the common Doukhobor cross represent?
> A. A narrow path, a voluntary sorrow, a life of a pilgrim, a life of poverty.

4 Although the Freedomite leader Stephan Sorokin (1950) published an autobiography called *Three Days and Three Nights in the Life beyond the Grave: What I Saw, Heard, and Endured When I was Tortured to Death by the Godless Authorities of the USSR*, Sorokin was not a Doukhobor and it is difficult to know how many Freedomites read the book.

5 There are wide stylistic variations in this text and, in some sections, Efanow's name is spelled "Echfanow." This suggests that Efanow's text, like the diary of Mike Chernenkoff and friends, could have had multiple authors and transcribers. Although this possibility invites more analysis of collective subjectivity in Freedomite diary writing, multiple authorship of Efanow's diary cannot be proven at this time.

6 I have not found written material by Freedomite women. This does not mean that Freedomite women were subjugated groups. As George Woodcock observes, historically Doukhobor protests have been led or instigated by women, who have traditionally resisted schooling and other attempts at assimilation more rigorously than have men. This could mean that literacy rates among Freedomite women were lower than were those of men. See Chapter 4 for transcribed oral accounts by Freedomite women.

7 See Chapter 1 for a discussion of Judith Butler's and Sidonie Smith's development of performatives and identity construction.

8 See Chapter 2 for a discussion of the *sobranie* meeting form.

9 Selections from this manuscript are from an unpublished translation.

10 Selections from Efanow's manuscript are from an unpublished translation.

11 Personal correspondence with Mike Chernenkoff.

12 Although this guard's name appears in *Prison Diary* as "Jovans," he is named "Jones" in Holt's *Terror in the Name of God*.

13 The vision actually marks the beginning of the diary in its present form, although the page number is 45. Some of this manuscript has been recopied and censored. It is unclear whether Efanow made these changes himself or whether someone else made them. Pagination in this manuscript refers to an unpublished translation.

14 See Holt (1964, 232-38). The rhetorical construction of many of Holt's questions lectures Davidoff: "Don't you feel this is a hard way of life for a child?" "Can you really believe in your heart that Peter Chistiakoff was good?" or "Couldn't you see the prophecy is wrong, the tool of an evil man?"

15 Doukhobors in Canada historically differentiate themselves from other people living in Canada by referring to all outsiders as *angliki* (the English) whether or not they spoke English and whether or not they were from England.

16 Letter to McClelland & Stewart, 27 January 1969, Davidoff papers, National Archive of Canada.

17 Strictly speaking, as he makes clear, Peter Maloff was not a Freedomite when he wrote this report. However, due to his former leadership position in the Sons of Freedom movement and the fact that he tells his story in response to a commission inquiring into the Sons of Freedom depredations, his narrative fits most readily into this chapter.

18 In the media, the Freedomite depredations were commonly known as the "Doukhobor Problem." Freedomites also referred to the situation the "Doukhobor Problem," but this was in reference to their need to migrate and their difficulties with the federal and provincial governments.

References

Adam, Ian. 1996. Oracy and Literacy: A Post-Colonial Dilemma? *Journal of Commonwealth Literature* 31 (1): 97-109.

Althusser, Louis. 1990. *For Marx*. Translated by Ben Brewster. London, New York: Verso.

Anderson, Benedict. 1983. *Imagined Communities: Reflections on the Origins and Spread of Nationalism*. London: Verso.

Andrews, William L. 1991. African-American Autobiography Criticism: Retrospect and Prospect. In *American Autobiography: Retrospect and Prospect*. Edited by Paul John Eakin. Madison, WI: University of Wisconsin Press.

–. 1993. Introduction to *African American Autobiography: A Collection of Critical Essays*. Englewood Cliffs, NJ: Prentice Hall.

Andrews, William L., ed. 1986. *To Tell a Free Story: The First Century of Afro-American Autobiography, 1760-1865*. Champaign-Urbana: University of Illinois Press.

Androsoff, Ryan. 2003. *Doukhobor Home Page*. <http://www.doukhobor-homepage.com>.

Ang, Ien. 1994. On Not Speaking Chinese: Postmodern Ethnicity and the Politics of Diaspora. *New Formations* 24: 1-18.

Appadurai, Arjun. 1996. *Modernity at Large: Cultural Dimensions of Globalization*. Minneapolis: University of Minnesota Press.

Arishenkoff, Nick D., and Cecil W. Koochin. 1974. Life in the Doukhobor Commune – (CCUB). Interview and translation by Jim Popoff. *Mir* 2 (3-6): 3-50.

Ashley, Kathleen. 1994. The Mark of Autobiography. In *Autobiography and Post-Modernism*. Edited by Kathleen Ashley, Leigh Gilmore, and Gerald Peters. Amherst: University of Massachussetts Press.

Bakhtin, M.M. 1981a. Discourse and the Novel. In *The Dialogic Imagination*. Edited by Michael Holquist, translated by Caryl Emmerson and Michael Holquist. Austin, TX: University of Texas Press.

–. 1981b. Forms of Time and Chronotope in the Novel. In *The Dialogic Imagination*. Edited by Michael Holquist. Translated by Caryl Emmerson and Michael Holquist. Austin, TX: University of Texas Press.

Barnes, Annie B. 1998. Doukhobor Women in the Twentieth Century. In *Spirit-Wrestlers' Voices*. Edited by Koozma J. Tarasoff. New York: Legas.

Bayoff, Vanya. 1908a. Execution. In *Dukhobortsy: sbornik razskasov, pisem, dokumentov i statei po religioznym voprosam*. Edited and transcribed by Alexander M. Bodianskii. *The Doukhobors: Collection of Narratives, Letters, Documents and Articles on Religious Questions*. Kharkov, 1908. Special Collections. University of British Columbia, Main Library.

–. 1908b. Babushka's Grief. In *Dukhobortsy: sbornik razskasov, pisem, dokumentov i statei po religioznym voprosam*. Edited and transcribed by Alexander M. Bodianskii. *The Doukhobors: Collection of Narratives, Letters, Documents and Articles on Religious Questions*. Kharkov, 1908. Special Collections. University of British Columbia, Main Library.

–. 1992. The Execution. In *Dukhobortsy: sbornik razskasov, pisem, dokumentov i statei po religioznym voprosam*. Edited and transcribed by Alexandr M. Translated by Ken Soroka. *The Doukhobors: Collection of Narratives, Letters, Documents and Articles on Religious Questions. Iskra* 1742 (12 February): 16-46.

Benjamin, Walter. 1969. The Task of the Translator. In *Illuminations*. Edited and translated by Hannah Arendt. New York: Schocken Books/Harcourt, Brace and World.

Benstock, Shari. 1988. Authorizing the Autobiographical. In *The Private Self: Theory and Practice of Women's Autobiographical Writings*. Edited by Shari Benstock. Chapel Hill, NC: University of North Carolina Press.

Benveniste, Emile. 1971. *Problems in General Linguistics*. Translated by Mary Elizabeth Meek. Coral Gables, FL: University of Miami Press.

Berger, Carl. 1970. *The Sense of Power: Studies in the Ideas of Canadian Imperialism, 1867-1914*. Toronto: University of Toronto Press.

Bergland, Betty. 1994. Postmodernism and the Autobiographical Subject: Reconstructing the "Other." In *Autobiography and Post-Modernism*. Edited by Kathleen Ashley, Leigh Gilmore, and Gerald Peters. Amherst: University of Massachussetts Press.

Beverly, John. 1992. The Margin at the Center: On *Testimonio* (Testimonial Narrative). In *De/Colonizing the Subject: The Politics of Gender in Women's Autobiography*. Edited by Sidonie Smith and Julia Watson. Minneapolis: University of Minnesota Press.

Bhabha, Homi K. 1990. The Third Space: Interview with Homi Bhabha. Interviewed by Jonathan Rutherford. In *Identity: Community, Culture, Difference*. Edited by Jonathan Rutherford. London, UK: Lawrence and Wishart.

–. 1994. *The Location of Culture*. London, UK: Routledge.

Blackman, Margaret B. 1991. The Individual and Beyond: Reflections of the Life History Process. *Anthropology and Humanism Quarterly* 16 (2): 56-62.

Bojey, Mrs. 1977. Interview with Mrs. Bojey. Sound Recording. Salmo, British Columbia. Special Collections, University of British Columbia, Main Library.

Bondareff, Bill (Vasil Vasilevich). 1977. Interview with Bill Bondareff. Sound Recording. Salmo, British Columbia. Special Collections, University of British Columbia, Main Library.

Bondoreff, Ivan G. 1975. The Named Doukhobors of Canada. *Mir* 2 (7-10): 12-13.

The Book of Life of the Doukhobors (The Living Book). 1978. Edited by Vladimir Bonch-Bruevich. Translated by Victor O. Buyniak. Doukhobor Societies of Saskatchewan, Saskatoon and Blaine Lake: Blaine Lake. Originally published in 1954 as *Zhivotnaia kniga Dukhobortsev*. Winnipeg: Union of Doukhobors of Canada.

Boyce Davies, Carole. 1992. Collaboration and the Ordering Imperative in Life Story Production. In *De/Colonizing the Subject: The Politics of Gender in Women's Autobiography*. Edited by Sidonie Smith and Julia Watson. Minneapolis: University of Minnesota Press.

Braxton, Joanne. 1989. *Black Women Writing Autobiography: A Tradition Within a Tradition*. Philadelphia: Temple University Press.

Brée, Germaine. 1986. Autogynography. *Southern Review* 22 (2): 223-45.

Breyfogle, Nicholas B. 1995. Building Doukhoboriia: Religious Culture, Social Identity, and Russian Colonization in Transcaucasia, 1845-1895. *Canadian Ethnic Studies* 27 (3): 24-51.

Brodzki, Bella, and Celeste Schenk. 1988. Introduction to *Life/Lines: Theorizing Women's Autobiography*. Edited by Bella Brodzki and Celeste Schenck. Ithaca, NY: Cornell University Press.

Bruce, Jean. 1976. *The Last Best West*. Toronto: Fitzhenry and Whiteside.

Bruss, Elizabeth W. 1976. *Autobiographical Acts: The Changing Situation of a Literary Genre*. Baltimore: Johns Hopkins University Press.

Buss, Helen. 2001. *Reproducing the World: Reading Memoirs by Contemporary Women*. Waterloo: Wilfrid Laurier Press.

Butler, Judith. 1990. *Gender Trouble: Feminism and the Subversion of Identity*. New York and London: Routledge.

–. 1993. *Bodies that Matter: On the Discursive Limits of "Sex."* New York: Routledge.

–. 1997a. *Excitable Speech: A Politics of the Performative*. New York and London: Routledge.

–. 1997b. *The Psychic Life of Power: Theories in Subjection*. Stanford, CA: Stanford University Press.

Butterfield, Stephen. 1974. *Black Autobiography in America*. Amherst: University of Massachussetts Press.

Calinescu, Matei. 1993. Orality in Literacy: Some Historical Paradoxes of Reading. *Yale Journal of Criticism* 6 (2): 175-91.

Canadian Museum of Civilization. 1998. 100 Years: The Spirit Wrestlers (The Doukhobors). 1997-98. Exhibit Pamphlet.

Certeau, Michel de. 1984. *The Practice of Everyday Life*. Translated by Stephen Rendall. Berkeley: University of California Press.

Chernenkoff, Mikhail, i drugie. 1993. *Tyuremnyi Dnevnik: sobytie i perezhivanie v Gornoi Tyurme Agassiz, BC, 1962-1969*. (Mike E. Chernenkoff and Friends. *Prison Diary: Events and Experiences in Mountain Prison, Agassiz, BC 1962-1969*.) Crescent Valley, BC: Steve Lapshinoff.

The Concise Oxford Dictionary. 1984. Edited by J.B. Sykes. 7th ed. London: Oxford University Press.

Crapanzano, Vincent. 1984. Life-Histories. *American Anthropologist* 86: 953-60.

Danahay-Reed, Deborah. 1997. *Auto/Ethnography: Rewriting the Self and the Social*. New York: Berg Press.

Davidoff, Fred Nicolas. 1964. Autobiography of a Fanatic. In Simma Holt's *Terror in the Name of God*. Toronto: McClelland & Stewart.

–. 1966. Autobiography of Fred Nicolas Davidoff, Books 1-6, BC Penitentiary, Box M. New Westminster, British Columbia. Unpublished manuscript. National Archives of Canada, Fred N. Davidoff fonds R5397-0-2-E, vols. 1-4.

de Lauretis, Teresa. 1986. Introduction: Feminist Studies/Critical Studies. In *Feminist Studies/Critical Studies*. Edited by Teresa de Lauretis. London: Macmillan.

–. 1987. *Technologies of Gender*. Bloomington: Indiana University Press.

de Man, Paul. 1979. Autobiography as De-facement. *MLN* 94: 919-30.

Derrida, Jacques. 1985. *The Ear of the Other: Otobiography, Transference, Translation*. Edited by Christie McDonald. Translated by Peggy Kamuf. New York: Shocken Books.

Dickinson, Peter. 1994. "Orality in Literacy": Listening to Indigenous Writing. *Canadian Journal of Native Studies*. 14 (2): 319-40.

Dorsey, Peter A. 1993. *Sacred Estrangement: The Rhetoric of Conversion in Modern American Autobiography*. University Park, PA: Pennsylvania State University Press.

Eakin, Paul John. 1985. *Fictions in Autobiography: Studies in the Art of Self-Invention*. Princeton, NJ: Princeton University Press.

Efanow, Alexander. 1930. Journal from Agassiz. Unpublished manuscript. Special Collections, University of British Columbia, Main Library. Anonymous submission to the UBC Library Special Collections.

Egan, Susanna. 1999. *Mirror Talk: Genres of Crisis in Contemporary Autobiography*. Chapel Hill: University of North Carolina Press.

Egan, Susanna, and Gabriele Helms. 2001. Introduction to Special Issue: Autobiography and Changing Identities. *Biography: An Interdisciplinary Quarterly* 24 (1): ix-xx.

Finnegan, Ruth. 1988. *Literacy and Orality*. Oxford, UK: Basil Blackwell.

Fischer, Michael M.J. 1994. Autobiographical Voices and Mosaic Memory. In *Autobiography and Post-Modernism*. Edited by Kathleen Ashley, Leigh Gilmore, and Gerald Peters. Amherst: University of Massachussetts Press.

Foster, Frances Smith. 1992. Autobiography after Emancipation: The Example of Elizabeth Keckley. In *Multicultural Autobiography: American Lives*. Edited by James Robert Payne. Knoxville, TN: University of Tennessee Press.

Freud, Sigmund. 1991. "Group Psychology and the Analysis of the Ego." In *Civilization, Society and Religion*. Vol. 12: *Selected Works*. Harmondsworth, UK: Penguin.

Friedman, Susan Stanford. 1988. Women's Autobiographical Selves: Theory and Practice. In *The Private Self: Theory and Practice of Women's Autobiographical Writings*. Edited by Shari Benstock. Chapel Hill, NC: University of North Carolina Press.

Friesen, John W., and Michael M. Verigin. 1989. *The Community Doukhobors: A People in Transition*. Ottawa: Borealis Press.

Frye, Northrop. 1957. *Anatomy of Criticism*. Princeton, NJ: Princeton University Press.

Gilmore, Leigh. 1994a. *Autobiographics: A Feminist Theory of Women's Self-Representation.* Ithaca, NY: Cornell University Press.

–. 1994b. Policing Truth: Confession, Gender, and Autobiographic Authority. In *Autobiography and Post-Modernism.* Edited by Kathleen Ashley, Leigh Gilmore, and Gerald Peters. Amherst: University of Massachussetts Press.

–. 2001. *The Limits of Autobiography: Trauma and Testimony.* Ithaca, NY and London: Cornell University Press.

Gilroy, Paul. 1996. Route Work: The Black Atlantic and the Politics of Exile. In *The Post-Colonial Question: Common Skies, Divided Horizons.* Edited by Iain Chambers and Lidia Curti. London/New York: Routledge.

Goldman, Anne E. 1996. *Take My Word: Autobiographical Innovations of Ethnic American Working Women.* Berkeley and Los Angeles: University of California Press.

Gunn, Janet Varner. 1982. *Autobiography: Toward a Poetics of Experience.* Philadelphia: University of Pennsylvania Press.

Gusdorf, Georges. 1975. De l'autobiographie initiatique à l'autobiographie genre littéraire. *Revue d'histoire littéraire de la France* 75: 954-57.

–. 1980. Conditions and Limits of Autobiography. In *Autobiography: Essays Theoretical and Critical.* Edited by James Olney. Princeton, NJ: Princeton University Press.

–. 1991. *auto-bio-graphie.* Paris: Éditions Odile Jacob.

Hagen, Susan K. 1990. *Allegorical Remembrance.* Athens: University of Georgia Press.

Hall, Stuart. 1996. Introduction: Who Needs "Identity"? In *Questions of Cultural Identity.* Edited by Stuart Hall and Paul de Gay. London: Sage Publications.

Haraway, Donna. 1995. Foreword: Cyborgs and Symbiants — Living Together in the New World Order. In *The Cyborg Handbook.* Edited by Chris Hables-Gray. New York and London: Routledge.

Harshenin, Alex N. 1965. Interview with Fred (Fedya) Zhikarov. Reel 16, Track 1. 11 June. Special Collections, University of British Columbia, Main Library.

Havelock, Eric. 1971. *Prologue to Greek Literacy.* Cincinnati: University of Cincinnati Press.

Heilbrun, Carolyn. 1988. *Writing a Woman's Life.* New York: Norton.

Holt, Simma. 1964. *Terror in the Name of God: The Story of the Sons of Freedom Doukhobors.* Toronto/Montreal: McClelland & Stewart.

Hutcheon, Linda. 1988. *The Canadian Postmodern: A Study of Contemporary English-Canadian Fiction.* Oxford: Oxford University Press.

Jacobus, Mary. 1984. The Law of/and Gender: Genre Theory and *The Prelude. Diacritics* 14: 47-57.

Janzen, William. 1990. *Limits on Liberty: The Experience of Mennonite, Hutterite and Doukhobor Communities in Canada.* Toronto: University of Toronto Press.

Jay, Paul. 1984. *Being in the Text.* Ithaca: Cornell University Press.

Jelinek, Estelle C., ed. 1980. Introduction to *Women's Autobiography: Essays in Criticism.* Bloomington: Indiana University Press.

Joint Doukhobor Research Committee. 1997. *Report of the United Doukhobor Research Committee in the Matter of Clarification of the Motivating Life-Concepts and the History of the Doukhobors in Canada (Symposium Meetings 1974-1982).* Transcribed, edited, and translated by Eli Popoff. Castlegar, BC: Selkirk College.

Kadar, Marlene, ed. 1992. *Essays on Life Writing: From Genre to Critical Practice.* Toronto: University of Toronto Press.

Kalmakoff, Jonathan J. 2003. *Doukhobor Genealogy.* <http://users.accesscomm.ca/doukhobor.genealogy/>.

Kaplan, Caren. 1992. Resisting Autobiography: Out-Law Genres and Transnational Feminist Subjects. In *De/Colonizing the Subject: The Politics of Gender in Women's Autobiography.* Edited by Sidonie Smith and Julia Watson. Minneapolis: University of Minnesota Press.

Kingwell, Mark, and Christopher Moore. 1999. *Canada: Our Century.* Toronto: Doubleday Canada.

Krupat, Arnold. 1991. Native American Autobiography and the Synecdochic Self. In *American Autobiography: Retrospect and Prospect.* Edited by Paul John Eakin. Madison, WI: University of Wisconsin Press.

Lang, Candace. 1982. Autobiography in the Aftermath of Romanticism. *Diacritics* 12: 2-16.

Lavie, Smadar, and Ted Swedenburg, eds. 1996. Introduction to *Displacement, Diaspora and Geographies of Identity*. Durham and London: Duke University Press.

Lejeune, Philippe. 1989. *On Autobiography*. Edited by Paul John Eakin. Translated by Katherine Leary. Minneapolis: University of Minnesota Press.

Lionnet, Françoise. 1989. *Autobiographical Voices: Race, Gender, Self-Portraiture*. Ithaca, NY: Cornell University Press.

Locke, John. 1980. *An Essay Concerning Human Understanding*. London, UK: Routledge.

McGowan, Sharon. 1998. *Soul Communion*. Video. Vancouver: Blue Heron Media Ltd.

McLaren, John. 1999. The Despicable Crime of Nudity: Law, the State and Civil Protest Among the Sons of Freedom Sect of Doukhobors, 1899-1935. *Journal of the West* 38 (3): 27-33.

McLuhan, Marshall. 1966. *Understanding Media: The Extensions of Man*. 2nd ed. Toronto: New American Library of Canada, Ltd.

Makhortoff, Vanya. 1987. Account of My Imprisonment. Translated by Mike G. Jmieff. *Iskra* 1648, 2: n.p.

Makortoff, Elaine J. 1974. Of Other Generations. *Mir* 2 (3-6): 44.

Malloff, Marjorie, ed. 1977. *Toil and Peaceful Life*. Vancouver: British Columbia Archives Oral History Series.

Maloff, Cecil C. 1992. A Tribute to the Original Doukhobors and Their Descendents. *Iskra* 1758 (21 October): 36-37.

Maloff, Marie. 1997. Letter to the Editor. *Iskra* 1831 (March): 27.

Maloff, P. 1957. *In Quest of a Solution (Three Reports on the Doukhobor Problem)*. 2nd ed. Trail, British Columbia. Special Collections, University of British Columbia, Main Library.

Marcus, Laura. 1994. *Auto/biographical Discourses: Theory, Criticism, Practice*. Manchester, UK: Manchester University Press.

–. 1995. Autobiography and the Politics of Identity. *Current Sociology* 43 (2-3): 41-52.

Markova, Anna Petrovna. 1974. An Interview with Anna Petrovna Markova. Interviewed by Jim Popoff. *Mir* 1 (7-10): 3-42.

Mason, Mary G. 1980. The Other Voice: Autobiographies of Women Writers. In *Autobiography: Essays Theoretical and Critical*. Edited by James Olney. Princeton, NJ: Princeton University Press.

Maude, Alymer. 1904. *A Peculiar People: The Doukhobors*. New York: Funk and Wagnalls.

Mauss, Marcel. 1985 [1938]. A Category of the Human Mind: The Notion of Person, the Notion of Self. In *The Category of the Person: Anthropology, Philosophy, History*. Edited by Michael Carrithers, Steven Collins, and Steven Lukes. Translated by W.D. Halls. Cambridge, UK: Cambridge University Press.

Melanya, Grandma. 1996. Grandma Melanya's Story. *Iskra* 1821 (25 September): 47.

Miller, Nancy K. 1991. *Getting Personal*. New York and London: Routledge.

Misch, Georg. 1950. *A History of Autobiography in Antiquity*. Translated by E.W. Dickes. 2 vols. London: Routledge and Kegan Paul. First published as *Geschichte der Autobiographie* in 1907.

Mishra, Vijay. 1995. Postcolonial Differend: Diasporic Narratives of Salman Rushdie. *Ariel* 26 (3): 7-45.

Murphy, Emily. 1910. *Janey Canuck in the West*. London: Cassell.

Neuman, Shirley. 1996. Introduction: Reading Canadian Autobiography. *Essays on Canadian Writing* 60 (Winter): 1-13.

Novokshyonov, Vanya. 1908. Turning Down the Post of Village Headman. In *Dukhobortsy: sbornik razskasov, pisem, dokumentov i statei po religioznym voprosam*. Edited and transcribed by Alexander M. Bodianskii. *The Doukhobors: Collection of Narratives, Letters, Documents and Articles on Religious Questions*. Kharkov, 1908. Special Collections. University of British Columbia, Main Library.

Nussbaum, Felicity. 1988a. Eighteenth-Century Women's Autobiographical Commonplaces. In *The Private Self: Theory and Practice of Women's Autobiographical Writings*. Edited by Shari Benstock. Chapel Hill, NC: University of North Carolina Press.

–. 1988b. Towards Conceptualizing Diary. In *Studies in Autobiography*. Edited by James Olney. New York: Oxford University Press.

Olney, James, ed. 1972. *Metaphors of Self: The Meaning of Autobiography*. Princeton, NJ: Princeton University Press.

–. 1980. Introduction. *Autobiography: Essays Theoretical and Critical*. Princeton, NJ: Princeton University Press.

–. 1988. Introduction. *Studies in Autobiography*. New York: Oxford University Press.

Ombudsman, Province of British Columbia. 1999. *Righting the Wrong: The Confinement of the Sons of Freedom Doukhobor Children*. Public Report No. 38. April, 1-76.

Ong, Walter J. 1982. *Orality and Literacy: The Technologizing of the Word*. New York: Routledge.

Oxford English Dictionary. 2001a. "Identity." Online edition. June. <http://dictionary.oed.com/>.

–. 2001b. "Subject." Online edition. June. <http://dictionary.oed.com/>.

Padilla, Genaro M. 1988. "The Recovery of Chicano Nineteenth-Century Autobiography." *American Quarterly* 40 (3): 286-306.

–. 1993a. The Mexican Immigrant as *: The (de)Formation of Mexican Immigrant Life Story. In *The Culture of Autobiography*. Edited by Robert Folkenflik. Stanford, CA: Stanford University Press.

–. 1993b. *My History, Not Yours: The Formation of Mexican American Autobiography*. Milwaukee, WI: University of Wisconsin Press.

Palmer, Howard. 1994. Anglo-Conformity. In *Immigration in Canada: Historical Perspectives*. Edited by Gerald Tulchinsky. Toronto: Copp Clark Longman.

Paredes, Raymund. 1992. Autobiography and Ethnic Politics: *Richard Rodriguez's Hunger of Memory*. In *Multicultural Autobiography: American Lives*. Edited by James Robert Payne. Knoxville, TN: University of Tennessee Press.

Pascal, Roy. 1960. *Design and Truth in Autobiography*. London: Routledge and Kegan Paul.

Perepelkin, Nikolai Nikolaevich. 1993. Grandfather Nikolai Nikolaevich Perepelkin's Recollections of Incidents from His Life in Canada. Edited and translated by Tim and Hazel Samorodin. *Iskra* 1778 (December): 24.

Pile, Steve, and Nigel Thrift, eds. 1995. Introduction to *Mapping the Subject: Geographies of Cultural Transformation*. London/New York: Routledge.

Plotnikoff, Vi. 1998. The Circle Journey. In *Spirit-Wrestlers' Voices*. Edited by Koozma J. Tarasoff. New York: Legas.

Podovinikoff, Joe, and Florence Podovinikoff. 1989. Former Saskatchewan Doukhobors Recall. *Iskra* (8 January): 18-20.

Popoff, D.E. (Jim). 1995. The Story of One Psalm. *Iskra* 1809 (22 November): 14-15.

Popoff, Helen. 1977. Interview with Helen Popoff. Sound Recording. Salmo, British Columbia. Special Collections, University of British Columbia, Main Library.

Popoff, Peter J. 1974. An Autobiographical Note. *Mir* 2 (1-2): 13-15, 42.

Popov, Vasily Ivanovitch. 1908. The Suffering of Vasily Ivanovich Popov for the True Way. *Dukhobortsy: sbornik razskasov, pisem, dokumentov i statei po religioznym voprosam*. Edited by A.M. Bodianskii. Transcribed by V.D. Bonch-Bruevich. *The Doukhobors: Collection of Narratives, Letters, Documents and Articles on Religious Questions*. Kharkov. Special Collections. University of British Columbia, Main Library.

Poznikoff-Koutny, Luba. 1996. Some "Thoughts From Luba." *Iskra* 1824 (6 November): 21-25.

Pratt, Mary Louise. 1992. *Imperial Eyes: Travel Writing and Transculturation*. London, UK: Routledge.

Rak, Julie. 2001. Doukhobor Autobiography as Witness Narrative. *Biography* 24 (1): 226-41.

Rimstead, Roxanne. 1996. Mediated Lives: Oral Histories and Cultural Memory. *Essays on Canadian Writing* 60 (Winter): 139-65.

Rodriguez, Richard. 1982. *The Hunger of Memory: The Education of Richard Rodriguez – An Autobiographyy*. Boston: D.R. Godine.

Rozinkin, William M. 1992. Let Us Remember. *Iskra* 1746 (15 April): 27-28.

Saldívar, Ramón. 1990. *Chicano Narrative*. Madison, WI: University of Wisconsin Press.

Sanders, Mark A. 1994. Theorizing the Collaborative Self: The Dynamics of Contour and Content in the Dictated Autobiography. *New Literary History* 25: 445-48.

Sayre, Robert. 1980. Autobiography and the Making of America. In *Autobiography: Essays Theoretical and Critical*. Edited by James Olney. Princeton, NJ: Princeton University Press.

Schenck, Celeste. 1988. All of a Piece: Women's Poetry and Autobiography. In *Life/Lines: Theorizing Women's Autobiography*. Edited by Bella Brodzki and Celeste Schenck. Ithaca, NY: Cornell University Press.

Sharpe, Jenny. 1995. Is the United States Postcolonial? Transnationalism, Immigration, and Race. *Diaspora* 4 (2): 181-99.

Smith, Paul. 1988. *Discerning the Subject*. Minneapolis: University of Minnesota Press.

Smith, Sidonie. 1987. *A Poetics of Women's Autobiography: Marginality and the Fictions of Self-Representation*. Bloomington and Indianapolis: Indiana University Press.

–. 1993. *Subjectivity, Identity, and the Body: Women's Autobiographical Practices in the Twentieth Century*. Bloomington and Indianapolis: Indiana University Press.

–. 1995. Performativity, Autobiographical Practice, Resistance. *a/b: Auto/Biography Studies* 10 (1): 17-33.

Smith, Sidonie, and Julia Watson, eds. 1992. Introduction to *De/Colonizing the Subject: The Politics of Gender in Women's Autobiography*. Minneapolis: University of Minnesota Press.

Sorokin, Stephan. 1950. *Tri Dniia i Tri Nochi v Zagrobnoi Zhizni: Chto Ya Videl, Slishal, i Perezhil, Kogda bil Ymiychen na Cmetr Bezbozhnimi C.C.C.P. [Three Days and Three Nights in the Life Beyond the Grave: What I Saw, Heard and Experienced When I was Tortured to Death by the Godless Authorities of the U.S.S.R.]* Crescent Valley [Krestova]: publisher unknown. Special Collections. University of British Columbia, Main Library.

Soukorev, Gregory Ivanovich. 1938. My Renunciation of Military Service. Translated by William Petrovich Sheloff. *Nelson Daily News*. 1 October 1938: 6. Instalment 9.

–. 1996a. My Renunciation of Military Service. Part 1. Translated by William Petrovich Sheloff. *Iskra* 1820 (19 June): 60-64.

–. 1996b. My Renunciation of Military Service. Part 2. Translated by William Petrovich Sheloff. *Iskra* 1821 (25 September 25): 40-42.

–. 1996c. My Renunciation of Military Service. Part 3. Translated by William Petrovich Sheloff. *Iskra* 1822 (16 October): 53-55.

–. 1996d. My Renunciation of Military Service. Part 4. Translated by William Petrovich Sheloff. *Iskra* 1823 (30 October): 26-29.

–. 1996e. My Renunciation of Military Service. Part 5. Translated by William Petrovich Sheloff. *Iskra* 1824 (13 November): 38-40.

–. 1996f. My Renunciation of Military Service. Part 6. Translated by William Petrovich Sheloff. *Iskra* 1825 (27 November): 9-10, 42.

–. 1996g. My Renunciation of Military Service. Part 7. Translated by William Petrovich Sheloff. *Iskra* 1826 (18 December): 95-97.

Spengemann, William C. 1980. *The Forms of Autobiography: Episodes in the History of a Literary Genre*. New Haven: Yale University Press.

Stanley, Liz. 1992. *The Auto/Biographical "I."* Manchester: Manchester University Press.

Stich, K.P., ed. 1988. *Reflections: Autobiography and Canadian Literature*. Ottawa: University of Ottawa Press.

Stone, Albert E. 1982. *Autobiographical Occasions and Original Acts*. Philadelphia: University of Pennsylvania Press.

Sturrock, John. 1977. The New Model Autobiographer. *New Literary History* 9: 51-65.

Sulerzhitsky, L.A. 1982. *To America with the Doukhobors*. Translated by Michael Kalmakoff, with an introduction by Mark Mealing. Regina, SK: Canadian Plains Research Centre.

Tarasoff, Koozma J. 1982. *Plakun Trava: The Doukhobors*. Grand Forks, BC: Mir Publication Society.

–. 1995. One Hundred Years of Doukhobors in Retrospect. *Canadian Ethnic Studies* 27 (3): 1-23.

Tarasoff, Koozma J., and Robert Klymasz, eds. 1995. Introduction to *Spirit Wrestlers: Centennial Papers in Honour of Canada's Doukhobor Heritage*. Hull, PQ: Canadian Museum of Civilization.

USCC Kootenay Men's Group. 1995. *"Vechnaya Pamyat"*: *A Guide to Traditional Customs and Procedures at Doukhobor Funerals*. Castlegar, BC: USCC Kootenay Men's Group.

Walker, Nancy. 1988. "Wider Than the Sky": Public Presence and Private Self in Dickinson, James, and Woolf. In *The Private Self: Theory and Practice of Women's Autobiographical Writings*. Edited by Shari Benstock. Chapel Hill, NC: University of North Carolina Press.

Williams, Raymond. 1976. *Keywords: A Vocabulary of Culture and Society*. London, UK: Croom Helm.

Wong, Hertha Dawn. 1992. *Sending My Heart Back across the Years: Tradition and Innovation in Native American Autobiography*. New York and Oxford: Oxford University Press.

Wong, Sau-Ling C. 1995. Denationalization Reconsidered: Asian American Cultural Criticism at a Theoretical Crossroads. *Amerasia Journal* 21 (1-2): 1-27.

Woodcock, George, and Ivan Avakumovic. 1977. *The Doukhobors*. Toronto: McClelland & Stewart.

Woodsworth, J.S. 1909. *Strangers within Our Gates*. Toronto: University of Toronto Press.

Yerbury, J.C. 1984. The "Sons of Freedom" Doukhobors and the Canadian State. *Canadian Ethnic Studies* 16 (2): 47-70.

Zubek, John, and Patricia Solberg. 1952. *Doukhobors at War*. Toronto: Ryerson Press.

Index

Markin, Anne, 79
Markova, Anna, 70-74, 89
Mason, Mary G., 21
Maude, Alymer, xii, 148n8
Mauss, Marcel, 7
Mead, Colonel F.J., 138
memoir, xiii, 11, 12, 13, 76, 122
Miller, Nancy K., 24
Mir: articles by members from all
  Doukhobor groups, 66; autobiographical
  writing in, 57-58; founding of, 52-53;
  Independent Doukhobors as authors,
  66; interpretation of interviews as lessons
  for current generation, 74; memoirs
  and interviews in, xiii, 63, 69-78, 89,
  104; publication of poem in, 55
Misch, Georg, 10-11, 13
Mishra, Vijay, 57-58, 61, 83
Moore, Christopher, 41
Murphy, Emily, xii, 41

Nelson Daily News, 78, 82
Neuman, Shirley, 33, 144
New Denver dormitory, 52, 116-18, 131,
  136
New Model theorists, 14-15
Novokshyonov, Vanya, 88, 93-96, 100,
  104
Nussbaum, Felicity, 21, 122

Oakalla prison, 130
Ogloff, Joe, 124
Ogloff, William, 110, 113
Oliver, Frank, 42; and the Doukhobor
  land dispute, 44-48
Olney, James, xii; advocacy of
  interdisciplinary approaches, 19-20;
  on auto-bio-graphe, 15, 32; as a liberal
  humanist critic, 9-10; his opposition to
  poststructuralism, 17
Ombudsman of British Columbia, 118
O'Neal, Hazel, xii
Ong, Walter J., 90-91
orality: as communal, 89; Doukhobors
  and, 90, 114, 119; and literacy, 85-86,
  89, 90-91, 109; and oracy, 89-90; and
  voice recordings, 88. *See also* oral
  accounts *under* Doukhobor; oral culture
  under Doukhobor

Padilla, Genaro, xii, xv, 27-28
Palmer, Howard, 43
Pascal, Roy, 12-14
Perepelkin, Nikolai, 63
person, 3; -hood, 7-8. *See also* individual;
  self

personal criticism, 24
Pile, Stephen, 5
Plotnikoff, Vi, 57, 149n12
Podmoroff, Paul, 123, 125
Podmoryov, Vasily, 113
Podovinikoff, Florence, 65-66
Podovinikoff, Joe, 65-66
Popoff, Eli, 109
Popoff, Helen, 106-8
Popoff, Jim, 52, 71, 74, 88
Popoff, Mae, 78
Popoff, Peter, 66-67
Popov, Vasily, 87, 89-90, 94-96
Poznikoff-Koutny, Luba, 68-69
Pratt, Mary Louise, 58

Rak, Julie, 146n1
Rimstead, Roxanne, 86, 92-93, 102
Rodriguez, Richard, 27

Saldívar, Ramón, 27
Samorodin, Hazel, 63
Samorodin, Tim, 63
Sanders, Mark, 85-86
Sayre, Robert F., 20
Schenck, Celeste, 21
self: the author's, 9; autobiography seen
  as reflection of, xii; connection to text,
  10; discourse of, 135, 143; fictions of,
  16; idea of in autobiography studies,
  2-3; as individual and free, 6; liberal
  view of, 143; and life, 119; and other,
  12, 32, 120-21; as private, 71; self-in-
  relation, 88; self-reflection, 121;
  self-reflexivity, 90; as unique and pre-
  existing, 119; as a Western institution,
  xiv, 119. *See also* individual
Sharpe, Jenny, 59
Sheloff, William, 78
Shumaker, Wayne, 12
Sifton, Clifford, 38, 42, 46
Smith, Sidonie: on alternate narratives,
  143; on autobiographical manifestos,
  146n1; autobiography as political, 30;
  critique of Olney, 10; and the feminist
  critique of "the universal subject," 22-
  24; on Gertrude Stein, 146n2; on
  performativity, 31-32, 33; on William
  Spengemann, 147n7; *Subjectivity,
  Identity, and the Body,* 3
Solberg, Patricia, 41
Sorokin, Stephan, xii, 51, 137, 152n4
Soukorev, Gregory, 78-82, 94
Stanley, Liz, 24
Stich, K.P., 33
Stone, Albert E., 20

Storgeoff, Frances, 52
Sturrock, John, 15
subject, xiv; bad subjects, viii-ix, 7, 8; as
  collaborative, 85; as diasporic, 60-61;
  discourse of the, 22, 83; formation as
  communal, 109; as hybrid, 87; and
  object, 18; positions, 19, 122; purified
  through suffering, 94-96; referentiality
  of, 20; singularity of, 74, 78, 81, 123; as
  speaking, 139; truth-telling, 138;
  universal, 23-24. *See also* subjectivity
subjectivity: alternative ways to represent,
  xiv; in autobiography theory, xiii, 1, 8;
  as collective, 121; Doukhobor, 56-57,
  63, 66, 71, 74, 89, 93-95, 106, 108-9,
  131; female, 22; Freedomite, 124;
  individual, 71, 74; liberal, 1; of a
  minority, 2; national, 57; non-
  poststructuralist vs. poststructuralist
  approaches to, 17; and performativity,
  30-31; in philosophy and psychology,
  2-5; as plural, 63, 74, 76-77, 95, 114;
  Romantic, 11; as split, 137; as a
  Western construct, 143. *See also*
  identity; individual; subject
Sulerjitskii, Leopold, xii, 148n7
Swetlishoff, Peter, 113-14, 151n19

Tarasoff, Koozma: for background on the
  Burning of Arms, 147n5; Chistiakov's
  migration model, 50; Doukhoborism as
  a social movement, 38; idea of *plakun
  trava,* xvi; Mae Popoff's recollections,
  78; press reaction to the Sons of God,
  40
Thrift, Nigel, 5
Tolstoy, Leo, xiv, 38; connected to
  Alexander Efanow's diary, 128; as
  diasporic, 55, 61-62; followers of, 38,
  39; in Gregory Soukorev's writing, 78;
  Nick Arishenkoff's appeal to, 76-77;
  and the novel *Resurrection,* 39; as part
  of Doukhobor oral tradition, 83, 85; as
  sacred, 127; *vechnaia pamit,*
  explanation of, xiii, 58
trek of 1902, 40, 112-13, 115, 121

Verigin, John J. (Ivan), 36, 71, 73; Fred
  Davidoff's interpretations of his
  commands, 137; and the Freedomites,
  52, 70; and Hazel Sookochoff's psalm,
  84; son of Anna Markova, 71-72;
  successor to Chistiakov, 51
Verigin, Michael, 53, 117
Verigin, Peter Chistiakov: in Alexander
  Efanow's diary, 126; assistants of, 91;

Cecil Koochin's recollections of, 75;
  dissolves the CCUB, 149n13; father of
  Anna Markova, 70-72; Joe and Florence
  Podovinikoff's recollections of, 65-66;
  leadership of, 50-51; Lucy Maloff's
  recollections of, 111-12; memories of,
  109; Mike Chernoff's recollections
  of, 110; his name, 148n12; Peter N.
  Maloff's relationship to, 139; and
  "the Doukhobor University," 85
Verigin, Peter Iestrobov (the Hawk), 51,
  71
Verigin, Peter Lordly: in Alexander
  Efanow's diary, 126-27; arrival in
  Canada, 39; assistants of, 91;
  Bondareff's recollections of, 104; and
  the CCUB, 41-42, 50; Cecil Koochin's
  recollections of, 75; changes to
  Doukhobor spiritual practices, 36-37;
  death of, 48; denounced by the Sons
  of Freedom, 48; exile of followers of,
  37; exile in Siberia, 39; followers of, 98;
  Fred Davidoff's court testimony about,
  130; instructions to live communally,
  39; Large Party of, 147n4; memories
  of, 109; his name, 147n3; naming of
  CCUB, 149n13; Novokshyonov's
  loyalty to, 94; obeying directives of,
  110; slogan of, 36; visit to Russia, 47;
  Zhikarov's recollections of, 101-2

Walker, Nancy, 21
Watson, Julia, 30, 143
Williams, Raymond, 3, 4
witness narrative, 79, 82, 93, 114, 122-26
Wong, Hertha Dawn, xii, 28-29
Wong, Sau Ling Cynthia, 60
Woodcock, George: conflict between
  federal government and the Freedomites, 116; conflict between the Sons
  of Freedom and Peter Lordly, 48; death
  of Peter Iestrobov, 71; on Doukhobor
  protest, 152n6; the Doukhobors and
  assimilation, 52; the Doukhobors as
  transients, 49; meaning of the term
  "Doukhobor," 35-37; the 1902 trek, 40;
  the success of the CCUB, 42
Woodsworth, J.S., 47; Ivan Bondoreff's
  recollections of, 67; and literacy, 43;
  Winnipeg mission of, 48

Yerbury, Colin, 147n2

Zhikarov, Fred, 101-3, 104, 108
Zubek, John, 41

Printed and bound in Canada by Friesens

Set in Stone by Brenda and Neil West, BN Typographics West

Copy editor: Joanne Richardson

Proofreader: Jillian Shoichet